D1645871

Gower College Swansea

Gorseinon : Swansea : SA4 6RD Tel: (01792) 890731
This resource is **YOUR RESPONSIBILITY** and is due for
return/renewal on or before the last date shown.

CLASS NO. 378.425   **ACC. NO.**   037150

RETURN OR RENEW - DON'T PAY FINES

CONTENTS

FOREWORD

" HAVING BEEN INVOLVED WITH UNIVERSITY ADMISSIONS FOR OVER TEN YEARS, I CAN SYMPATHISE WITH THE ANXIETIES AND HOPES OF PROSPECTIVE CANDIDATES. THE COMPETITION FOR A PLACE AT OXFORD OR CAMBRIDGE HAS NEVER BEEN MORE FIERCE.

Many school leavers feel that the odds are stacked against them and that only those who have privileged access can ever be successful. Extra tests and the prospect of an interview can make potentially successful candidates give up before they begin. They feel that there is some secret formula or hidden key that is denied to them. This is entirely untrue: anybody with the right qualifications has an equal chance of success, and what may seem from the outside to be a system slanted in favour of those who can buy success, is in fact a system designed to select the best candidates regardless of their background. If you want to apply and have the appropriate grades, you have as good a chance as anyone else.

In the admissions tests and at interview you are treated as an individual and not a statistic and it is a level playing field for all candidates. The universities do not have any hidden agenda or favoured type of candidate. All they want are the students who perform best in the application process, taking into account their work in the admissions tests and at interview. And by 'best', they don't mean the person with the most crammed knowledge – they are looking for all-round intellectual ability alongside academic curiosity and commitment. Nobody can obtain these things over the counter: they are intrinsic to an individual who is prepared to stretch themselves to the limit and aim for the highest. Background is irrelevant.

The competition for places continues to grow as more candidates attain high grades at A level. Exam boards now have to differentiate between A grades by awarding A★s as marks of distinction, and a typical Cambridge offer, as well as for some subjects at Oxford, includes at least one A★. From 2015, Cambridge will be raising their offers for science subjects to include two A★s. The universities are also attaching more importance to the tests they set for applicants at interview, as they do their best to sift through a highly talented pool of candidates in as fair and efficient a way as possible. All this makes the interview even more important in the selection process. A difficult situation inevitably arises: at interview the universities want to gauge those things which the A level and UCAS form cannot properly reveal – things like potential and motivation. These are things which cannot be prepared for – innate qualities that haven't been taught and which can't be bought by those with greater access to facilities or specialist teaching.

Candidates can expect to be given some unseen material to be discussed at their interview, which is usually given to them just before the interview itself. These tasks will tend to concentrate on how you apply your mind rather than your ability to recall facts, and how you can think under pressure. All candidates (and parents), however, will of course ask themselves 'how can I prepare for these extra hurdles?' It is clear that at one level the answer is: 'You can't, nor should you be able to.' That is, you cannot suddenly improve your academic and intellectual potential overnight. What you can do is consult those whose experience can help you to show yourself as you are now to your best possible advantage. This is what the education consultancy Oxbridge Applications and the authors of this book are aiming to do. Nobody is offering that secret formula because none exists. What is on offer is a wide range of expertise to help you both play to your strengths and avoid the pitfalls into which so many students fall that prevent the interviewer from getting a true impression of their abilities.

It's important to realise that the interview is intended to discover what is unique about you, not how you fit into some pre-conceived mould. Your UCAS form will have shown how much you know about the basics of the subject you have chosen to study, so the interview is unlikely to concentrate entirely on this. More important is showing how you react to unexpected academic and intellectual challenges: the interviewer will want to judge how much you are likely to develop over three or four years. You need to be able to show that you are a committed and engaged candidate; if you aren't, you shouldn't be entering the competition!

This is not a conveyor belt – the admissions process is about individuality rather than conformity – and there is no brain-washing or attempting to beat the system: as explained, that would be as unethical as it is impossible. What is possible is for you to raise your game through sensible discussion and advice. It has been a pleasure to see so many candidates from a variety of backgrounds improve their chances through this common-sense approach, and the success rate suggests that it has been a valuable experience for many. But remember: anyone can offer advice, but only you can turn advice into success. ❞

BARRY WEBB

Introduction:
SO YOU WANT TO GO OXBRIDGE?

──────────── ☸ ────────────

WITH ALL CHALLENGES IN LIFE, THERE IS A MIXTURE OF ABILITY, FOCUS, PREPARATION AND SHEER DETERMINATION THAT LEADS TO SUCCESS. YES, THE GENIUSES WILL GET THEIR PLACES, BUT WHAT ABOUT THE REST OF US?

We want to help you perform at your best throughout the selection process, which is all any rational and reasonable admissions tutor can wish to see. For them to miss students of ability – just because they are not confident or lack the right insights into what tutors are looking for – is a real shame.

We find that there are three ways students approach the application process. Firstly, there's the group that pretend they don't care about the result. They treat their application as someone else's project ('oh, I'm just applying because mum/dad wants it, but really I'm not that bothered'). They would rather not take responsibility for their own application and don't put in the hard work (extra reading, thinking about their personal statement, interview preparation). If they fail to get an offer, there are almost always feelings of what could have been.

The second group makes getting an Oxbridge offer the be-all and end-all of their existence. This is extremely unhealthy to say the least. Not only does it make for a more anxious applicant (and therefore one less likely to succeed), but if the contents of the envelope aren't positive, their whole reason for academic existence (i.e. to get into Oxbridge) is undermined. This can have negative consequences in the run up to A2 exams.

Finally, the most successful group: they are honest that, as they have applied to Oxbridge, they therefore would like a place. However, this group recognises the elements beyond their control (the quality of the other applicants that particular year, how they feel on interview day, the mood of the interviewer). They do everything they possibly can to make their application exceptional. Then, whatever the result, they know they have given it their best. They also know that the work they put into applying to Oxbridge will make their whole UCAS application stronger and, even if they don't get into Oxbridge, they will still go to another Times Top 20/Russell Group university.

Having worked with over 60,000 applicants we think that, if you do apply, all anyone can ask is that come the January after you have submitted your application forms, sat an admissions test and hopefully been invited to interview, you have done everything you possibly could do to excel. Whether you end up at Oxford, Cambridge or another good university, your mind can rest easy that you have no regrets.

What do successful applicants do?

Firstly, they really want to study their chosen course at their chosen university. They understand what the course entails and why it's a good fit for them. They then apply every realistic ounce of effort and energy to achieving that goal. They delve further into their subject area, not because they have to, but because they have a genuine love for their subject – they want to do it and in so doing, show tutors they are capable of independent learning.

They take time over their application to prepare for the various hurdles that present themselves, from the UCAS form to an admissions test, from written work to selecting the right college. Why do they do this? Because they're convinced that studying that course at that university is right for them.

Finally, they focus on the interview: a key aspect of the Oxbridge admissions process. They accept that this is a relatively new experience for them. The idea of being in new surroundings, with unfamiliar people, talking about challenging academic material is, understandably for many, a nerve-racking prospect.

They realise that, like any examination, they can prepare for this experience. They think about what tutors are looking for and practise approaching hard questions and structuring arguments using examples when they don't know the answer. They take on feedback in the run up to the interview about how they can improve and have the humility to understand how they might come across to a stranger – be that too shy or even over confident. Successful applicants understand that the person sitting across from them is making a decision about whether they want to teach that person for three years and potentially more.

No guarantees and no regrets

Of course, there are no guarantees and even if you do all of the above, that offer may still prove elusive. With nearly five of the best-qualified students going for each available place, the need for motivation, enthusiasm, talent, commitment and a real interest in your subject beyond the curriculum is as high as ever. For many, the Oxbridge application process may be the first time they do not succeed academically and for some this is a difficult pill to swallow.

We've written this book to gather advice and information from thousands of students who've been through the process. We've heard the regrets, 'I wish I hadn't been so nervous', 'I wish I'd read those books on my personal statement', 'I wish I'd brushed up on my school work' and, as much as possible, we want to help you to make your application a positive experience.

So you want to go to Oxbridge? Tell me about a banana... has been written by people who want to give you the advice and guidance to help your application reflect its true potential.

We wish you the very best of luck.

The Oxbridge Applications Team

1 CHOOSING A COURSE

- QUESTIONS TO CONSIDER WHEN CHOOSING THE COURSE THAT MOST INSPIRES YOU

- WE EXPLORE THE UNDERGRADUATE COURSES ON OFFER AT CAMBRIDGE AND OXFORD

What am I enjoying about my current studies?

Interest is the first rung on the ladder towards demonstrating real motivation and potential for your chosen subject. If you want to secure a place, your interviewer will need to know that you already enjoy interacting with your subject and that you'll continue to do so in tutorials and supervisions. What topics do you love studying in class to the extent that you carry on exploring ideas and reading outside of school because you're keen to gain a greater understanding of related issues?

❛❛ Physics applies maths, logic and experience to help understand the universe and all its machinations. Why wouldn't you want to study that?! Beyond its intrinsic value, studying Physics is also a great way to train your mind to formulate creative solutions to quantitative puzzles. Almost everything that can be measured can also be modelled using insights from Physics. ❜❜

Tom, Physics at Oxford

Do I understand the course I'm applying for?

Your interviewers will expect you to have a clear understanding of what the course entails and to be prepared for each aspect. For example, a number of students might like the sound of Philosophy at Cambridge, but may not be prepared to grapple with the mathematical nature of logic, as you have to in the admissions test you sit at interview and then in the first year of study. If you don't have a core understanding of what logic is or how to approach it, you may find the application process and, if you're successful, your first year, quite tough – so make sure you know what you're getting yourself into! Likewise, applicants for E&M (Economics & Management) at Oxford and Economics at Cambridge will need to be able to solve mathematical problems confidently, and be expected to have an understanding of the macro-economic situation in Britain. In previous years, applicants have been asked to prove Pythagoras' Theorem algebraically, as well as explain quantitative easing and discuss GDP growth. Be sure to read the full course prospectus so that you can see what you will potentially be studying each year in detail.

" I chose English because I love the process of teasing out the depth of meaning in a text through close reading. It fascinates me to see how much more there is to understanding a sentence than just reading words – how structure, tradition and association, rhythm, metre, mimesis – a million elements all contribute to a writer communicating complex thought. "

Olivia, English at Oxford

What do I excel at?

The enjoyment factor is not the only thing to consider – you need to have the ability too. As two of the top universities in the world, Oxford and Cambridge are looking for the best and brightest. All-round academic achievement is extremely important, and you need to have the grades on paper (at GCSE and A level or equivalent) to match your desire to study the subject. This means top UMS scores for a Cambridge application and strong GCSEs for Oxford.

Do I have the right qualifications?

Most subjects require you to have certain qualifications in order to apply. This is to ensure that you have a certain level of knowledge to build on when you start the course – or training in the skills that will allow you to succeed (for example the ability to write an analytical essay). If you're applying for Physics or Engineering, it's worth taking the Further Maths A level or equivalent to strengthen your application. For Medicine, in reality you're going to need both Biology and Chemistry to make a competitive application: all of the successful applicants we surveyed in 2014 had this combination.

Have I considered a subject I haven't studied before?

Many university courses apply academic skills that you've already developed at school to different subject disciplines, such as Engineering with its use of Maths and Physics. If you enjoy History, Classical Civilisation or Human Geography, for example, you may enjoy learning about the development of society and culture in the Archaeology & Anthropology course at Oxford or HSPS (Human, Social & Political Sciences) at Cambridge. Alternatively, if Physics, Chemistry and Maths are your preferred subjects, would you consider studying their application to our planet with a degree in Earth Sciences at Oxford? The interviewers are looking for keen amateurs and students who have taken the initiative to explore their chosen subject independently.

Have I compared similar courses at Oxford and Cambridge?

While there are obvious similarities between the two universities, there are key differences between the courses at each institution. Cambridge courses tend (generally speaking) to allow students more flexibility and the chance to explore less traditional areas of the subject: courses are split into Parts I and II. Part I allows you to gain a broad knowledge and understanding of your subject, before choosing your own modules in Part II, which gives you the opportunity to devise your own course of study.

Oxford courses tend to be more rigidly structured with a more traditional approach. Undergraduates usually engage with their subject in more depth from the outset. If you compare Natural Sciences (Physical) at Cambridge, with its nearest equivalent, Physics at Oxford, Oxford Physicists get an earlier induction into the specifics of their chosen subject. In contrast, Cambridge Physical Natural Scientists gain a wide view of the available options in their first year before settling on one subject.

Do I really care about my subject?

Be sure to consider how different a university course will be from A level (or equivalent) subjects. Just because you're good at a subject at school, doesn't necessarily mean that you will enjoy it when you study it at university. The style of learning and the topics that you will cover may be completely different – and the only way to find out whether your ability and enjoyment will translate is to spend time doing your research. And don't be tempted to plump for the course that you think will give you the best chance of getting an offer – you'll need to convince the admissions tutors at interview that you are genuinely enthusiastic about your subject!

What do I want to do after university?

It's worth bearing in mind that you don't necessarily need a vocational undergraduate degree to go into certain fields. Many applicants feel compelled to apply for courses such as Law and Medicine because they fear that, if they don't, they will miss out on the option of those careers forever. If you feel this pressure, you should remember that a Law conversion course only takes one year longer than the equivalent qualification for a Law student, and that Magic Circle firms now take almost half of their trainees from non-Law backgrounds – some recruiters actually prefer to take graduates in different subjects who have done a law conversion so that they can bring a different approach to the profession. There is also a graduate fast-track programme for Medicine, reducing the five year training to four years for those with the relevant Science at A level. Similarly, many applicants believe that without an Economics-based degree, a career in the City will be beyond reach. But bear in mind there are many successful graduates from disciplines as varied as History, Engineering, Maths and Land Economy, who are now excelling in the financial world.

If you already know you want to be a heart surgeon or a chemical engineer, you should look to choose the most suitable course to give you the necessary qualifications and experience to achieve that goal. Our advice, however, is that you should only apply if you feel absolutely certain about your choice. Not only do these courses tend to be among the most competitive, admissions tutors are likely to test your total commitment and understanding of the profession at interview.

Now it's time to research your options…

There's no substitute for good research. A great place to start is with the university prospectuses and then the university and course Open Days. These days give you a fantastic opportunity to meet with tutors and current students and ask lots of questions. Current students are usually open to discussing their studies with potential applicants – after all, they enjoy what they're doing! A faculty tour is a brilliant insight into the workings of the department, and many will host a lecture to give you a taste of the working life of a student. After visiting the departments, you will probably have a gut feeling as to which subject you could envisage yourself studying at Oxbridge. There is also a wealth of information on the Oxford and Cambridge websites.

Read our course profiles

To help inspire your journey of course discovery, we've put together profiles of courses currently available at Oxford and Cambridge written by graduates who have read those courses. These pages will give you a taster of the key elements of the course, as well as past interview questions and reading recommendations. We've also included suggestions of similar courses you might like to consider at the bottom of each course page.

Once you've decided on the right course for you, head to Chapter 8: Approaching Questions to delve into example interview questions for your subject. We've enlisted recent graduates to talk you through how best to approach these.

Which courses require which test?

- **BMAT: BioMedical Admissions Test** Oxford Medicine and Biomedical Sciences, Cambridge Medicine and Veterinary Medicine (also used by Imperial, Royal Veterinary College, UCL, LKC, Brighton and Sussex and Leeds)

- **CAT: Classics Admissions Test** Oxford Classics and joint schools

- **ELAT: English Literature Admissions Test** Oxford English and joint schools

- **HAT: History Aptitude Test** Oxford History and joint schools

- **LNAT: National Admissions test for Law** Oxford Law (also used by Birmingham, Bristol, Durham, Glasgow, King's, Nottingham, SOAS and UCL)

- **MAT: Mathematics Admissions Test** Oxford Mathematics, Computer Science and joint schools (also used by Imperial)

- **MLAT: Modern Languages Admissions Test** Oxford Modern Languages, Linguistics and joint schools

- **OLAT: Oriental Languages Aptitude Test** Oxford certain Oriental languages

- **PAT: Physics Aptitude Test** Oxford Engineering, Materials Science and Physics

- **STEP: Sixth Term Examination Paper** Cambridge Maths. Some colleges may use STEP for Computer Sciences, Economics, Engineering and Natural Sciences (also used by Warwick)

- **TSA Cambridge: Thinking Skills Assessment** Some Cambridge colleges may use it for Computer Sciences, Economics, Engineering, HSPS, Land Economy, Natural Sciences and PBS

- **TSA Oxford: Thinking Skills Assessment** Oxford E&M, Experimental Psychology, Geography, PPE, PPL

ASNaC (Anglo-Saxon, Norse & Celtic)
Three years

Past interview questions to get you thinking:

• How could you go about dating an unknown manuscript?
• What is the difference between history and literature, especially in the context of the Anglo-Saxon period?
• How will your choice of A levels benefit your study of ASNaC?

The ASNaC course combines the study of literature, language and history of the early medieval period. It is unique to Cambridge, and allows students to work on a range of disciplines in great depth. No specific subjects are required, but language and humanities A levels are preferred. Most colleges will require you to **submit written work** to demonstrate your ability to structure material and argue your point of view, and some will set their own **admissions test** at interview.

" The amount of choice is amazing – essentially you can design your own degree, and the dissertation allows you to contribute towards the field of scholarship. **"**

Harriet, ASNaC graduate

Interested? Why don't you explore. . .

Beowulf translation by Seamus Heaney – one of the most important works of Anglo-Saxon literature and a set text on the course.

The Sagas of Icelanders: A Selection by Robert Kellogg – a particularly good introduction to Old Norse literature.

Anglo-Saxon England by Frank Stenton – a core history text covering the period prior to the Norman Conquest.

Not the course for you? Take a look at **Classics, English** or **History** at Cambridge or Oxford.

Architecture
Three years

Past interview questions to get you thinking:

• What would you say is the most important building of the 20th Century?

• What are your views on the combining of modern and historical architecture?

• What are the social implications of architecture?

The course provides a wide-ranging education in the principles of architectural design and its theoretical background. It is one of the few subjects that combines the intellectual challenge of a Cambridge Tripos with the opportunity for creative design. All applicants are expected to show a **portfolio of recent work** at interview but this needn't be of an architectural nature. Some colleges set their own **admissions test or preparatory studies**. Mathematics, Physics or Art A levels are preferred, but no specific subjects are required.

❝ The course is a great mix of science and design. I liked having the flexibility to study many sub-topics alongside the design, and I found the studio projects challenging and exciting. ❞

Chloe, Architecture graduate

Interested? Why don't you explore. . .

Invisible Cities by Italo Calvino – a beautiful novel of 'city description'.

Towards a New Architecture by Le Corbusier – a classic modernist architectural text.

The Timeless Way of Building by Christopher Alexander – proposes a new theory of architecture that relies on the understanding of design patterns.

Not the course for you? Take a look at the **Engineering** and **History of Art** courses at Oxford and Cambridge, or **Materials Science** or **Fine Art** at Oxford.

Asian & Middle Eastern Studies

Four years (with the third year spent abroad)

Past interview questions to get you thinking:

• How would life in the Gulf be transformed if its oil supplies ran out?
• What are the advantages of studying a foreign culture from an outsider's perspective?
• Why did the Cultural Revolution not happen in England?

Asian & Middle Eastern Studies is not only a language course. It also covers history, philosophy, literature and current affairs, and the course works towards a complete understanding of Asian culture and tradition. You can choose to study Arabic, Chinese, Hebrew, Japanese or Persian. All Asian and Middle Eastern languages are taught from scratch, so no specific subjects are required but a modern or ancient language A level is desirable. Most colleges will require you to **submit written work**, and some will set an **admissions test** to be sat at interview.

❝ The sense of achievement you get from studying a completely new language and culture from scratch certainly makes the course worthwhile. ❞

Andrew, Asian & Middle Eastern Studies graduate

Interested? Why don't you explore. . .

The Rise of Civilization in East Asia by Gina L. Barnes – charts the development of China, Korea and Japan.

Wild Swans: Three Daughters of China by Jung Chang – a compelling account of three generations of women living in 20th century China.

A History of the Arab Peoples by Albert Hourani – a comprehensive history covering Arab culture, society and politics.

Not the course for you? Check out **MML (Modern & Medieval Languages)** at Cambridge or **Modern Languages** or **Oriental Studies** at Oxford.

Classics

Three years (four if you don't already have Latin or Greek A level)

Past interview questions to get you thinking:

• How civilised was the Roman world?
• Are history and myth compatible?
• Is the ending of the *Iliad* useful?

The course encompasses the study of the literature, history, culture, philosophy and language of the classical world. Less traditional than the Oxford course, Classics at Cambridge gives you the opportunity to explore a rich and expansive volume of Latin and Greek texts. For the three-year course, a Latin A level is essential. However, if you haven't studied a classical language before, you can opt for the four-year degree. Most colleges will require you to **submit written work**, and some will set an **admissions test**.

❝ Very few courses offer you the opportunity to study two languages to a very high standard whilst also studying the history and culture of the people whose language you are learning. ❞

May, Classics graduate

Interested? Why don't you explore. . .

The Iliad – Homer's works are the bedrock of all Classical literature.

Classics: A Very Short Introduction by Mary Beard & John Henderson – this is an excellent book for understanding the breadth of Classics.

The Latin Love Poets from Catullus to Horace by R.O.A.M. Lyne – surveys the poetry of the major Latin practitioners.

Not the course for you? Try **Classics** at Oxford, **ASNaC (Anglo-Saxon, Norse & Celtic)** at Cambridge or **CAAH (Classical Archaology & Ancient History)** at Oxford.

Computer Science
Three years, with an optional fourth year

Past interview questions to get you thinking:

- What is the fundamental difference between a spreadsheet and a database?
- What factors contribute to the accuracy of the Global Positioning System (GPS)?
- How would you ensure security between two people, A and B?

The course is partly mixed with other sciences, making it very flexible, with a wide range of project and practical work. Cambridge was the first university to offer a Computer Science course, and the world's first fully programmable computer, EDSAC, was built there. **A level Mathematics** is essential, and Further Mathematics is highly desirable. The **TSA Cambridge** is required by most colleges, while others may set their own **admissions test** at interview.

❝ I enjoyed mastering something that is so fundamental, but which few people really take the time to investigate. **❞**

Alexandra, Computer Science graduate

Interested? Why don't you explore. . .

The Mythical Man-Month by Fred Brooks – this book is focused on quite a bit in first year lectures.

The Emperor's New Mind by Roger Penrose – this book uses the physics of computing to explore the concept of artificial intelligence.

Computer Science: A Modern Introduction by Les Goldschlager & Andrew Lister – an introductory overview.

Not the course for you? Try **Computer Science** at Oxford, or **Mathematics** or **Engineering** at Oxford or Cambridge.

Economics
Three years

Past interview questions to get you thinking:
- What is the point of privatisation?
- Why is climate change Economics and not Chemistry?
- Compare Keynesian and classical macroeconomics.

The course will give you a solid understanding of the core features of Economics, both pure and applied, with compulsory micro- and macroeconomics papers. It also allows considerable breadth, giving you the opportunity to consider topics from an inter-disciplinary perspective, taking in history, sociology, maths, statistics and philosophy. **A level Mathematics** is essential, and Economics and Further Maths are desirable. Some colleges will ask you to **submit written work**, some will require you to sit the **TSA Cambridge and/or STEP**, and others will ask you to complete a **preparatory study** at interview.

❝ The course offers a lot of variety, which enabled me to focus on the specific aspects of Economics that most interested me. ❞

Rebecca, Economics graduate

Interested? Why don't you explore. . .
Black Swan by Nassim Nicholas Taleb – a very good book on the current, flawed economic system.

The Ascent of Money by Niall Ferguson – an accessible history of money, banking and credit systems.

Too Big to Fail: Inside the Battle to Save Wall Street by Andrew Ross Sorkin – widely regarded as the definitive history of the banking crisis.

Not the course for you? Try **Land Economy, History** or **Mathematics** at Cambridge or **PPE (Philosophy, Politics & Economics)** or **E&M (Economics & Management)** at Oxford.

Education
Three years

Past interview questions to get you thinking:
- What are the current issues facing educational practitioners today?
- What makes a good teacher?
- What should be the government's involvement in education?

The course aims to provide an understanding of education through its four foundation disciplines: history, philosophy, psychology and sociology. Cambridge's unique approach allows you to combine the academic study of education with another subject, effectively offering you a joint honours degree, and you must have an **A level in your chosen area** of specialism. Some colleges will require you to **submit written work**, and some will set an **admissions test or preparatory study** at interview.

❝ The course provides an excellent basis not only for teaching, but also for further academic study. ❞
Debra, Education Studies graduate

Interested? Why don't you explore. . .
Fifty Modern Thinkers on Education ed. by Joy Palmer – accessible summaries of great educators and their impact and influence.
Philosophy of Education: The Key Concepts by John Gingell & Christopher Winch – a good reference book.
How Children Think and Learn by David Wood – an important study in developmental psychology.

Not the course for you? Check out the specialist subjects **(Biological Sciences, Classics, English, Geography, History, Mathematical Sciences, Modern Languages, Music** or **Theology)** on their own at either Oxford or Cambridge.

Engineering
Four years

Past interview questions to get you thinking:
- Explain one of the following to someone with no knowledge of Physics: force, momentum, power.
- Sketch a velocity time graph for a skydiver jumping out of a plane.
- Why does a bullet spiral?

Year one provides a broad education in Engineering and furnishes you with the necessary analytical, design and computing skills to take on your specialisation in Part II. You're required to complete eight weeks of industrial experience by the end of your third year. **A level Mathematics** and **Physics** are essential. Further Mathematics is strongly encouraged. Most colleges will ask you to sit the **TSA Cambridge and/or STEP**, some will ask you to sit a different test at interview, while others make an assessment on interview alone.

❝ The practical side of the course gives a real-life understanding of what you learn. I loved being able to explain the results that were generated through theory in lab sessions. **❞**

Charlie, Engineering graduate

Interested? Why don't you explore. . .
Mathematical Methods for Science Students by George Stephenson – this is the main set text for the course.

Cats' Paws and Catapults by Steven Vogel – an introduction to biomechanics.

The New Science of Strong Materials: Or Why You Don't Fall Through the Floor by J. E. Gordon – explores the general properties of all materials.

Not the course for you? Try **Natural Sciences (Physical)** or **Mathematics** at Cambridge, or **Engineering**, **Materials Science** or **Physics** at Oxford.

English
Three years

Past interview questions to get you thinking:

- Why do you think English is important?
- When reading a novel or poem, how important is its historical context?
- Can a play just be read, or must it be seen on stage to be understood?

First and second year papers are broad in their scope and you can generally choose what you want to study within a given period, with the option to study a European language and its literature. The backbone of the course is Practical Criticism, which is the close analysis of unseen texts. You can be quite creative with this, and will usually be asked to discuss an unseen passage at interview. Writing style is incredibly important, which is why most colleges will ask you to **submit written work** before coming up to interview, and nearly all colleges will set a **written test**. An **English A level** is required.

66 English is such a discursive subject, so it really helps having intelligent people around who challenge your ideas and force you to think more deeply and creatively. *99*

Claudia, English graduate

Interested? Why don't you explore. . .

The Wheel of Fire by G. Wilson Knight – classic critical essays on Shakespeare's tragedies which will stand you in good stead for the compulsory Shakespeare paper.

The Poetry Handbook by John Lennard – this will arm you with the necessary vocabulary to approach unseen texts.

Literary Theory: An Introduction by Terry Eagleton – a good place to start to get you thinking about English as an academic discipline.

Not the course for you? Try **English** at Oxford, **Philosophy** at Cambridge or **Modern Languages**, **History** or **Classics** at Oxford or Cambridge.

Geography
Three years

Past interview questions to get you thinking:
- Is climate change a man-made phenomenon?
- What is the role of maps in a modern-day society?
- Define the term 'globalisation'.

The first year covers topics from globalisation through to environmental economics and historical geography. You will also take the Geographical Skills and Methods paper to equip you with numerical and spatial data analysis skills, survey and fieldwork techniques. There are no specific A level requirements, but you will need strong analytical skills and a good writing style, so most colleges will require you to **submit written work**. Some colleges will also ask you to sit a **preparatory study** at interview.

❝ The Geography course prompted me to question why humans consider our world, society and landscape the way we do. It was a transformative course for me as I began to look at everyday problems more analytically. ❞

Jim, Geography graduate

Interested? Why don't you explore. . .

Human Geography: an Essential Anthology ed. by John Agnew – a vital resource.

Glaciers and Glaciation by Douglas Benn & David Evans – a comprehensive overview of the nature and history of glaciers.

The City in History by Lewis Mumford – this award-winning book traces the origins of the sprawling cities we know today.

Not the course for you? Take a look at **Land Economy**, **Economics** or **Natural Sciences (Physical)** at Cambridge or **Geography** or **PPE (Philosophy, Politics & Economics)** at Oxford.

History
Three years

Past interview questions to get you thinking:

- What is the difference between modern history and modern politics?
- Do you think that all of history is a history of thought?
- Is it a historian's job to look for cycles in history?

History at Cambridge offers the chance to study a hugely diverse range of topics from British Economic History, to Ancient Greece, the History of the USA or even the History of Political Thought. The compulsory Themes and Sources paper allows you to take on a broad theme in comparative history and trace its changes over time (e.g. gender). There are no specific subjects required, although A level History is highly desirable. Most colleges will ask you to **submit written work** and some will set an **admissions test** at interview.

" I loved the freedom to pursue my own interests. I was never told to stick to a certain topic, but always encouraged to go beyond reading lists and go beyond traditional approaches. **"**

Esther, History graduate

Interested? Why don't you explore. . .

A Little History of the World by E.H. Gombrich – a classic piece of historical writing, chronicling human development through the ages.

The Art of War by Sun Tzu – this razor-sharp ancient Chinese treatise gives an interesting insight into military strategy and, on a more fundamental level, how humans make decisions.

Guns, Germs and Steel by Jared Diamond – an engaging book on human history, which takes into account environmental factors in the development of societies.

Not the course for you? Check out **ASNaC (Anglo-Saxon, Norse & Celtic)** or **HSPS (Human, Social & Political Sciences)** at Cambridge, or **Classics** or **History of Art** at Oxford or Cambridge.

History of Art
Three years

Past interview questions to get you thinking:
• How does art reflect its society?
• How would you account for there being such a vast quantity of art based on religious subject matter?
• What do you believe makes something a piece of art?

History of Art is for you if you are interested in studying works of art and understanding them in their historical and social context. The course makes first-hand use of the wealth of resources found in Cambridge; for example the excellent Fitzwilliam Museum, illuminated manuscripts, stained-glass windows as well as the architecture and sculptures by distinguished artists such as Henry Moore. A level requirements aren't specific, but arts and humanities subjects are recommended. Most colleges will ask you to **submit written work** and some will set an **admissions test** at interview.

❝ The course develops your understanding of the world and art. I spent a great deal of my time learning about history and literature, the other two areas that I would have really enjoyed studying. **❞**

Jade, History of Art graduate

Interested? Why don't you explore. . .
The Story of Art by E.H. Gombrich – this gives a very good overview.
Studies in Iconology by Erwin Panofsky – a useful introduction to symbolism and how to read into works of art.
This is Modern Art by Matthew Collings – another good introductory book, this time to the world of contemporary art.

Not the course for you? **History of Art** is also offered at Oxford. You might also wish to consider **Fine Art** at Oxford, or **History** at Oxford or Cambridge.

Human, Social & Political Sciences (HSPS)
Three years

Past interview questions to get you thinking:
- What is class?
- What aspect of the US government is not democratic?
- How is Trafalgar Square a symbol?

This is one of two new courses available since 2012[*], broadly replacing **Politics, Psychology & Sociology** and **Archaeology & Anthropology.** The course is huge in its scope, allowing you to explore a variety of subjects (such as International Relations or Biological Anthropology), before tailoring the course to suit your specialised area of interest in the second and third years. There are no specific A levels required. Most colleges will ask you to **submit written work** and some will set an **admissions test at interview**.

[*] see Psychological & Behavioural Sciences (PBS) on page 40.

❝ My main reason for picking the course was an unwillingness to pin myself down to a narrow topic. The course gave a broad scope for study in a wide range of disciplines. **❞**

Tim, Archaeology & Anthropology graduate

Interested? Why don't you explore. . .

Setting the People Free: The Story of Democracy by John Dunn – traces the Ancient Greek roots of democracy through to the modern age.

Why Humans Have Cultures by Michael Carrithers – a firm foundation for the study of culture, society and history.

The Culture of the New Capitalism by Richard Sennett – looks at the social implications of the new-economy model.

Not the course for you? Take a look at **PPE (Philosophy, Politics & Economics), Archaeology & Anthropology** or **EP (Experimental Psychology)** at Oxford. Or try **Economics, PBS (Psychological & Behavioural Sciences)** or **Philosophy** at Cambridge.

Land Economy
Three years

Past interview questions to get you thinking:
- Why is the USA a country when Europe isn't?
- How do towns grow?
- Why are wages higher in London?

The course is predominantly a mix of Law and Economics, and looks at how these disciplines interact and are applied to the built and natural environment. Less theoretical than an Economics degree, Land Economy gets to grips with solving real-world issues, such as sustainable housing and rural conservation. No particular A levels are required, but Economics, Mathematics and Geography are desirable. Some colleges will require you to **submit written work,** some will require you to sit the **Cambridge TSA** or other **test at interview,** while others make an assessment on interview alone.

❝ The course offers a wide range of paper choices, and there's a lot of freedom to make Land Economy into your own subject. ❞

Henry, Land Economy graduate

Interested? Why don't you explore. . .
Economics by John Sloman – a comprehensive introduction, particularly useful for those without an Economics A level.
Economics: Principles and Policy by William J Baumol & Alan S Blinder – a vital guide to land law and economics.
The World is Flat by Thomas Friedman – examines the influences shaping business in the technological age.

Not the course for you? Take a look at **Geography** or **Economics** at Cambridge or **Geography, E&M (Economics & Management)** or **PPE (Philosophy, Politics & Economics)** at Oxford.

Law
Three years

Past interview questions to get you thinking:
- How do you think the House of Lords should be reformed?
- What do you think is more important, actions or motives?
- Is international law the first step to a single legal system and would it be possible?

Law students are challenged to think in a deeply analytical way, approach problems from a logical position and defend their arguments against criticism. Although you will primarily study English law, there are opportunities to study other legal systems, including EU or international law. Most students haven't studied Law at school and no specific A level subjects are required. Most colleges will ask you to sit the **Cambridge Law Test**, as well as a **preparatory study** at interview, and some will ask you to **submit written work**.

" I enjoyed learning the set rules of law and then exploring the room for interpretation within them. **"**

Cara, Law graduate

Interested? Why don't you explore. . .
The Times Law Supplement – essential reading as it helpfully summarises all the week's legal events and issues.
Learning the Law by Glanville Williams – an accessible introduction to the core basics of law.
Discipline and Punish by Michel Foucault – evaluates the changes in western penal systems in the modern age.

Not the course for you? Take a look at **Land Economy** at Cambridge. **Law (Jurisprudence)** is also available at Oxford, with the option to take **Law with Law Studies in Europe**.

Linguistics
Three years

Past interview questions to get you thinking:

* Discuss the ambiguities in this sentence: 'I bumped into a woman carrying flowers'.
* Do you agree with the Chomskyan theory of a 'universal grammar'?
* How do you think babies learn languages differently to older people?

Linguistics is the systematic study of human language. The course is interdisciplinary, drawing on methods and knowledge from a wide range of subjects, such as Philosophy, Biology and Psychology. No specific A level subjects are required, although a language or English A level does serve as good preparation. Most colleges will ask you to **submit written work**, and a handful will ask you to sit a **test at interview**.

** The study of different accents and dialects is to me the most interesting part of the course. **

Sarah, Modern Languages & Linguistics graduate

Interested? Why don't you explore. . .

The Language Instinct by Steven Pinker – lucidly explains everything you need to know about language learning.

The Articulate Mammal by Jean Aitchison – an excellent introduction to the field of psycholinguistics.

Syntactic Structures by Noam Chomsky – a key text in linguistics, and Chomsky's first published book.

Not the course for you? You might be interested in **English** or **MML (Modern & Medieval Languages)** at Cambridge. Or check out **PPL (Psychology, Philosophy & Linguistics)** or **Modern Languages & Linguistics** at Oxford.

Mathematics
Three years, with an optional fourth year

Past interview questions to get you thinking:

- Is mathematics a language?
- Describe a complex number to a non-mathematician.
- How many ways are there of arranging 'n' objects and why?

In your first year you will choose between two paths: Pure & Applied Mathematics or Mathematics with Physics. Both will teach you the fundamentals of higher mathematics. There is the chance to specialise as you progress, with optional computational projects in your second and third years. You may be invited to complete a fourth year of study if you achieve a first or high II.i. **A level Mathematics and AS level Further Mathematics** are essential. All colleges will require you to sit the **STEP** and some will set an **additional test** at interview.

❝ The thing that I enjoyed most about my course was the challenging aspect, and there is no doubt that the Cambridge Tripos is the most challenging mathematical undergraduate degree in the country. ❞

Tahar, Mathematics graduate

Interested? Why don't you explore. . .

The Mathematical Tourist by Ivars Peterson – a journey through important mathematical concepts, told in accessible language.

Alice in Numberland by J Baylis & R Haggerty – this is recommended by tutors as preparation for the course.

Fermat's Last Theorem by Simon Singh – an interesting read on one of the most notorious mathematical problems.

Not the course for you? Take a look at **Mathematics** at Oxford, which offers several joint school degrees, or **Computer Sciences** or **Engineering** at either university.

Medicine

Three years pre-clinical, followed by a three-year clinical degree

Past interview questions to get you thinking:

• What are the challenges to be faced by the NHS in the near future?

• What would life be like without enzymes?

• What do you know about Parkinson's disease and its treatment?

The course involves a combination of intensive scientific teaching and practical training to equip you with the skills to deal with patients effectively. The pre-clinical years are taught through lectures, practical classes and supervisions, with emphasis shifting during the clinical years, when you will be learning in clinical environments such as hospitals. You will need to have a solid scientific understanding, which is why **A level Chemistry and a further two of the following subjects: Biology/Human Biology, Physics, Mathematics** are required. All applicants are required to sit the **BMAT** and how well you do in this is an important factor in the selection process.

‟ The first three years are essentially an academic biological sciences degree, which gave me a good grounding in pre-clinical concepts. ”

Jules, Medicine graduate

Interested? Why don't you explore. . .

Human Physiology by Gillian Pocock & Christopher Richards – covers most of the major physiological systems in a clinically relevant way.

Principles of Evolutionary Medicine by Peter Gluckman, Alan Beedle & Mark Hanson – a good review of advances in the field of evolutionary biology.

The Man Who Mistook His Wife for a Hat by Oliver Sacks – details the strangest neurological conditions Sacks has treated as a clinical neurologist.

Not the course for you? Check out **Natural Sciences (Biological)** at Cambridge or **Medicine** or **Biomedical Sciences** at Oxford.

MML (Modern & Medieval Languages)
Four years (with the third year spent abroad)

Past interview questions to get you thinking:
• Why do some languages have genders when others don't?
• Can you only understand or analyse a text properly in its original language?
• What is the role of a translator?

You'll study two languages, one of which you can learn from scratch. The course is very literary in its focus, although slightly more balanced with language work in your first year. By the second year you'll be expected to be fluent and the focus is on the culture and literature of your chosen language, with less emphasis on oral skills. You'll get the chance to pick this up again during the compulsory third year abroad. An **A level in at least one of your chosen languages** is essential. Most colleges will ask you to **submit written work** and undertake both a **preparatory study** and **test at interview.**

❝ I got to try so many new things, from language exchanges and foreign film nights, to living and working abroad. ❞

Steph, Modern & Medieval Languages graduate

Interested? Why don't you explore. . .
Through the Language Glass by Guy Deutscher – an extremely readable study of how language influences the way we view the world.
Foreign newspapers, such as *Le Monde, El Pais, Die Welt* – it's a good idea to keep up to date with current affairs in the languages you're applying for. Reading the headline articles of the major newspapers of that language will be helpful and may provide content for discussion at interview.

Not the course for you? You might be interested in **English, Linguistics** or **Classics** at Cambridge. Or take a look at the selection of **Modern Languages** joint school degrees on offer at Oxford.

Music
Three years

Past interview questions to get you thinking:

- Is an awareness of context necessary to appreciate a composer's works?
- Why do you think the jazz tradition branched off from popular music?
- Is music an art incomparable to history in that history cannot be performed?

The Music course is highly regarded amongst academic musicians for the advanced level of training it offers in harmony, counterpoint, fugue and analysis. Although largely academic in its scope, there is now a growing emphasis on performance skills within the Cambridge course, with a recital examination now an option for second and third year students. **A level Music** is essential. Most colleges will ask you to **submit written work** and undertake both a **preparatory study** and **test at interview**.

" The course gave me a broad awareness of chronology, as well as a detailed knowledge of my specific areas of interest. It also provides great training for practical skills. "

Joanna, Music graduate

Interested? Why don't you explore. . .

The Norton Anthology of Western Music by J. Peter Burkholder & Claude V. Palisca – extremely readable and a good starting point.

The Dynamics of Harmony by George Pratt – a short book packed full of information on tonal composition and harmony.

A Guide to Musical Analysis by Nicholas Cook – an important introduction to analytical processes and terminology.

Not the course for you? Try **Music** at Oxford.

Natural Sciences (Biological)
Three years, with an optional fourth year

Past interview questions to get you thinking:
• What evidence is there to suggest that humans are still evolving?
• How could you prove chloroplasts used to be free-living organisms?
• Why is carbon of such importance in living systems?

The course (also known as Biological NatSci) offers a wide range of science subjects for you to choose from. Biological NatSci covers everything concerned with living things: Zoology, Plant Sciences, Molecular Biology, Physiology and Pharmacology, as well as less obvious subjects like Geology or Psychology. The breadth of the course reflects the increasingly multi-disciplinary nature of modern scientific research. **At least two science/mathematics A levels** are essential, and a third is desirable. The **Cambridge TSA** is required by some colleges and is sat at interview. Other colleges may set their own **admissions test**.

66 Few universities offer the breadth and depth of the Natural Sciences course. It was an added bonus that we only specialised in our third and fourth year, allowing us the first two years to figure out what area of science was our passion. **99**

Henry, Natural Sciences (Biological) graduate

Interested? Why don't you explore. . .
The Greatest Show on Earth: The Evidence for Evolution by Richard Dawkins – a popular and controversial read, which should help you to form your own opinions on evolution.
How Animals Work by Knut Schmidt Nielson – a good analysis which will help you to grasp comparative physiology.
The Diversity of Life by Edward O. Wilson – a great overview of biodiversity.

Not the course for you? You might be interested in **Biomedical** or **Biological Sciences**, **Biochemistry** or **EP (Experimental Psychology)** at Oxford.

Natural Sciences (Physical)
Three years, with an optional fourth year

Past interview questions to get you thinking:

• Explain Schrödinger's cat.

• How does sound come from a flute?

• What is the photoelectric effect?

Physical NatSci includes modules in Physics, Chemistry, Earth Sciences and Materials Science. There is more practical focus in the second and third year, with significantly more lab work. If the option of combining several different scientific disciplines appeals to you, then this is a great course choice, as it is much more varied and multidisciplinary than a combined honours degree at another university. This is why **at least two science/mathematics A levels** are essential, and a third is desirable. The **Cambridge TSA** is required by some colleges and is sat at interview. Other colleges may set their own **admissions test**.

❝ I loved being able to discuss science across the board with friends, from chatting about semiconductors with engineers to discussing primate behaviour with anthropologists. ❞

Matthew, Natural Sciences (Physical) graduate

Interested? Why don't you explore. . .

Warped Passages: Unravelling the Universe's Hidden Dimensions by Lisa Randall – an accessible read on theoretical physics.

A Brief History of Time by Stephen Hawking & Leonard Mlodinow – this gives a good overview of physical cosmology, whilst explaining some difficult maths.

Why Chemical Reactions Happen by James Keeler & Peter Wothers – a good overview of chemical processes, to help you think like a chemist.

Not the course for you? Take a look at the many science courses available at Oxford, such as **Physics**, **Chemistry**, **Materials Science** or **Engineering Science**.

Philosophy
Three years

Past interview questions to get you thinking:
* Is happiness a basis for morality?
* How would you define consciousness?
* Give an example of an argument with false premises but a true conclusion.

In your first year, you'll acquire the reasoning skills to enable you to tackle general philosophical problems, such as the nature of reality and the basis of knowledge. There is also a compulsory logic paper. The main emphasis of the current undergraduate course continues in the analytic tradition of previous Cambridge philosophers, Bertrand Russell and Ludwig Wittgenstein. No particular subjects are required at A level, however, a combination of arts and science subjects is considered useful. All colleges will set a **test at interview,** and some will require you to **submit written work.**

" The Cambridge Philosophy Tripos was an excellent choice for me, largely because it's so intense that you manage to learn an extraordinary amount of philosophy over the course of three years. **"**
Jamie, Philosophy graduate

Interested? Why don't you explore. . .
Ethics and the Limits of Philosophy by Bernard Williams – a must read for those interested in broadening their understanding of moral philosophy.
Meditations by Descartes – Descartes is hugely influential, and easy to read.
Practical Ethics by Peter Singer – an excellent and accessible introduction to the field of applied ethics.

Not the course for you? Take a look at the many joint school Philosophy degrees on offer, or **PPE (Philosophy, Politics & Economics)** at Oxford. You might also like to consider **Theology** at either university.

PBS (Psychological & Behavioural Sciences)
Three years

Past interview questions to get you thinking:
• Do you know why we have two eyes and two ears?
• What do you believe is the best parenting strategy?
• Design an experiment to test the effect of cortisol on healing time.

Introduced in 2012, PBS offers a broad degree covering all aspects of psychology, from social relations to neurological processes. There are two compulsory papers in your first year, which will give you a solid grounding in psychology and psychological research methods. From here you will be able to choose which direction you want to go in, and how much lab and project work you would like to do. No specific A levels are required, but Mathematics, science and humanities subjects are considered useful. Most colleges will ask you to **submit written work** and some will set a **test at interview.** some colleges may ask you to sit the **TSA Cambridge**.

Interested? Why don't you explore. . .

Psychology: The Science of Mind and Behaviour by Richard Gross – a key reference book which covers all the main areas of psychology across 50 chapters.

Developmental Social Psychology by Kevin Durkin – provides a good introduction to the subject and the themes and topics that will come up in lectures.

The Language Instinct by Steven Pinker – lucidly explains everything you need to know about language learning.

Not the course for you? Try **EP (Experimental Psychology)** or **PPL (Psychology, Philosophy & Linguistics)** at Oxford.

Theology & Religious Studies
Three years

Past interview questions to get you thinking:

• How would you define faith?
• Would having a personal faith help or hinder the study of Theology?
• What did Kant say about proving God's existence?

As well as covering a broad range of religions, you will have the opportunity to consider how religious convictions have been expressed through time, drawing on cultural, historical and philosophical sources. The course offers you the chance to branch out at an early stage. One of the four scriptural languages (Greek, Hebrew, Sanskrit or Arabic) must be studied in the first year, though no prior knowledge is required. No specific A levels are required, but English, Religious Studies, History or languages are considered useful. Most colleges will ask you to **submit written work**, and some will set a **preparatory study** at interview.

66 Theology at Cambridge is taught as an inter-disciplinary and dynamic subject within the modern world. **99**

Misbah, Theology graduate

Interested? Why don't you explore. . .

The Puzzle of Evil and *The Puzzle of God* by Peter Vardy – these books offer an interesting and accessible introduction to theology and philosophy.

Christian Theology: An Introduction by Alister McGrath – an introduction to important theological concepts.

Genealogy of Morality by Friedrich Nietzsche – a key text on ethics.

Not the course for you? Take a look at **Philosophy, History, English** or **Classics** at Cambridge. **Theology** is also available at Oxford.

Veterinary Medicine
Six years

Past interview questions to get you thinking:
- How are diseases able to spread between species?
- Why do 80% of racehorses have stomach ulcers?
- Explain the oxygen dissociation curve.

During the three year pre-clinical course you will undertake a thorough scientific programme of study, with the option to pursue an interest in a specialised topic in your third year, from Pathology to Philosophy. This opportunity is unique to the Cambridge vet school. You will need to have a solid scientific understanding, which is why **Chemistry to at least AS level** and a further **two of the following subjects: Biology/Human Biology, Physics, Mathematics** are required. All applicants are required to sit the **BMAT** and how well you do in this is an important factor in the selection process.

❝ I liked that we were thoroughly schooled in the fundamentals before we were let loose on the clinical course. **❞**

Freya, Veterinary Medicine graduate

Interested? Why don't you explore. . .
The Textbook of Veterinary Anatomy by Dyce, Sack and Wensing – this is known as 'the Vets' Bible' and it's a vital read.

Getting into Veterinary School by John Handley – useful guide which includes application tips and interview advice.

Veterinary Ethics: An Introduction by Giles Legood – this book will help you to frame opinions on ethical issues.

Not the course for you? You might like to consider **Natural Sciences (Biological)** at Cambridge, **Biomedical Sciences** at Oxford, or **Medicine** at either Oxford or Cambridge.

Archaeology & Anthropology
Three years

Past interview questions to get you thinking:
- Some people say that in 100 or 200 years we will have one global culture. What do you think about this?
- What is the point of archaeology?
- How would you define 'ritual'?

Commonly referred to as Arch & Anth, the course will give you a broad overview of past and contemporary human societies. This is through social, biological and material perspectives, covering almost every aspect of human behaviour. No specific A level subjects are required, although a combination of arts and sciences is useful. You will be asked to **submit two pieces of written work**, plus a **300-word statement** on the relationship between archaeology, social and cultural anthropology, and biological anthropology, so that the admissions tutors can assess your understanding of, and passion for, the subject.

❝ The course has the perfect combination of science (biological anthropology) and social science (social and cultural anthropology) for me. **❞**

Tom, Archaeology & Anthropology graduate

Interested? Why don't you explore. . .

The Origin of Species by Charles Darwin – this text is central to evolutionary biology.

The Selfish Gene by Richard Dawkins – an excellent complementary text for *The Origin of Species*, to get you up to speed with a more modern look at evolution.

Orientalism by Edward Said – this classic text about definition through opposition sets up some of the major themes of anthropology.

Not the course for you? Check out **CAAH (Classical Archaeology & Ancient History)** or **Human Sciences** at Oxford. You might also like to consider **HSPS (Human, Social & Political Sciences)** at Cambridge.

Biochemistry (Molecular & Cellular)
Four years

Past interview questions to get you thinking:
- When does science become technology?
- What is the significance of the human genome project?
- Why are there only twenty amino acids?

Biochemistry is the study of living things at a molecular level. The course involves a lot of essay writing in a way that other science degrees such as Physics or Chemistry do not, in addition to many practical requirements. An important aspect of the Oxford Biochemistry course is its fourth-year project, (lasting 18 weeks full time), which allows you to explore both laboratory-based research and specific recent advances in biochemistry in detail. **A level Chemistry, with another science or Mathematics**, is essential.

❝ I enjoyed the fact that Biochemistry is such a fast-moving subject with so many advances being made all the time. ❞

Padma, Biochemistry graduate

Interested? Why don't you explore. . .
Genome by Matt Ridley – will give you short introductions to various areas of genetics and evolution.

Foundations of Organic Chemistry by Michael Hornby & Josephine Peach – a short book, which covers some important concepts really well.

Power, Sex, Suicide: Mitochondria and the Meaning of Life by Nick Lane – a very interesting read on the subject of cell biology.

Not the course for you? Check out **Biological Sciences, Biomedical Sciences, Chemistry** or **Human Sciences** at Oxford. You might also want to take a look at the **Natural Sciences (Biological)** course at Cambridge.

Biological Sciences
Three years

Past interview questions to get you thinking:
- What are the arguments for preserving biodiversity?
- How does the immune system recognise invading pathogens as foreign cells?
- Discuss ways in which plants are adapted to dry conditions.

Biological Sciences is a rapidly developing subject area. It is an immensely diverse subject, and you will be studying cutting edge topics from evolutionary biology to molecular genetics. There is a lot of essay writing required, but the main emphasis is on practical laboratory work, preparing you for your third-year research project. There is the option to carry out your project in the field, either in the UK or in the tropics. **A level Biology** is essential and another science or Mathematics is considered helpful.

❝The course is very well designed – it allows you to get a solid foundation in the first year, start specialising in the second year and then really immerse yourself in your chosen specialisations in the third year. ❞

Sally, Biological Sciences graduate

Interested? Why don't you explore. . .

The Single Helix by Steve Jones – a witty and engaging writer, this is a collection of his essays on popular science.

The Secret Life of Trees by Colin Tudge – everything you need to know about trees, covering botany, reproductive techniques and their historical importance.

The Beak of the Finch by Jonathan Weiner – an account of a 20-year study of Darwin's finches in the Galapagos, which shows how we can watch evolution happen in real-time.

Not the course for you? Try **Biochemistry** or **Biomedical Sciences** at Oxford. Alternatively, take a look at the **Natural Sciences (Biological)** course on offer at Cambridge.

Biomedical Sciences
Three years

Past interview questions to get you thinking:
- Why is the heart on the left-hand side of the body?
- Why is Physics less relevant to Biomedical Sciences than Chemistry?
- How does immunisation work?

The smallest (in terms of intake) of the three Biology courses on offer at Oxford, Biomedical Sciences is for you if you're fascinated by the human body and how it works. Understanding how cells, organs and systems function within the human body promotes your understanding of human diseases, and you will be studying a range of areas from molecular biology to neurophysiology. The course enables you to study human biology from a medical perspective, without having to commit to a medical career. **Two of the following A levels are essential: Biology, Chemistry, Physics** or **Mathematics**, and all colleges will require you to sit the **BMAT**.

❝ I considered Experimental Psychology before deciding on Biomedical Sciences – I chose the latter because it enables the in-depth study of more than one organ! **❞**

Rena, Biomedical Sciences graduate

Interested? Why don't you explore. . .

Biomedicine and the Human Condition by Michael G. Sargent – traces developments in biomedicine, and how they have improved human life.

Incognito by David Eagleman – an engaging popular science book, which explores the unconscious workings of the mind.

The Man Who Mistook His Wife for a Hat by Oliver Sacks – details the strangest neurological conditions Sacks has treated as a clinical neurologist.

Not the course for you? Check out **Medicine** at either university. Or take a look at **Biochemistry, Biological Sciences** or **Experimental Psychology** at Oxford. You may also be interested in **Natural Sciences (Biological)** at Cambridge.

Chemistry
Four years

Past interview questions to get you thinking:

- What happens to the mobility of Group 1 elements going down the periodic table?
- What makes some chemicals explosive?
- How does a glow stick work?

The focus of the first year is on three core areas of Chemistry: Organic, Inorganic and Physical. If you have a scientific approach, and Chemistry is your favourite subject, this course is ideal, with far less emphasis on essay writing than Biochemistry. What makes this course unique is the inclusion of a compulsory fourth year, entirely dedicated to original research, which will enable you to develop your critical awareness of developments in the field and your ability to carry out independent research. **A levels in both Chemistry** and **Mathematics** are essential. Another science or Further Mathematics is considered helpful.

" The course enabled me to develop my analytical skills and to continue with the mathematical concepts of science. **"**

Clemmie, Chemistry graduate

Interested? Why don't you explore. . .

Chemistry Review – this quarterly review, edited by academics at the University of York, is a great resource covering A level topics and beyond.

Foundations of Organic Chemistry by Michael Hornby & Josephine Peach – a short book, which covers important concepts clearly.

The Periodic Table: A Very Short Introduction by Eric R. Scerri – an engaging history of the evolution of the periodic table.

Not the course for you? Check out **Biochemistry**, **Biomedical Sciences**, **Earth Sciences (Geology)** or **Materials Science.** You might also like to consider the **Natural Sciences** courses on offer at Cambridge.

CAAH (Classical Archaeology & Ancient History)
Three years

Past interview questions to get you thinking:
• Why do you think ancient history is important?
• When would you start a book about the history of England?
• What are the advantages and disadvantages of removing artefacts?

The course looks at the societies and cultures of the Ancient World, centred on Greece and Rome, through their written texts, visual art and material remains. Although it is primarily a historical and non-linguistic degree, there is the chance to study ancient languages as part of the course. Designed to give an integrated, interdisciplinary approach to the topics studied, this combination is unique to Oxford. No specific A levels are required, but a classical language, Classical Civilisation or Ancient History can be helpful. You will be asked to **submit written work**.

❝ My favourite module was the museum or site report, which gives you complete freedom to choose the topic you research. ❞

Harry, CAAH (Classical Archaeology & Ancient History) graduate

Interested? Why don't you explore. . .
Love, Sex and Tragedy; How the Ancient World Shapes Our Lives by Simon Goldhill – very readable, with good ideas on why the classical era is relevant today.
The Roman World by Martin Goodman – an illuminating view of the Roman world and its people.
The Archaeology of Ancient Greece by James Whitley – a thoroughly researched overview of Ancient Greece.

Not the course for you? Take a look at **Archaeology & Anthropology** at Oxford or **Classics** and its joint honours or **History** and its joint honours.

Classics
Four years

Past interview questions to get you thinking:

• What were Plato's and Aristotle's views of women?
• Did the Romans or the Greeks leave a more notable impression on the culture of today?
• What are the gods' main roles in the *Iliad*?

Classics is a varied and interdisciplinary subject, enabling you the opportunity to study the literature, philosophy, linguistics, history and archaeology of ancient Greek and Roman civilisations. You will also develop a good reading knowledge of Latin and Greek. In order to fit in such a broad range of study, the Oxford Classics course lasts four years, and is split into two. If you have studied Ancient Greek or Latin, you are admitted into Course I. However, if you will be studying these languages from scratch, you should apply for Course II. You will be asked to **submit written work**, and you will be required to sit the **Classics Admissions Test**.

❝ I loved the challenge of deciphering ancient texts, in particular Greek comedy. ❞

Jack, Classics graduate

Interested? Why don't you explore. . .

The Iliad – Homer's works are the bedrock of all Classical literature.

Classics: A Very Short Introduction by Mary Beard & John Henderson – this is an excellent book for understanding the breadth of Classics.

The Latin Love Poets from Catullus to Horace by R.O.A.M. Lyne – surveys the poetry of the major Latin practitioners.

Not the course for you? Take a look at **Archaeology & Anthropology**, at Oxford or **Classics**, **History** or **Philosophy** and their joint honours. **Classics** is also offered at Cambridge.

Classics & English
Three years (four if you don't have Latin or Greek A level)

Past interview questions to get you thinking:

• What role did the chorus have in Greek plays and how well do they translate into a modern context?

• Is it fair that Ted Hughes won a literary prize for a translation of an Ovid poem?

• What is tragedy?

Classics & English is as much a degree in comparative literature as it is a joint honours degree and the course is unique in this approach. English may be taken with Latin or Greek or both. If you already have Latin or Greek A level, this is a three-year course (Course I). If you do not have either language, you can take Course II, which involves a preliminary year learning either Latin or Greek, with some study of classical literature. An **English A level** is essential. You will be asked to **submit written work**, and you will sit two tests: both the **ELAT** and the **CAT.**

❝ I loved the variety of being able to switch between different disciplines, including translation, commentary, research and essay writing. ❞

Mike, Classics & English graduate

Interested? Why don't you explore. . .

I, Claudius by Robert Graves – a modern novel written in the form of Claudius' biography.

The Classical World: An Epic History from Homer to Hadrian by Robin Lane Fox – an excellent overview of the classical era.

The Bible – so much of English literature draws on ideas and language from the Bible. Dip into sections, e.g. Revelations, Job, the Gospel, Genesis, and Exodus.

Not the course for you? Try **Classics** or **English** at Oxford or Cambridge. Alternatively, you might be interested in **ASNaC (Anglo-Saxon, Norse & Celtic)** at Cambridge.

Classics & Modern Languages

Four years (five if you don't have Latin or Greek A level. The third year is spent abroad in both cases)

Past interview questions to get you thinking:

- How does the literature you have read affect your opinion of that society?
- What is the difference between historical books and books written in the past?
- Can you think of examples in poetry or in literature where tone or meaning has been lost in translation?

The Classics & Modern Languages course provides the opportunity to study one language (Celtic, Czech (with Slovak), French, German, Modern Greek, Italian, Portuguese, Russian or Spanish), along with Latin and/or Ancient Greek. The main focus of both parts of the course is on literature and language, and as you progress you will get the opportunity to study linguistics and ancient history as well. You may need an **A level in your chosen language**, depending on which language you choose. You will be asked to **submit written work**, and will have to sit both the **CAT** and the **MLAT**.

❝ The joy of the course is the opportunity it affords to study a diverse range of subjects in one degree. ❞

Amy, Classics & Modern Languages graduate

Interested? Why don't you explore. . .

Classics: A Very Short Introduction by Mary Beard & John Henderson – this is an excellent book for understanding the breadth of Classics.

Greek Tragedy by Albin Lesky – a masterful overview of tragic theatre in Greece.

Through the Language Glass by Guy Deutscher – an extremely readable study of how language influences the way we view the world.

Not the course for you? Try **Classics** and **Modern Languages** on their own, or **Classics & Oriental Studies**. You may also be interested in **MML (Modern & Medieval Languages)** or **Classics** at Cambridge.

Classics & Oriental Studies

Four years (three if you opt out of spending the third year abroad and Oriental Studies is your main subject)

Past interview questions to get you thinking:

• What links can be drawn between ancient Egyptian and other ancient languages?

• What underlying cultural differences separate Japan from the West?

• If Bach is conducted by an Arab person, is it Western or Eastern music?

This course allows you to combine the study of an Oriental language and culture with Latin or Greek and the study of the ancient world. There are two options: Classics with Oriental Studies and Oriental Studies with Classics. In each case the first subject becomes the main focus, comprising approximately two thirds of the degree and the second subject forms the remaining third. You will be required to **submit written work** and to sit the **CAT**. Some candidates must also sit the **OLAT**, depending on which subject you decide to focus on. Latin and/or Greek at A level are also highly recommended.

66 Studying Classics with Oriental Studies allowed me to focus on the aspects of each course I enjoyed. **99**

Olivia, Classics & Oriental Studies graduate

Interested? Why don't you explore. . .

Orientalism by Edward Said – this classic text explores the concept of definition through opposition.

The Location of Culture by Honi Bhabha – a difficult but interesting study in culture and national identity.

The Ancient Orient by Wolfram von Soden – a comprehensive presentation of ancient Near Eastern civilization.

Not the course for you? Check out both **Classics** and **Oriental Studies** on their own, or **Classics** and its other joint honours. You might also like to consider **Asian & Middle Eastern Studies** or **Classics** at Cambridge.

ing Science

ew questions to get you thinking:

a pendulum work, bearing in mind that the amplitude of
tions increases over time rather than decreases?

cceleration against velocity graph to describe the motion
are in a lift.

a bullet spiral?

Science encompasses a vast range of subjects, from
nics to offshore oil platforms, which will give you a solid
oundation. In the third and fourth years you can specialise
x branches of engineering: Biomedical, Chemical, Civil,
formation and Mechanical. In the fourth year you will
major research project in the field of your choice and at
is broad-based four-year course, you will graduate with a
ster of Engineering. **A level Mathematics and Physics**
and you will be required to sit the **PAT**.

e way lectures complemented the laboratory work. There
of opportunities to apply what you had learned to practical

Thakoon, Engineering Science graduate

Why don't you explore. . .

Design: How Engineers Get from Thought to Thing by Henry
oks at the engineering design processes behind objects,
buildings.

Catapults by Steven Vogel – an introduction to biomechanics.

nce of Strong Materials: Or Why You Don't Fall Through the
Gordon – explores the general properties of all materials.

se for you? You might be interested in **Engineering** at
Materials Science or **Physics** at Oxford.

56

Computer Science
Three years, with an optional fourth year

Past interview questions to get you thinking:

- Tell me about binary searches and their efficiency.
- What are the possible ways of making a secure transfer?
- What is the fundamental difference between a spreadsheet and a database?

Computers are among the most complex products created by humans; Computer Science is about understanding their programs, networks and systems. The course, largely theoretical in its approach, will develop your understanding of the underlying principles of programming. Oxford offers two courses in Computer Science: a 3-year BA degree and a 4-year Masters degree, though there is no distinction between them on applying. **A level Mathematics** is required, and Further Mathematics or a science is recommended. You will also be required to sit the **MAT**.

❝ The Computer Science course at Oxford is highly regarded in the industry that I have gone on to work in. **❞**

Jenny, Computer Science graduate

Interested? Why don't you explore. . .

An Introduction to Algorithms by Thomas H. Cormen et al. – this is quite tricky, but getting your head around the content is likely to impress.

The Emperor's New Mind by Roger Penrose – this book uses the physics of computing to explore the concept of artificial intelligence.

Computer Science: A Modern Introduction by Les Goldschlager & Andrew Lister – an introductory overview.

Not the course for you? Take a look at the **Computer Science & Philosophy** course on the Oxford website (introduced for 2013 entry). Alternatively, try **Computer Science** at Cambridge, or **Mathematics** or **Engineering** at either university.

53

Earth Sciences (Geology)
Three years, with an optional fourth year

Past interview questions to get you thinking:
- How would you go about calculating the total amount of energy reaching the Earth's surface?
- How does the age of ice change as you walk up a glacier?
- List a number of different possible methods for dating a rock specimen.

This course offers a multidisciplinary approach to the study of the Earth, embracing an enormous range of topics, including: the evolution of life; the nature of planetary interiors; Earth-surface processes; and the origin and behaviour of oceans and atmosphere. The emphasis of the course is on understanding the underlying physical principles of geological processes. Oxford offers two courses: a BA in Geology and an MEarthSc in Earth Sciences, which are exactly the same for the first three years. You can then choose to continue with the four-year Earth Sciences course or leave with a BA in Geology. **A level Mathematics** as well as either **Physics** or **Chemistry** are essential.

❝ I enjoyed applying the theory to the real environment, and seeing in front of me, either out in the field or in the lab, things that I had learnt in lectures. **❞**

Robert, Earth Sciences (Geology) graduate

Interested? Why don't you explore. . .

Earth: Evolution of a Habitable World by Jonathan I. Lunine – an outstanding history of the evolution of Earth.

Igneous Petrology by Anthony Hall – comprehensive treatment of all aspects of igneous rocks.

Global Geomorphology by Michael Summerfield – an in-depth study into surface processes and landforms.

Not the course for you? You might also like to consider **Geography, Human Sciences, Materials Science** or **Physics**. Or try **Natural Sciences (Physical)** at Cambridge.

E&M (Economics & Manaς
Three years

Past interview questions to get y
- Are large or small companies mc
- What are the arguments for and
- Should a Walmart store be open

The highly competitive E&M
the world we live in: namely h
turn, how organisations function
broader understanding of the ec
all organisations operate; manager
frameworks of those organisatio
E&M is that it combines academ
Mathematics A level is essentia
TSA Oxford.

❝ I enjoyed the fact that as one of
relevant for the world in which we

Jac

Interested? Why don't you exp

Scale and Scope: The Dynamics of In
– a thorough analysis of the orig

Rise of the Corporate Economy by L
in the formulation of the moder

The Ascent of Money by Niall Fer:
giving great insights into the bir

Not the course for you? Take a lo
an option to take **Management**
also like to consider **History 8**
Politics & Economics) at Ox

Enginee
Four years

Past interv
- How does
  the oscilla
- Draw an a
  when you
- Why does

Engineering
microelectro
theoretical f
in one of si
Electrical, In
undertake a
the end of th
degree of M
are essential,

❝ I loved th
were plenty
scenarios. **❞**

Interested?

Invention by
Petroski – lo
machines and
Cats' Paws and
The New Scie
Floor by J. E.

Not the cour
Cambridge, N

Computer Science
Three years, with an optional fourth year

Past interview questions to get you thinking:
* Tell me about binary searches and their efficiency.
* What are the possible ways of making a secure transfer?
* What is the fundamental difference between a spreadsheet and a database?

Computers are among the most complex products created by humans; Computer Science is about understanding their programs, networks and systems. The course, largely theoretical in its approach, will develop your understanding of the underlying principles of programming. Oxford offers two courses in Computer Science: a 3-year BA degree and a 4-year Masters degree, though there is no distinction between them on applying. **A level Mathematics** is required, and Further Mathematics or a science is recommended. You will also be required to sit the **MAT**.

❝ The Computer Science course at Oxford is highly regarded in the industry that I have gone on to work in. **❞**

Jenny, Computer Science graduate

Interested? Why don't you explore. . .

An Introduction to Algorithms by Thomas H. Cormen et al. – this is quite tricky, but getting your head around the content is likely to impress.

The Emperor's New Mind by Roger Penrose – this book uses the physics of computing to explore the concept of artificial intelligence.

Computer Science: A Modern Introduction by Les Goldschlager & Andrew Lister – an introductory overview.

Not the course for you? Take a look at the **Computer Science & Philosophy** course on the Oxford website (introduced for 2013 entry). Alternatively, try **Computer Science** at Cambridge, or **Mathematics** or **Engineering** at either university.

Earth Sciences (Geology)
Three years, with an optional fourth year

Past interview questions to get you thinking:

- How would you go about calculating the total amount of energy reaching the Earth's surface?
- How does the age of ice change as you walk up a glacier?
- List a number of different possible methods for dating a rock specimen.

This course offers a multidisciplinary approach to the study of the Earth, embracing an enormous range of topics, including: the evolution of life; the nature of planetary interiors; Earth-surface processes; and the origin and behaviour of oceans and atmosphere. The emphasis of the course is on understanding the underlying physical principles of geological processes. Oxford offers two courses: a BA in Geology and an MEarthSc in Earth Sciences, which are exactly the same for the first three years. You can then choose to continue with the four-year Earth Sciences course or leave with a BA in Geology. **A level Mathematics** as well as either **Physics** or **Chemistry** are essential.

" " I enjoyed applying the theory to the real environment, and seeing in front of me, either out in the field or in the lab, things that I had learnt in lectures. **" "**

Robert, Earth Sciences (Geology) graduate

Interested? Why don't you explore. . .

Earth: Evolution of a Habitable World by Jonathan I. Lunine – an outstanding history of the evolution of Earth.

Igneous Petrology by Anthony Hall – comprehensive treatment of all aspects of igneous rocks.

Global Geomorphology by Michael Summerfield – an in-depth study into surface processes and landforms.

Not the course for you? You might also like to consider **Geography, Human Sciences, Materials Science** or **Physics**. Or try **Natural Sciences (Physical)** at Cambridge.

E&M (Economics & Management)
Three years

Past interview questions to get you thinking:

• Are large or small companies more successful?
• What are the arguments for and against a minimum wage?
• Should a Walmart store be opened in the middle of Oxford?

The highly competitive E&M course examines issues central to the world we live in: namely how the economy functions, and in turn, how organisations function within it. Economics provides the broader understanding of the economic environment within which all organisations operate; management in turn analyses the goals and frameworks of those organisations. The key advantage of studying E&M is that it combines academic vigour with vocational worth. A **Mathematics A level** is essential and you will be required to sit the **TSA Oxford**.

❝ I enjoyed the fact that as one of Oxford's most modern degrees, it was relevant for the world in which we live. **❞**

Jack, Economics & Management graduate

Interested? Why don't you explore. . .

Scale and Scope: The Dynamics of Industrial Capitalism by Alfred Chandler – a thorough analysis of the origins of large corporations.

Rise of the Corporate Economy by Leslie Hannah – looks at crucial periods in the formulation of the modern corporate system.

The Ascent of Money by Niall Ferguson – a brilliant history of banking, giving great insights into the birth of globalisation.

Not the course for you? Take a look at **Economics** at Cambridge, with an option to take **Management Studies** in your final year. You might also like to consider **History & Economics** or **PPE (Philosophy, Politics & Economics)** at Oxford.

Engineering Science
Four years

Past interview questions to get you thinking:

• How does a pendulum work, bearing in mind that the amplitude of the oscillations increases over time rather than decreases?

• Draw an acceleration against velocity graph to describe the motion when you are in a lift.

• Why does a bullet spiral?

Engineering Science encompasses a vast range of subjects, from microelectronics to offshore oil platforms, which will give you a solid theoretical foundation. In the third and fourth years you can specialise in one of six branches of engineering: Biomedical, Chemical, Civil, Electrical, Information and Mechanical. In the fourth year you will undertake a major research project in the field of your choice and at the end of this broad-based four-year course, you will graduate with a degree of Master of Engineering. **A level Mathematics and Physics are essential, and you will be required to sit the PAT.**

❝ I loved the way lectures complemented the laboratory work. There were plenty of opportunities to apply what you had learned to practical scenarios. **❞**

Thakoon, Engineering Science graduate

Interested? Why don't you explore. . .

Invention by Design: How Engineers Get from Thought to Thing by Henry Petroski – looks at the engineering design processes behind objects, machines and buildings.

Cats' Paws and Catapults by Steven Vogel – an introduction to biomechanics.

The New Science of Strong Materials: Or Why You Don't Fall Through the Floor by J. E. Gordon – explores the general properties of all materials.

Not the course for you? You might be interested in **Engineering** at Cambridge, **Materials Science** or **Physics** at Oxford.

English Language & Literature
Three years

Past interview questions to get you thinking:
• How would you judge a work to be canonical?
• Do you think there is any point to reading criticism?
• Is literature useful when studying a specific time in history?

You will study the full breadth of English literature from its Anglo-Saxon origins to the present day, working through seven different historical periods. Alongside this you'll also be introduced to the conceptual and technical approaches you need to study literature. You will have a lot of freedom to choose authors within each paper as there are no set texts, as well as exploring your interests further through three coursework papers. Good writing skills are key, so you'll be asked to **submit written work** before coming up to interview, and to sit the **ELAT**. An **English A level** is required.

❝❝ It was a good course for me because although it covered the major authors in each time period, esoteric interests were also permitted which made the course more interesting. ❞❞

George, English Language & Literature graduate

Interested? Why don't you explore. . .

The Art of Fiction by David Lodge – a series of critical readings of classic texts, which are easy to dip into and cover complex ideas.

The Short Oxford History of English Literature – this will give you a chronological overview of English literature since the Middle Ages and is a great guide to choosing preparatory reading from each period.

The Genius of Shakespeare by Jonathan Bate – this book will get you thinking more carefully about literary works in context, be it authorial, social or historical.

Not the course for you? Try **English & Modern Languages** or **History & English**. You may also like **History, Modern Languages**, **Theology**, **Classics**, **History of Art** or you could consider **English** at Cambridge.

English & Modern Languages
Four years (with the third or fourth year spent abroad)

Past interview questions to get you thinking:

- What are the differences between English literature and the literature of the language which you want to study?
- Do you think learning a language is obsolete due to English being spoken internationally?
- Should a work in translation stay true to the original text or be altered to represent a different culture?

Alongside tutorial work on a choice of English literary periods from the Anglo-Saxon era to the present day and selected texts in your foreign language, you'll work on your practical language skills. The course is very flexible and allows you to pick and choose modules from both degree courses, as well as linking the two through comparative literature papers. You will need to sit both the **MLAT** and the **ELAT**. You'll also be asked to submit one piece of **written work for each subject**. **English A level** is required and usually an **A level in the language** you wish to study.

  ❝ I loved the year abroad, and the two disciplines that gave me two sets of friends, two faculties, two different approaches to books and two cultures to steep myself in. **❞**

Maya, English & French graduate

Interested? Why don't you explore. . .

Through the Language Glass by Guy Deutscher – an extremely readable study of how language influences the way we view the world.

Foreign newspapers, such as *Le Monde, El Pais, Die Welt* – reading the headline articles of the major newspapers of that language will be helpful and may provide content for discussion at interview.

Not the course for you? Consider studying either subject on its own, or with **History, Classics, Linguistics** or **Philosophy.** You might also like the **English** or **MML (Modern & Medieval Languages)** courses at Cambridge.

EP (Experimental Psychology)
Three years

Past interview questions to get you thinking:
• How do you measure emotions?
• What use is psychological study for society?
• How can genetics be used in determining an individual's intelligence?

The course is scientific and you will learn to test ideas through experiments and observation rather than introspection. You will spend the first two years studying a broad range of core fields, such as Neurophysiology or Statistics, as well as optional topics, such as Social Psychology or Language and Cognition. In your third year you get the opportunity to complete your own research project and follow your special interests through a choice of more optional courses. Due to the scientific focus of the course you'll normally need **one or more science or Mathematics A level**, and you'll sit the **TSA Oxford**.

f f The structure meant that you had a thorough understanding of everything that you could possibly need within the first two years, and then you are let loose to do whatever you want with your final year. **7 7**

Caroline, EP (Experimental Psychology) graduate

Interested? Why don't you explore. . .

Statistics Without Tears by Derek Rowntree – this book explains statistics using words instead of numbers and is excellent for building your confidence in working with them.

Mindwatching by H J & M W Eysenck – a good introduction to a number of areas in psychology, including experiments.

The Man Who Mistook His Wife for a Hat by Oliver Sacks – interesting short stories about strange neurological conditions..

Not the course for you? Try **Human Sciences, PPL (Psychology, Philosophy & Linguistics), Biological Sciences** or **Medicine**. You might also be interested in **PBS (Psychological & Behavioural Sciences)** at Cambridge.

Fine Art
Three years

Past interview questions to get you thinking:

- Discuss restoration and conservation. Are they good or bad?
- If you had to save one piece of art in the world, what would it be and why?
- What is the definition of prehistory?

The course combines practical studio work and art history with theory and criticism, and is designed to prepare students to become artists. You will participate in regular workshops to learn techniques and approaches and you'll be assessed through a mixture of studio projects, submitted essays and written exams. In your third year you will also work towards a final exhibition with a portfolio of work made over the final two years of your studies, alongside writing a linked extended essay. You're strongly encouraged to take **Art A level** and an **Art Foundation Course**, and you'll be asked to submit a **portfolio** to demonstrate your ability and interests, and take a **practical test at interview.**

❝ The course is a perfect combination of theory and practice, which is quite unusual for a BA course in Fine Art in the UK. The staff are very interesting and inspiring and the opportunity to be in an art school and at the same time part of a large university is very unique. **❞**

Anja, Fine Art graduate

Interested? Why don't you explore. . .

Art in Theory 1900-2000: An Anthology of Changing Ideas ed. by Charles Harrison & Paul Wood – a good way to get to grips with both new research and different critical frameworks over the 20th Century.

Keep up to date with contemporary trends by going to current art exhibitions.

Broaden your interests by having a look at Art House cinema, including films by directors such as Chris Marker and Werner Herzog.

Not the course for you? Try **History of Art** at either Oxford or Cambridge.

Geography
Three years

Past interview questions to get you thinking:
- What is the relevance of physical geography to human geography?
- Why should we conserve?
- If you were the policy makers of your home town, what would you do to improve the area?

The course focuses on the relevance and diversity of Geography and you will approach it from a range of directions – as a social science, a natural science and an arts discipline. You'll also have opportunities to study how Geography relates to other subjects, such as Anthropology or Biology. The first year papers cover the full range of geographical topics, preparing you to follow up your interests in optional papers and research over the course of the second and third years. Fieldwork is a key element of the course and trips are part of core study. Good knowledge, analytical skills and the ability to argue coherently are key. Applicants will have to sit the **TSA Oxford** before interview. **Geography A level** is highly recommended.

❝ I most enjoyed my special options in second and third year. The field trip to Tunisia was a highlight – the best part about Geography is seeing it in action, after all. ❞

Max, Geography graduate

Interested? Why don't you explore. . .
The Great Divergence by Kenneth Pomeranz – this book will help you to get to grips with the making of the modern world economy.
The Geographical Tradition by David Livingstone – a great introduction to the development of geographical thought.
Earth's Climate: Past and Future by William Ruddiman – detailed projections and insight into the causes of long term climate change.

Not the course for you? Try **Earth Sciences** or **Human Sciences** at Oxford, or have a look at **Geography** and **Natural Sciences** at Cambridge.

History
Three years

Past interview questions to get you thinking:

* Do you think History is an art?
* Do you think the concept of nationalism is useful when considering European History before the 18th Century?
* How do we know anything in the past happened at all?

From the outset of the course you will pick and choose options ranging chronologically from the end of the Roman Empire to the present day, and geographically from the British Isles to Africa. You will focus on honing your skills in using source materials and develop sensitivity to the issues that affect your interpretation of history. Independent research is an important focus for second- and third-year students, and you'll produce two extended pieces of written work. Strong analytical and written skills are essential, so you will be asked to **submit one piece of written work** and to sit the **HAT**. **History A level** is highly recommended.

❝ I loved that I didn't have to just study the normal political and economic history we had done at school, I got to delve into the lives of peasants, gender history, cultural history – a whole spectrum that I had never really known to exist. **❞**

Louise, History graduate

Interested? Why don't you explore. . .

The Penguin History of Britain series – an excellent way to get an overview of any given period and to help you identify what to read to find out more.

What is History Now? ed. by David Cannadine – a response to E H Carr's *What is History?* which will give you an overview of developments of historical thinking over the past few decades.

Developments in Modern Historiography ed. by Henry Kozicki – a good overview of 20th Century historical approaches.

Not the course for you? Have a look at **History** combined with **Politics, English** or **Economics**. You could also try **English, Classics** or **PPE (Philosophy, Politics & Economics)**.

History (Ancient & Modern)
Three years

Past interview questions to get you thinking:
• How does a historian gather information?
• What is the difference between prehistory and history?
• Why do you prefer older history to more modern history or vice versa?

The Ancient & Modern History course gives you the chance to study the Bronze Age to the present day, and from Ancient Greece to Latin America. You can choose modules from both the History and Classics faculties, and in your second and third year it will be up to you to decide whether you want to spend more time on Ancient or Modern History. There is also the chance to carry out independent research for two pieces of extended written work. **History A level** is highly recommended and a classical language, Classical Civilization and Ancient History are also useful choices. Written skills and analytical ability are important, so you'll be asked to sit the **HAT** and **submit one piece of written work** when you apply.

❝ I loved being able to combine my study of the Ancient World with more recent history. ❞

David, History (Ancient & Modern) graduate

Interested? Why don't you explore. . .
A Little History of the World by E.H. Gombrich – a classic piece of historical writing, chronicling human development through the ages.

The Penguin History of Britain series – an excellent way to get an overview of any given period and to help you identify what to read to find out more.

The History of the Ancient World: From the Earliest Accounts to the Fall of Rome by Susan Wise Bauer – traces the chronological rise and demise of ancient civilisations.

Not the course for you? Have a look at modern **History** or consider combining **History** with **Politics**, **English** or **Economics**. Alternatively, try a **Modern Language**, **Theology**, **English** or **Classics**.

History & Economics
Three years

Past interview questions to get you thinking:

• Would it be feasible to have an economy entirely based on the service sector?

• Why does labour move to towns rather than capital to the country?

• How can you define a revolution?

The range of module options will equip you to view real-world issues from the contrasting angles of both historian and economist, and you will learn to apply the methods and analysis of both disciplines. Though students continue to study core papers in History and Economics throughout the degree, in your second and third year you will also have some freedom to decide to weight your studies more heavily towards one subject if you wish. You will be asked to **submit one piece of History and one piece of Economics written work**, and to sit both the **HAT** and an Economics test. **History and Mathematics A level** are highly recommended.

❝ I loved learning about British economic history. It's given me a much fuller understanding of current economic issues. ❞

Natalie, History & Economics graduate

Interested? Why don't you explore. . .

The Ascent of Money by Niall Ferguson – an engaging history of banking which explains how globalisation happened.

Marx: A Very Short Introduction by Peter Singer – this will help you get to grips with how History and Economics overlap.

Black Swan by Nassim Nicholas Taleb – a pertinent book on the failure of economic science to predict the most recent financial collapse.

Not the course for you? Consider **History** on its own, or have a look at **History** combined with **Politics** or a **Modern Language**. Alternatively, try **PPE (Philosophy, Politics & Economics)**.

History & English
Three years

Past interview questions to get you thinking:
• Why did imperialism happen?
• What are the connections between language and culture?
• Is literature useful when studying a specific time in history?

History & English is designed to equip you with the skills to study literature and history as interrelated disciplines through the study of historical periods and authors. However, the course also leaves you the freedom to simply pick and choose unrelated options from both courses should you prefer variety. Study of the relationship between History and English is built into each year of the course, but you will also have the scope to weight your modules towards either subject. To convince tutors from both departments that you have the ability to succeed in this course, you will be asked to **submit three pieces of written work, one piece for History and two for English**, and to sit the **HAT** (but not the ELAT).

❝ The subjects complement each other perfectly. I loved being able to combine the study of literary texts with the in-depth study of their historical context. **❞**

Lewis, History & English graduate

Interested? Why don't you explore. . .
Witnesses of War by Nicholas Stargardt – this book uses a range of surprising sources to document the effect of WWII on European children.
The Short Oxford History of English Literature by Andrew Sanders – an excellent way to get an overview of the literature of any given period.
Literary Theory: An Introduction by Terry Eagleton – if you are new to reading criticism and literary theory this is an excellent place to start as it introduces you to many different critical frameworks and their application.

Not the course for you? Have a look at the individual **History** and **English** courses, or try **Classics, Modern Languages, Philosophy & Theology**.

History & Politics
Three years

Past interview questions to get you thinking:
• Why do we need government?
• How do you organise a successful revolution?
• Differentiate between power and authority.

The History & Politics course will teach you to understand the historical context of modern-day political problems, and equip you with an understanding of political science that will enlighten your study of historical events. The course is unusual in allowing students to choose very varied modules across both subjects, so you might find yourself studying history from 300AD alongside contemporary American politics. In your third year you'll have the choice of researching and writing a thesis on either an historical or a political topic. **History A level** is highly recommended. Good analytical thinking skills are important, so tutors will ask you to **submit one piece of written work** and to sit the **HAT**.

❝ I enjoyed the freedom we were given to study subjects of our choice in depth, and the intellectual challenge of tutorials. I met some great tutors who were very giving with their time and expertise. ❞
Luke, History & Politics graduate

Interested? Why don't you explore. . .
A History of Political Thought by Bruce Haddock – a lively history of Western political ideas.
The State We're In by Will Hutton – an intriguing analysis of how Britain has become socially, economically and politically out of date.
The Economist – keep yourself up to date on current affairs in major world powers in particular and most importantly, work out what you think.

Not the course for you? Have a look at **History & Economics**, **PPE (Philosophy, Politics & Economics)** or **Law**. You might also like to consider **HSPS (Human, Social & Polical Sciences)** at Cambridge.

History of Art
Three years

Past interview questions to get you thinking:
• Do you think the written word is more valuable than visual images?
• What is style?
• What do you think are the main factors in dividing different art movements?

History of Art at Oxford offers you the chance to study a broader range of global art than most UK courses. You'll get a strong grounding in more traditional 'fine art' and 'western art' history, but you'll also learn to interpret the making, function, cultural reception and history of almost anything designed by human beings. The Oxford course tends to focus less on architecture than the Cambridge course. You will need to **submit a piece of written work** and to demonstrate your artistic engagement and sensitivity by writing **a response to a piece of art, architecture or design**. You should have taken an **essay-based subject at A level**. Fine Art, History of Art or English may be useful.

❝ The extended reading and the influx of images in the course has immensely changed the way I look at and appraise art. History of Art is so interdisciplinary that it has been a joy to examine historical, social, political and anthropological aspects of contextual evidence. ❞

Rosy, History of Art graduate

Interested? Why don't you explore. . .
Art in Theory, 1900-2000 by Charles Harrison – a good place to start getting to grips with conceptual approaches to art through the 20th Century.
Ways of Seeing by John Berger – this very influential book will get you thinking critically about how we see the world around us.
The Penguin Dictionary of Art and Artists by Peter & Linda Murray – this will help you get a good overview and identify areas of particular interest.

Not the course for you? Try **Fine Art**, **History** or **Archaeology & Anthropology** at Oxford, or **History of Art** at Cambridge.

Human Sciences
Three years

Past interview questions to get you thinking:
- Design an experiment to show whether monkeys' behaviour is innate or learnt.
- What is the greatest threat to humankind?
- What use can scientists make of a 19th Century skeleton?

The core of this course is the study of human life, but throughout your studies you'll approach it from numerous and varied perspectives: biological, social and cultural. Human Sciences is designed to equip students to understand, and go on to address, contemporary issues facing humans from disease to population growth to conservation. You'll study a broad range of modules over the course of your first and second years before following your interests by choosing two optional modules and writing a dissertation. There are no required A levels, but Biology and Mathematics are useful.

66 I now have a broad approach to everything and can look at things from other points of view, generally with an evolutionary underpinning to why people act the way they do. 99

Mary, Human Sciences graduate

Interested? Why don't you explore. . .
Journal of Human Evolution – it's useful to keep up to date with new theories and discoveries in biological anthropology.

Collapse: How Societies Choose to Fail or Succeed by Jared Diamond – an interesting look at why past civilizations have failed or flourished.

Genes, Peoples and Languages by L. Cavalli-Sforza – an excellent introduction to how genetics, languages and archaeology can be used to study human evolution before written records.

Not the course for you? You might prefer **Biological Sciences, Archaeology & Anthropology,** or **EP (Experimental Psychology).** Alternatively, try **HSPS (Human, Social & Political Sciences)** at Cambridge.

Law (Jurisprudence)
Three years

Past interview questions to get you thinking:
- If a man is stuck in a burning building and he shouts that he will give you all his money if you put a nearby ladder by the window for him to climb to safety, is he obliged to keep his promise?
- What is the difference between intention and foresight?
- What do you think is more important, actions or motives?

The course is designed to give students a firm foundation for further legal training. You'll get this grounding by studying Jurisprudence, the branch of philosophy concerned with the Law and the principles behind it. You will train your skills of analysis, comprehension and presentation to a high level. Over three years of study you cover all the major branches of Law as well as choosing two further optional modules, and unusually you'll normally be assessed only by exam. There are no required A level subjects for Law but you do need at least a **C grade in GCSE Mathematics**. Tutors are looking for students with good communication and reasoning skills, so to help them decide who to invite for interviews you'll be asked to sit the **LNAT**.

ᏝᏝLaw offers the chance to combine practical and academic elements – I developed my argument, analytical and academic abilities in a very practical context.ᏠᏠ

Darren, Law graduate

Interested? Why don't you explore. . .
Learning the Law by Glanville Williams – an accessible introduction.
The Times Law Supplement – read this regularly to keep up to date on current legal issues.
Eve Was Framed by Helena Kennedy – this is an interesting and unusual critique of the legal system to get you thinking from new perspectives.

Not the course for you? You might prefer **PPE (Philosophy, Politics & Economics)** or **History & Politics**. Have a look at **Law** at Cambridge too.

Law with Law Studies in Europe
Four years (with the third year spent abroad)

Past interview questions to get you thinking:

- A man is lost in the desert and falls asleep. A second man comes along and empties the water from his bottle. A third man comes along and fills it with poison. Who killed the first man?
- Would it be possible to have one legal system for the whole world?
- What is the difference between fault, responsibility and cause?

Three years of this course have exactly the same structure and content as the Oxford Law degree, but students spend their third year abroad studying the Law of another European country, in France, Germany, Italy or Spain. Alternatively, you can choose to study European and international law in the Netherlands. The latter is a course taught in English, but for all other countries you'll need to have studied the **relevant foreign language A level** (there is an exceptions for Italian). As with straight Law, you need at least a **C grade in GCSE Mathematics**. Tutors are looking for students with good communication and reasoning skills, so to help them decide who to invite for interviews you'll be asked to sit the **LNAT**.

❝ Essentially, it is a course that demands hard thinking and problem solving, which I have always enjoyed. **❞**

Helen, Law with Law Studies in Europe graduate

Interested? Why don't you explore. . .

What About Law by Catherine Barnard – this will give you an accessible introduction to legal reasoning and the legal system.

Just Law by Helena Kennedy – a good discussion of current legal issues surrounding civil liberties and especially relevant if you are interested in Human Rights.

The Times Law Supplement – read this regularly to keep up to date on current legal issues.

Not the course for you? Consider **Law** on its own, or **Modern Languages**.

Materials Science
Four years

Past interview questions to get you thinking:
- If I place a cube in water, what shape does it make on the surface?
- Can you think of a logical reason why stress concentrates on the bottom of a crack when you stretch a material?
- If a human being was doubled in size would he jump higher or less high?

Materials Science is the study of modern advanced materials, from silicon microchips to bone replacement materials. This makes it an extremely varied course which encompasses elements of Physics, Chemistry, Engineering and Industrial Manufacturing. Over your first two years of study you'll focus on understanding the properties, structure and application of materials before undertaking a group design project in your third year and an independent research project in your fourth year. To show tutors that you can cope with the scope of Materials Science you'll need strong logical reasoning skills and be able to apply them to a range of physical science problems. You will be required to sit the **PAT** before interview. **A level Mathematics and Physics** are essential for this course and Chemistry is highly recommended.

❝ The most enjoyable year is almost certainly the fourth year, with flexibility to research nearly anything. ❞
Ben, Materials Science graduate

Interested? Why don't you explore…
The New Science of Strong Materials: or Why You Don't Fall Through the Floor by J.E. Gordon – a great introduction to modern materials science.
An Introduction to Metallurgy by A. Cottrell – this will give you a taster of first-year study.
Structures: or Why Things Don't Fall Down by J.E. Gordon – an excellent place to start getting to grips with engineering.

Not the course for you? Try **Engineering Science** or **Physics** at Oxford. Alternatively, have a look at **Natural Sciences (Physical)** or **Engineering** at Cambridge.

Mathematics
Three years, with an optional fourth year

Past interview questions to get you thinking:
• Which is bigger: 'e to the power of pi' or 'pi to the power of e'?
• Describe a complex number to a non-mathematician.
• How do you predict a Pythagorean triple?

The first year consists of core courses in Pure and Applied Mathematics and includes an Introduction to Statistics. You will complete the core part of the degree in the first term of the second year, introducing complex analysis and ideas from topology and number theory. You will be taught to think mathematically, in order to approach problems like the intricacies of quantum theory and relativity, or study the mathematics of financial derivatives. **A level Mathematics** is essential, and **Further Mathematics** or a science is strongly recommended. You will also be required to sit the **MAT**.

❝ I enjoyed the third and fourth years the best as we had free reign over what options we could choose. ❞

Laura, Mathematics graduate

Interested? Why don't you explore. . .
A Mathematician's Apology by G. H. Hardy – an engaging memoir written in 1940, extolling the pleasures of mathematical invention.
The Mathematical Tourist by Ivars Peterson – a journey through important mathematical concepts, told in accessible language.
Fermat's Last Theorem by Simon Singh – an interesting read on one of the most notorious mathematical problems.

Not the course for you? **Mathematics** can also be studied jointly with **Computer Science**, **Philosophy** and **Statistics**. You might also like to consider **Physics** or **Engineering** at Oxford, or check out the **Mathematics** course at Cambridge.

Mathematics & Computer Science
Three years, with an optional fourth year

Past interview questions to get you thinking:
- Why is the number 2.7182818... used in mathematics?
- Tell me about the efficiency of binary searches.
- Explain briefly the difference between science and technology.

The course focuses on the areas where Mathematics and Computing are most relevant to each other, emphasising the bridges between theory and practice. Combining the study of both subjects will enable you to develop a deeper understanding of the mathematical foundations of Computer Science, whilst the Computer Science element will give you the chance to apply your mathematical knowledge practically. In the second year you will get the chance to take part in an industry-sponsored group practical. **A level Mathematics** is essential, and **Further Mathematics** or a science is strongly recommended. You will also be required to sit the **MAT**.

❝ My tutors were wonderful. They were experts in their fields, had written the textbooks, and yet still had time to answer my questions. ❞

Ben, Mathematics & Computer Science graduate

Interested? Why don't you explore. . .

In Code: A Mathematical Journey by Sarah Flannery – an account of the way in which Flannery improved public-key encryption.

An Introduction to Algorithms by Thomas H. Cormen et al. – this is quite tricky, but getting your head around the content is likely to impress.

The Emperor's New Mind by Roger Penrose – this book uses the physics of computing to explore the concept of artificial intelligence.

Not the course for you? **Mathematics** can be studied on its own, or in combination with **Philosophy** or **Statistics**. You might also like to consider **Computer Science** or **Engineering** at either Oxford or Cambridge.

Mathematics & Philosophy
Three years, with an optional fourth year

Past interview questions to get you thinking:

* Is Mathematics a language?
* Each room in a house has an even number of doors leading out of it. Prove that the exterior of the house has an even number of doors.
* Can faith in quantum physics and invisible forces tie in with faith in an invisible God?

Historically, there have been strong links between Mathematics and Philosophy; logic, an important branch of both subjects, provides a natural bridge between the two. The study of Mathematics raises very interesting philosophical questions about the nature of the subject and the reasoning which forms its basis. This course was constructed with the belief that the parallel study of these two related disciplines will significantly enhance your understanding of each. **A level Mathematics** is essential, and **Further Mathematics** is strongly recommended. You will also be required to sit the **MAT**.

66 **The unique and varied nature of the course means that I found it constantly fascinating.** 99

Seb, Mathematics & Philosophy graduate

Interested? Why don't you explore. . .

The Mathematical Tourist by Ivars Peterson – a journey through important mathematical concepts, told in accessible language.

Think by Simon Blackburn – an engaging overview of the study of Philosophy.

Thinking about Mathematics by Simon Shapiro – an excellent introduction to the philosophy of Mathematics.

Not the course for you? **Mathematics** can also be studied on its own or in combination with **Statistics** or **Computer Science**. You might also like to consider the **Philosophy** course at Cambridge.

Mathematics & Statistics
Three years, with an optional fourth year

Past interview questions to get you thinking:

- Prove 'e' is irrational.
- Why do you think people buy lottery tickets when the chances of winning are extremely small?
- Differentiate x to the power of x.

Statistics is primarily the analysis of data, involving advanced mathematical ideas and modern computational techniques. If you are interested in this combination of mathematically grounded method-building, and wide-ranging applied work with data, this could be the course for you. For the first four terms the Mathematics & Statistics course is identical to straight Mathematics, and then you will follow core second-year courses in probability and statistics. **A level Mathematics** is essential, and **Further Mathematics** is strongly recommended. You will also be required to sit the **MAT**.

❝I enjoyed the time spent getting to grips with the Maths software – I found my computational skills developed dramatically.**❞**

Amy, Mathematics & Statistics graduate

Interested? Why don't you explore. . .

From Here to Infinity by Ian Stewart – a brilliant introduction to modern Mathematics.

The Man Who Loved Only Numbers by Paul Hoffman – a biography of the mathematical genius, Paul Erdos.

Mathematics: From the Birth of Numbers by Jan Gullberg – a huge historical overview of the subject.

Not the course for you? Check out **Mathematics** on its own at either university.

Medicine
Three years pre-clinical, followed by a three-year clinical degree

Past interview questions to get you thinking:
- Why is high blood sugar a problem in diabetes?
- How do bacteria develop antibacterial resistance?
- If you had to choose between being a nurse or a scientist, which would you be?

Medicine is an applied science, but it is equally about human interaction and dealing sympathetically with individuals. The aim of the course is to produce doctors with solid scientific knowledge, who have had the necessary training to pursue a career either in hospitals or in general practice. There is a clear distinction between the pre-clinical and clinical years, with the option to move to another hospital for the clinical years. **A level Chemistry** and a further **two of the following subjects: Biology, Physics and Mathematics** are required and you will need to sit the **BMAT**. How well you do in this is an important factor in the selection process.

❝ Now when I read about a new drug development I critically appraise it before considering prescribing it. Oxford taught me to challenge all of the information that is put in front of me. ❞

Robert, Medicine graduate

Interested? Why don't you explore. . .
Human Physiology by Gillian Pocock & Christopher Richards – covers most of the major physiological systems in a clinically relevant way.
Principles of Evolutionary Medicine by Peter Gluckman, Alan Beedle & Mark Hanson – a good review of advances in the field of evolutionary biology.
The Rise and Fall of Modern Medicine by James Le Fanu – a lively account of medical history.

Not the course for you? Check out **Biomedical Sciences** at Oxford, or **Medicine** or **Natural Sciences (Biological)** at Cambridge.

Modern Languages

Four years (with the third year spent abroad)

Past interview questions to get you thinking:

- Why do some languages have genders when others don't?
- Can you think of examples in poetry or in literature where tone or meaning has been lost in translation?
- What is the difference between poetry and prose?

The course is structured to allow you to attain spoken fluency, as well as develop the ability to write essays and produce translations both into and out of your chosen language(s). The course has a clear focus on literature, and over the four years you will study a wide range of literary texts. The skills required for translation are very different from those needed for writing literary essays, and this dual focus makes studying Modern Languages at Oxford stimulating and rewarding. **An A level in at least one of your chosen languages** is usually required. All colleges will ask you to **submit written work** in both English and the language that will be studied, and you will be required to sit the **MLAT**.

❝ I loved the variety. The course combines the study of the language itself with literature, culture and philosophy – understanding what makes a country tick. **❞**

Suzy, Modern Languages graduate

Interested? Why don't you explore. . .

Through the Language Glass: Why The World Looks Different In Other Languages by Guy Deutscher – an extremely readable study of how language influences the way we view the world.

Foreign newspapers, such as *Le Monde, El Pais, Die Welt* – reading the headline articles of the major newspapers of that language will be helpful and may provide content for discussion at interview.

Not the course for you? **Modern Languages** can also be studied jointly with **Linguistics, English, Classics** or **History**. You might also like to consider **MML (Modern & Medieval Languages)** at Cambridge.

Modern Languages & Linguistics
Four years (with the third year spent abroad)

Past interview questions to get you thinking:

• Do you think teaching a child their first language is the same as teaching someone a second language?

• How can language be scientific?

• How does grammar govern tone and style in literature?

One half of your course will be half of the Modern Languages course, whilst the other will focus on linguistics, the study of language itself. For this, you will be analysing the nature and structure of human language across a range of topics, from how words are formed, to how language is organised in the brain. The two subjects fit perfectly, enabling you to apply your linguistics knowledge to the study of your modern language. You will need an **A level in your chosen language,** unless you are applying for Italian or Portuguese. All colleges will require you to **submit written work** as for Modern Languages, and to sit the **MLAT**.

❝ I loved the combination of rigorous, technical analysis of language with the more conceptual study of literature and culture. **❞**

Claire, Modern Languages & Linguistics graduate

Interested? Why don't you explore. . .

Through the Language Glass by Guy Deutscher – an extremely readable study of how language influences the way we view the world.

The Language Instinct by Steven Pinker – lucidly explains everything you need to know about language.

Limits of Language by Mikael Parkvall – an enjoyable exploration of linguistics, filled with interesting facts.

Not the course for you? **Modern Languages** can also be studied on its own, or with **English, Classics, History** or **Philosophy**. You might also like to consider **MML (Modern & Medieval Languages)** or **Linguistics** at Cambridge.

Music
Three years

Past interview questions to get you thinking:
- What periods are you interested in and why?
- Can the listener and their attitude change the music they hear?
- Is music a language?

The compulsory papers in your first year will allow you to cover the key areas in music including its history, analysis, techniques of composition and keyboard skills. You can then opt to do a Performance, Extended Essay or Composition Portfolio. Although broad in its base, there is plenty of opportunity to specialise as you progress through the course, and performance options become more prominent in your finals. **A level Music is required**, and **keyboard ability** to ABRSM Grade V or above is highly recommended. You will be asked to **submit written work** and to **perform a prepared piece** on your chosen instrument/voice at interview.

❝ I left Oxford with a better understanding of world politics, culture and history as a result of this course. ❞

Chloe, Music graduate

Interested? Why don't you explore. . .

The Oxford History of Western Music by Richard Taruskin – a several-volume history by a revered musicologist. It would be worthwhile focusing on one or two chapters.

Nineteenth-Century Music by Karl Dahlhaus – an important figure in musical history writing, his book gives a fantastic overview of the 19th Century.

A Guide to Musical Analysis by Nicholas Cook – an important introduction to analytical processes and terminology.

Not the course for you? Take a look at **Music** at Cambridge.

Oriental Studies
Four years (three for Egyptology)

Past interview questions to get you thinking:
• What is the difference between a language and a dialect?
• How does culture influence our lives today?
• How filial is Western society?

Oriental Studies is an umbrella term that encompasses courses in Egyptology & Ancient Near Eastern Studies, Arabic, Chinese, Hebrew & Jewish Studies, Japanese, Persian, Sanskrit and Turkish. The course is broadly divided into two parts: the study of the language of your chosen area, and the study of its history and culture. The course draws upon many disciplines, including art and archaeology, history, literature, philosophy, religion and modern social studies, in order to introduce you to civilisations that are radically different from the Western world. A language A level can be helpful, but there are no specific requirements. All applicants are required to **submit written work**, and some will need to sit the **OLAT**.

❝ The four years fully immersed me in the study of a completely different culture. ❞

Nick, Oriental Studies graduate

Interested? Why don't you explore. . .

Islam in the World by Malise Ruthven – an introduction to the Islamic world and the challenges it presents to western society.

The Search for Modern China by Jonathan Spence – covers more than four centuries of Chinese history.

The Japanese Today: Change & Continuity by Edwin O. Reischauer – explores politics, history, religion and education.

Not the course for you? You can combine **Oriental Studies** with **Theology.** Alternatively, check out **Asian & Middle Eastern Studies** or **MML (Modern & Medieval Languages)** at Cambridge.

Philosophy & Modern Languages
Four years

Past interview questions to get you thinking:
- How does the literature you have read affect your opinion of that society?
- What are the similarities between ancient playwrights and ancient philosophers?
- 'This bench is long.' What does this mean?

Philosophy & Modern Languages brings together some of the most important approaches to understanding language, literature and ideas. You can choose whether you want to weight your final degree towards either Philosophy or the Modern Language you have chosen, or split the papers evenly. There is also the option to study papers that overlap across the two disciplines. Depending on your chosen language, you **may need a language A level**, and you will be required to sit the **MLAT and a Philosophy test**. You will also be required to **submit written work**.

❝ The academic independence of my thesis was the best part of the degree, I loved the freedom I had to explore the areas I found most interesting. ❞ Sarah, Philosophy & Modern Languages graduate

Interested? Why don't you explore. . .
Through the Language Glass by Guy Deutscher – an extremely readable study of how language influences the way we view the world.
Meditations by Descartes – Descartes is a hugely influential philosopher, and easy to read.
Whatever Happened to Good and Evil? by Russ Shafer-Landau – an excellent introduction to meta-ethics.

Not the course for you? You might be interested in **Modern Languages, PPL (Psychology, Philosophy & Linguistics)**, or **PPE (Philosophy, Politics & Economics)** at Oxford. You might also like to consider **MML (Modern & Medieval Languages)** or **Philosophy** at Cambridge.

PPE (Philosophy, Politics & Economics)
Three years

Past interview questions to get you thinking:
* Is society greater than the individual?
* Differentiate between power and authority.
* What is the point of privatisation?

The combination of Philosophy, Politics and Economics (known as PPE) forms a very popular and extremely diverse degree, which probes why people think the way they do, and explains how systems relate to theoretical principles. You are allowed to drop one of the subjects after your first year, and most students do. The course comprises a great mix of timeless human debates and modern-day economic and political problems. It's a great subject to study because it combines these analytical tools with real-world evidence and case studies. Although not formally required, the vast majority of successful applicants in 2013 had **Mathematics to at least AS level**. You will be required to sit the **TSA Oxford.**

❝The people I studied with were sharp, fun and interesting – I think that PPE attracts individuals with a lot of verve. **❞**

Mark, PPE graduate

Interested? Why don't you explore. . .
Political Philosophy: A Guide for Politicians and Students by Adam Swift – a good thematic overview of the key areas in modern political thought.

Anarchy, State and Utopia by Robert Nozick – a key text in political philosophy, which argues in favour of a minimal state.

Keynes: The Return of the Master by Robert Skidelsky – a recently published biography which reopens relevant economic discussions.

Not the course for you? Try **Economics** or **HSPS (Human, Social & Political Sciences)** at Cambridge. Or check out **E&M (Economics & Management)** or **History & Politics** at Oxford.

Philosophy & Theology
Three years

Past interview questions to get you thinking:
- What is the difference between Theology and Philosophy?
- Is atheism a religion?
- What did Kant say about proving God's existence?

Philosophy & Theology brings together some of the most important approaches to understanding and assessing the intellectual claims of religion, and in particular of Christianity. You will look at Theology from a philosophical perspective, bringing critical thinking to the study of God and religion, while you approach Philosophy from a theological angle, debating arguments for and against God's existence. Throughout the course you'll touch upon many key thinkers in both spheres, and develop a solid critical appreciation of the debates surrounding religion and philosophy. There are no A level requirements, although Religious Studies can be helpful. You will be required to **submit written work** and sit the **Philosophy Test**.

" There are some quite arcane options in the further reaches of the Philosophy & Theology prospectus, which turned out to be fascinating. "

Lucy, Philosophy & Theology graduate

Interested? Why don't you explore. . .
Nicomachean Ethics by Aristotle – one of the most influential philosophical texts, it is also a great basis for Christian theology.
Principles of Christian Theology by John Macquarrie – a very systematic outline of basic, and more complex, Christian doctrine.
Science and Wonders by Russell Stannard – an examination of science, theology and philosophy of religion.

Not the course for you? Take a look at **Theology** on its own at either university. Cambridge also offers straight **Philosophy**.

Physics
Three years, with an optional fourth year

Past interview questions to get you thinking:

• What is the equation for the motion of a pendulum?

• Explain how a hot air balloon works.

• How would the ratio of elements change in a radioactive substance over time?

Although Physics is a fundamental science it is also a very practical subject. The first year will provide you with a solid foundation in mathematics, before progressing on to papers including Electromagnetism and Quantum Physics in your second year. **A level Physics and Mathematics** are essential and you will be asked to sit the **PAT**.

66 Physics applies Maths, logic and experience to help understand the Universe and all its machinations. Why wouldn't you want to study it? **99**

Tom, Physics graduate

Interested? Why don't you explore. . .

In Search of Schrödinger's Cat by John Gribbin – an enjoyable read explaining quantum physics.

E=mc2 by David Bodanis – a 'biography' of Albert Einstein's famous formula.

The End of Time by Julian Barbour – an important contribution to the theory of time.

Not the course for you? You might be interested in **Physics & Philosophy** or **Mathematics** or **Engineering Science** at Oxford. You might also like to consider **Natural Sciences (Physical)** or **Engineering** at Cambridge.

Physics & Philosophy
Four years

Past interview questions to get you thinking:
- How would you define infinity?
- Explain Newton's three laws of motion.
- Is it a matter of fact or knowledge that time travels in only one direction?

This is a course for you if you have an inquisitive and deeply analytical mind. You will learn the theories of Physics – and the Maths on which they are based – to an advanced technical level, whilst also developing your abstract analytical skills through the study of modern philosophy. The bridging subject, Philosophy of Physics, is studied in each of the first three years of the course. There is the option to complete a fourth year, specialising in either Physics or Philosophy, or continuing to study both disciplines and their interrelations. **A level Physics and Mathematics** are essential and you will be asked to sit the **PAT**.

❝ I loved thinking philosophically about theories in Physics and trying to understand what they could be saying about the world. ❞

Nia, Physics & Philosophy graduate

Interested? Why don't you explore. . .
An Invitation to Philosophy by Martin Hollis – a wonderful introductory text on the subject of philosophy.

The Philosophy of Time ed. by Robin Le Poidevin & Murray MacBeath – a collection of important essays on the philosophy of time.

Warped Passages: Unravelling the Universe's Hidden Dimensions by Lisa Randall – an accessible read on theoretical physics.

Not the course for you? **Physics** can also be studied on its own. You might also like to consider the **Philosophy** course at Cambridge.

PPL (Psychology, Philosophy & Linguistics)
Three years

Past interview questions to get you thinking:
- How do we solve the nature vs. nurture debate?
- Does a snail have consciousness?
- What is the relevance of philosophy in science?

Introduced in 2013, PPL is slightly updated from the former Psychology & Philosophy course. You must apply for one of three combinations: Psychology & Philosophy, Psychology & Linguistics or Philosophy & Linguistics. After your second term, you'll have the option to study all three subjects as a tripartite degree, subject to your college's approval. Psychology at Oxford is essentially a scientific discipline, which works through experiments and systematic observation, therefore **a science or Mathematics A level** is expected for Psychology courses. All three courses options will require you to sit the **TSA Oxford**. If you're applying for a Linguistics course, you'll also need to take the **MLAT**.

❝ I enjoyed the diversity of the course. Managing my time to cope with both a science and humanities subject was challenging and rewarding. **❞**

Sam, Psychology & Philosophy graduate

Interested? Why don't you explore. . .

Psychology: The Science of Mind and Behaviour by Richard Gross – a key reference book which covers all the main areas of psychology.

What Does it all Mean? by Thomas Nagel – this short book gives an excellent summary of basic philosophical themes.

The Problems of Philosophy by Bertrand Russell – a more challenging read by a highly influential philosopher.

Not the course for you? Check out **EP (Experimental Psychology)**. You might also be interested in **Philosophy** or **PBS (Psychological & Behavioural Sciences)** at Cambridge.

Theology & Religion
Three years

Past interview questions to get you thinking:
• How should a modern theologian use the Bible?
• How large a role do you think church history has in Theology?
• Is the relationship between religion and science fragile?

Theology was one of the first subjects offered at Oxford University, and remains relevant to the modern student. However secular Britain feels today, the world is still shaped by the forces of religion. The course concentrates mainly on the origins and development of Christian theology, but appeals to students from any faith background. In engaging with the many different aspects of the course, you will develop your analytical, literary-critical and language skills. A Religious Studies A level is considered helpful, and you will be required to **submit written work**.

❝ Studying Theology made me question notions I had taken for granted all my life, and helped me to understand my own beliefs better. ❞

Sophie, Theology graduate

Interested? Why don't you explore. . .
The Early Church by Henry Chadwick – a great summary of the earliest Christian history.
The Shadow of the Galilean by Gerd Theissen – a novelistic look at Christ's own time – highly recommended.
Science and Wonders by Russell Stannard – an examination of science, theology and philosophy of religion.

Not the course for you? Check out **Theology** with **Philosophy** or **Oriental Studies**. Alternatively, take a look at **Theology** at Cambridge.

Theology & Oriental Studies
Three years

Past interview questions to get you thinking:
- What is meant by 'self' in Buddhism?
- Do you think religion has a place in today's modern world?
- What is Fundamentalism?

Oriental Studies complements the study of Theology through combining an in-depth look at a number of the world's religions including Buddhism, Hinduism, Islam and Judaism with the study of Christianity (mainly undertaken in the Theology Faculty). Over the course of the three years, you will develop a much broader understanding of the history and nature of religions that in some cases are radically different from those in Western societies, and also their similarities. You will need to demonstrate the ability to analyse historical and literary texts critically and an understanding of the histories and cultures of the different religions, which is why you are required to **submit written work.** You may also be required to take the **OLAT.**

Interested? Why don't you explore. . .

The BBC Radio 4 archives of the *'In Our Time'* program, especially the Religion and Philosophy archives.

Christian Theology: An Introduction by Alister McGrath – an introduction to important theological concepts.

Eastern Religions & Western Thought by S. Radhakrishnan – traces the influence of Indian philosophy and religion upon Western thought from classical times.

Not the course for you? Check out **Theology & Philosophy** at Oxford. Alternatively, take a look at **Theology** at Cambridge.

2 CHOOSING A COLLEGE

WE TAKE A LOOK AT THE DIFFERENCES BETWEEN COLLEGES AND HOW YOU CAN GO ABOUT FINDING THE ONE THAT'S RIGHT FOR YOU

With over sixty colleges between Oxford and Cambridge, it can be hard to know where to begin. The majority of your teaching at Oxford (tutorials) and Cambridge (supervisions) takes place in your college and it has a big impact on your social environment, so it's a key element of the application.

College 'entz' (entertainment) reps will organise parties called 'bops' in the college bar alongside other events such as arts weeks and theatre productions. You will live in the college grounds for at least one year, and possibly for your entire degree. Whilst living in college accommodation, you'll be looked after by the college staff: the porters, hall staff and the lovely people who come to clean your room and check on you if you're ill (Scouts at Oxford and Bedders at Cambridge).

Colleges are communities which shape your time at university, and for many graduates, they hold a special place in their heart long after leaving. Many students return each year for dinners organised by the clubs and societies they belonged to during their time there and some even return to get married in the college chapel.

So... how do you choose?

Having spoken to lots of applicants, it's clear that everyone has their own point of view on how to choose a college. The reasons they chose their individual colleges vary greatly. Emma, who graduated from Trinity College, Oxford, came to the conclusion that its location between the lecture hall and the centre of town made it the perfect college for her. Nick chose Corpus Christi at Cambridge because he felt the small, close-knit community would make a refreshing change after years at a rather large northern state school. Kate picked Wadham because, after meeting her tutor at an Open Day, she knew she'd enjoy exploring her subject under his guidance in her weekly tutorials. As for John, who graduated from Oxford, he didn't actually choose his college. He was pooled by the university when he went up to interview and ended up spending four happy years at Lady Margaret Hall reading Classics.

You don't even have to choose a college; if you really don't mind and have decided to focus your attentions on your subject instead, you can put in an open application. The university computers will randomly assign you to a college – and that college will not know whether you chose it or not.

Remember that everyone at Oxford and Cambridge loves their college and wouldn't go anywhere else, whether they applied to the college originally or not. You will make friends, receive excellent tuition and look back with happy memories at your time at Oxford or Cambridge. Choosing where to spend the next three years can be a little daunting, but it's very difficult to make a bad decision.

The Pooling System

The college you choose may not necessarily be the college you get an offer from: both Oxford and Cambridge will pool you to other colleges if they think you're a strong applicant but don't have space for you, or if they think you'd be better suited to another college. Around 27% of successful Oxford candidates for 2013 entry were placed at a college they hadn't applied to, and this is usually the case for 20% of Cambridge applicants. You should never think that you are a second-class applicant if you have been pooled. Oxford and Cambridge tutors are looking for the best applicants and will do their utmost to ensure good candidates get offers from the university.

Oxford

The Oxford Pooling System is an ongoing process which operates alongside regular interviews in December. Oxford colleges will be in constant communication with each other throughout the interview period, distributing applicants amongst them. This is one of the reasons why you'll usually be required to stay up in Oxford for more than one day if you apply there. Certain subjects (e.g. Medicine) and certain colleges operate a policy whereby every applicant will interview at a second college to level the playing field and give you a second chance to impress. 51% of Oxford applicants we surveyed in 2013 who made it to interview at their first choice college were then subsequently interviewed elsewhere.

Cambridge

The Cambridge Winter Pool doesn't come into effect until the January following your interview, as and when a college makes a decision about whether or not they would like to offer you a place. If your chosen college considers you to be strong, but they're unable to offer you a place in that particular year, they will write to you in January to notify you that you have been put in the Winter Pool. Once in the Pool, you might be offered a place outright by another college who likes your application on paper; you might be called to interview at another college in mid-January (and subsequently offered a place, or rejected); or you could be rejected if by 31st January no other college has scooped you up. Only a third of applicants in the Winter Pool go on to be successful.

To help you work out which college is for you or whether you will make an open application, here are a few questions that can help you reach that decision:

Does the college offer my course?

This is the fundamental first step to choosing a college. There are a number of colleges that do not have supervision/tutorial provision for every course. You may have fallen in love with Emmanuel College's stunning grounds and the ducks that you met on your Open Day, but if you are applying for Land Economy then, alas, it is not meant to be. The university websites are there to guide you on these matters.

What are the tutors like?

If you can, try to visit your college at an Open Day and, if they are around, speak to the tutors who will be interviewing you and later teaching you. It's really important that you feel comfortable with them – and that you think you will enjoy the tutor-student relationship. You're at university to learn about your subject, so it's a bonus if you like the people who are going to teach you. However, please be aware that tutors move on and there's no guarantee that the same tutor will be there when you arrive in December.

Will I need to sit an admissions test?

For certain subjects at Oxford, you'll have to sit an admissions test wherever you choose to apply, but at Cambridge, whether you have to sit an admissions test depends on the college to which you apply. For example, if you are applying for Natural Sciences at Cambridge (for 2015 entry), at St John's College you will be required to sit the TSA Cambridge. In contrast, Jesus College does not require this test and makes decisions based on interviews alone, whereas King's College sets its own test at interview. If you're generally good at tests, it might be worth applying to a college which requires it – it will give you an extra chance to shine! You can find out more about admissions tests in Chapter 6.

Would I like to spend the next few years of my life here?

What's important to you academically and personally? Is the college located centrally? How big is it? How rich is it? How academic is it? Think about your own personality, interests and ambitions. Do you want to be the next hot-shot hack or rugby superstar? Do you want to wave the socialist flag from the dreaming spires or lead a team to create the best Oxbridge Summer Ball yet? From here, you can move on to more practical contemplations: Do you thrive in a small, close-knit community or would you prefer a larger sporty college such as Keble College, Oxford? Do you like to laze by the river in the sun or would you prefer to be nearer to the lecture hall and have an extra five minutes in bed?

OUR COLLEGE QUIZ

We've designed this quiz as a bit of fun to get you thinking about which of the colleges might best suit your personality. Enjoy!

1) **Where would you most like to be based during your time at Oxford or Cambridge?**
   a. Away from the hustle and bustle – somewhere with its own little community
   b. In the oldest part of the city – where I can live in beautiful, historic surroundings
   c. Somewhere convenient for everything I need to do, but not too noisy or crowded
   d. Somewhere with enough room for me to stretch out and relax
   e. Slap bang in the middle where I can make my mark

2) **What would you most like to achieve from your time at university**
   a. Excellent friends I will know for the rest of my life
   b. A unique experience I couldn't have anywhere else
   c. A first-class education with a fantastic degree result
   d. Fond memories of all the super new things I tried
   e. A first-rate network and an impressive CV that will get me noticed

3) **What kind of environment would you most like in your college?**
   a. Friendly and caring – where everyone looks out for one another
   b. Small and cosy – I'd like to know everyone in my college
   c. Work hard, play hard – I'd like everyone to share in the same goals of having a great time and excelling in their academics
   d. Adventurous – I want to be around people who get involved in new things – and for my college to recognise the importance of this
   e. Inclusive and exciting – I want to be part of a big group and to always have loads of friends wherever I go

4) What is your favourite item of clothing in your wardrobe?

a. My jeans – they're great for just hanging out

b. A straw boater – it reminds me of eating strawberries and cream in the sunshine

c. My trainers – they don't make any noise in the library

d. A great vintage piece I picked up as a bargain

e. A very sharp dinner jacket/my showstopper little black dress

5) What's the least important factor you'd consider when choosing your college

a. The alumni

b. The extra-curricular activities and facilities

c. The college buildings

d. The location

e. The competition for places

6) What's your favourite London building?

a. The Tate Modern

b. The Houses of Parliament

c. The British Library

d. The Roundhouse

e. The National Portrait Gallery

7) What would be an ideal Saturday afternoon for you?

a. Relaxing with friends

b. Getting dressed up and going to the races

c. Chatting over tea with a renowned expert in my subject

d. Putting the finishing touches to an original new project I've been working on

e. Supporting my school team to go on to win a national competition

8) Which of these notable Oxbridge alumni do you most admire?

a. Germaine Greer

b. Stephen Fry

c. Sir Isaac Newton

d. Sir Ian McKellen

e. Boris Johnson

9) It's 11 o' clock on a Friday night. What are you doing?

a) I'm hitting the clubs tonight, and I'm hitting them hard

b) I've just had a formal dinner

c) Debating the finer points of a philosophical concept in the pub with my friends

d) Hanging out in a friend's room with pizza and a film

e) It's the opening night of my play

Mostly As... Breaking the Oxbridge mould

For you, a place at Oxford or Cambridge is more than just dreaming spires, ancient traditions and punting down 'the Backs'. You're looking for a college with its own slightly different personality, ethos and values. You might be interested in the newer colleges, which have a reputation for modernity – as well as excellent facilities and pastoral care.

When you visit Cambridge, pop into... Churchill, Fitzwilliam, Girton, Homerton, Murray Edwards, Newnham and Robinson

A lucky pick that might just be perfect... King's – although founded in 1441, King's is more modern in its approach and gives its students an alternative Cambridge experience – with the King's Affair (their answer to the traditional May Ball) a pleasant break from the pomp and ceremony elsewhere.

When you're up in Oxford, check out... Harris Manchester, St. Anne's, St. Catherine's, St. Hilda's, St. Hugh's, St. Peter's and Somerville

A lucky pick that might just be perfect... Mansfield – a one-time Permanent Private Hall, Mansfield is one of the smallest and friendliest colleges in the university and is forging ahead with a modern, access-focused admissions policy – and reaping the rewards with outstanding results.

Mostly Bs... Oxbridge with all the trimmings

Unlike some of your peers, you're looking forward to revelling in all the traditions that an ancient university has to offer. You want a unique experience – from regular formal hall, Latin grace and the odd secret society founded by a now very famous alumnus. You'll be looking at the older, often smaller colleges, with a long history and a deep-rooted respect for the past.

When you visit Cambridge, pop into... Corpus Christi, Gonville & Caius, Magdalene, Peterhouse and Trinity

A lucky pick that might just be perfect... Queens' – although Queens' doesn't have as many time-honoured traditions as other colleges, there is a real sense of college identity – and later generations of students have been able to leave their mark on the college: the myths about the Mathematical Bridge, for example.

When you're up in Oxford, check out... Brasenose, Exeter, Oriel, Queen's, St. Edmund Hall and Trinity

A lucky pick that might just be perfect... Corpus Christi – the college has some fun new traditions including the Pelican Cup, a sports day with Corpus Christi in Cambridge, and the annual Oxford Tortoise Race.

Mostly Cs... Brains over brawn

You're looking forward to everything university has to offer, but your number one priority is to take advantage of the opportunities to explore your subject. You want to be somewhere where people work hard and play hard – and where your college will give you everything you need to achieve. You could look at the academic league tables, the Tompkins Table (Cambridge) and Norrington Table (Oxford), to see which colleges get the best results.

When you visit Cambridge, pop into… Christ's, Clare, Emmanuel, Gonville & Caius, Selwyn, Trinity and Trinity Hall

A lucky pick that might just be perfect… Churchill – although it's a more modern college, the focus on the sciences, impressive numbers of Nobel laureates and high admissions requirements show that they mean business when it comes to academics.

When you're up in Oxford, check out… Corpus Christi, Hertford, Magdalen, Merton, New College and St. John's

A lucky pick that might just be perfect… Christ Church – better known for Harry Potter and Brideshead Revisited than for its academic excellence, Christ Church has dominated the top of the academic league tables for the last few years, proving that beautiful surroundings can help you learn.

Mostly Ds… Laid back and liberal

You want your time at university to be full and well-rounded. You're looking for lots of opportunities to get involved in different areas from sport to music and debating to drama – but also some chances to relax with your friends. You'll be looking for one of the more laid-back colleges, which may be less well known beyond Oxford and Cambridge, but whose students have nothing but the best to say.

When you visit Cambridge, pop into… Fitzwilliam, Homerton, Jesus, King's, Newnham, Pembroke, St. Catharine's and Sidney Sussex

A lucky pick that might just be perfect… Robinson – with its newer buildings and location slightly outside the city centre, Robinson students have access to excellent facilities, as well as the chance to get involved in a wide range of clubs and societies – from Chess to Cheese.

When you're up in Oxford, check out… Balliol, Jesus, Lady Margaret Hall, Lincoln, Pembroke, University College and Wadham

A lucky pick that might just be perfect... Somerville – easy access to Jericho (a village-like area full of cafes, restaurants and an independent cinema that shows foreign language films) and to Oxford's beautiful Port Meadows means students have plenty to do and a quick escape route from study.

Mostly Es... Grand and glorious

You're looking for the wow factor when it comes to your college. You want power and prestige, whether it be cheering on the college rugby team as they win the final (again), impressing tourists as you stroll through your college gates or even just basking in everyone else's college envy. You'll be looking at the biggest, oldest and most famous colleges.

When you visit Cambridge, pop into... Clare, Downing, King's, Queens', St. John's and Trinity

A lucky pick that might just be perfect... Jesus – slightly off the beaten track, Jesus' impressive buildings and power on the sports field – not to mention their own sculpture garden – means you'll get the benefits of a 'big' college, without the side helping of tourists.

When you're up in Oxford, check out... Balliol, Christ Church, Magdalen, New College, Queen's, Trinity and Worcester

A lucky pick that might just be perfect... Keble – built entirely out of redbrick, Keble is located a little further from the city centre than the other big colleges, but with its large student body it's a force to be reckoned with in the sporting stakes and its impressive architecture makes it a grand college, with an interesting twist.

Christ's College

—————————————— \☙/ ——————————————

Founded – 1505

Size – Medium (420 undergraduates, 170 postgraduates)

Academic Ranking – 2013 Tompkins Table = 8/29

Words that best describe it – Friendly, supportive, central, welcoming, green, academic

Suitable for – Those in search of academic excellence in the heart of Cambridge

You'll write home about...
Its central location
The extensive gardens
The good clubs and societies

It might not be for you if...
You like to party – Christ's is a serious, academic college

Churchill College

—————————————— \☙/ ——————————————

Founded – 1960

Size – Large (470 undergraduates, 300 postgraduates)

Academic Ranking – 2013 Tompkins Table = 5/29

Words that best describe it – Friendly, informal, recreational, open, sporty

Suitable for – Those looking for an escape from Cambridge's formalities

You'll write home about...
Everyone living on site
The dedicated theatre/cinema
The on-site playing fields

It might not be for you if...
You're looking for ancient splendour – the sixties architecture is not in the traditional style of Cambridge

Clare College

Founded – 1326

Size – Large (510 undergraduates, 300 postgraduates)

Academic Ranking – 2013 Tompkins Table = 11/29

Words that best describe it – Musical, informal, welcoming, popular, fun

Suitable for – History buffs wanting the picture-postcard experience

You'll write home about...
The great crypt music venue under the Chapel
The beautiful Fellows' Gardens
Ancient architecture
Decent external accommodation

It might not be for you if...
You're looking for a relaxed environment – its beauty is a little intimidating and it's a competitive college

Corpus Christi College

Founded – 1352

Size – Small (260 undergraduates, 220 postgraduates)

Academic Ranking – 2013 Tompkins Table = 16/29

Words that best describe it – Friendly, small, historic, convivial

Suitable for – Those looking for a small community

You'll write home about...
The Corpus Christi Playroom
The Parker Library
The outdoor swimming pool
The location

It might not be for you if...
You are not on track for top grades (when you get there) – the room ballot is academically weighted

Downing College

Founded – 1800

Size – Medium (425 undergraduates, 258 postgraduates)

Academic Ranking – 2013 Tompkins Table = 12/29

Words that best describe it – Spacious, convenient, friendly, beautiful, supportive, sporty

Suitable for – Sports players, sports fans

You'll write home about...
The many sporting victories
Huge, rolling lawns
The sheer amount of space

It might not be for you if...
You've got lots of friends at other colleges – you have to sign guests into the bar

Emmanuel College

Founded – 1584

Size – Large (473 undergraduates, 220 postgraduates)

Academic Ranking – 2013 Tompkins Table = 4/29

Words that best describe it – Fun, beautiful, central, open-minded, academic

Suitable for – Those who want to work hard and play hard

You'll write home about...
The famous duck pond
The outdoor swimming pool
Active music and drama societies
The bar
The unique laundry service

It might not be for you if...
You like cooking – there are limited facilities in college

Fitzwilliam College

———————————————— ☙ ————————————————

Founded – 1869 (full college status granted in 1966)

Size – Large (450 undergraduates, 308 postgraduates)

Academic Ranking – 2013 Tompkins Table = 20/29

Words that best describe it – Relaxed, unpretentious, friendly, fun

Suitable for – Those involved in university-level activities

You'll write home about...
The state-school-friendly approach
The lovely grounds
The brand new library and computer centre
The 250 seat auditorium

It might not be for you if...
You want to be central – Fitz is a little out of the way

Girton College

———————————————— ☙ ————————————————

Founded – 1869

Size – Large (520 undergraduates, 200 postgraduates)

Academic Ranking – 2013 Tompkins Table = 21/29

Words that best describe it – Distant, sprawling, pleasant, close-knit, unpretentious, easy-going

Suitable for – People who enjoy cycling

You'll write home about...
The huge grounds
The on-site sports facilities
The heated indoor swimming pool
The tasty food

It might not be for you if...
You're not into travelling – Girton is a bit of a trek from the centre of Cambridge

Gonville & Caius College

—————————————————— ⚭ ——————————————————

Founded – 1348

Size – Large (530 undergraduates, 250 postgraduates)

Academic Ranking – 2013 Tompkins Table = 17/29

Words that best describe it – Traditional, supportive, academic, energetic, sporty

Suitable for – Energetic types who want to work and play

You'll write home about...
Stephen Hawking having studied there
The central location
The strong boat club

It might not be for you if...
You want flexibility at meal times – there is compulsory Hall most nights

Homerton College

—————————————————— ⚭ ——————————————————

Founded – 1895 (full college status granted in 1976)

Size – Huge (570 undergraduates, 600 postgraduates)

Academic Ranking – 2013 Tompkins Table = 26/29

Words that best describe it – Friendly, open, modern, unpretentious, warm, communal

Suitable for – Slightly more relaxed characters

You'll write home about...
The space
The on-site sports facilities
The beautiful gardens
The lack of academic pressure

It might not be for you if...
You want to be centrally located

Jesus College

Founded – 1496

Size – Large (496 undergraduates, 310 postgraduates)

Academic Ranking – 2013 Tompkins Table = 6/29

Words that best describe it – Friendly, historic, beautiful, secluded

Suitable for – Fans of sculpture and people who like old buildings (without a side helping of tourists)

You'll write home about...
The architecture
Being five minutes from the centre of town
The on-site sports facilities
The statues

It might not be for you if...
You want to cook your own food – the kitchen fixed charge is expensive

King's College

Founded – 1441

Size – Medium (430 undergraduates, 280 postgraduates)

Academic Ranking – 2013 Tompkins Table = 14/29

Words that best describe it – Open, different, fun, impressive, accessible, liberal

Suitable for – Those looking for an alternative experience

You'll write home about...
The architecture
The King's Affair (King's May Ball alternative)
The location
The Mingles (large parties held at the end of the autumn and spring terms)

It might not be for you if...
You don't like tourists

Magdalene College

——————————————— ☯ ———————————————

Founded – 1428 or 1542, depending on who you ask

Size – Small (334 undergraduates, 235 postgraduates)

Academic Ranking – 2013 Tompkins Table = 15/29

Words that best describe it – Small, old, welcoming, close-knit, supportive

Suitable for – Traditionalists

You'll write home about...
The river bank
The Cambridge-style traditions
The Pepys Library
Its super-central location

It might not be for you if...
You want to keep yourself to yourself – the small community can mean gossip spreads like wildfire

Murray Edwards College

——————————————— ☯ ———————————————

Founded – 1954

Size – Medium (360 undergraduates, 130 postgraduates)

Academic Ranking – 2013 Tompkins Table = 24/29

Words that best describe it – Modern, dynamic, inspiring, diverse

Suitable for – Women who want a quieter, cleaner place to study

You'll write home about...
The luxurious second and third year accommodation
Beautiful lawns you can sit on
Free parking for students
The peace and quiet due to the non-central location

It might not be for you if...
Cycling uphill is an uphill struggle

Newnham College

Founded – 1871

Size – Medium (370 undergraduates, 285 Postgraduates)

Academic Ranking – 2013 Tompkins Table = 23/29

Words that best describe it – Sociable, safe, pretty, comfortable, peaceful, convenient

Suitable for – Those in need of an escape

You'll write home about...
The gardens (which you are allowed to sit in)
The proximity to many humanities departments
The on-site sports facilities
The food

It might not be for you if...
You're messy – there is no one to clean your room for you

Pembroke College

Founded 1347

Size – Medium (430 undergraduates, 250 postgraduates)

Academic Ranking – 2013 Tompkins Table = 2/29

Words that best describe it – Friendly, relaxed, central, inclusive, beautiful

Suitable for – Aspiring thesps and aesthetes

You'll write home about...
Being bang in the middle of Cambridge
The drama scene
The opportunities to go abroad with the college in the holidays
The lovely gardens

It might not be for you if...
You're hoping for a career in politics – the JCR is not politically active

Peterhouse

Founded – 1284

Size – Small (246 undergraduates, 110 postgraduates)

Academic Ranking – 2013 Tompkins Table = 10/29

Words that best describe it – Intimate, close-knit, relaxed, supportive, old, quaint

Suitable for – Those looking for a small community

You'll write home about...
Candlelit dining
The Deer Park
The accommodation

It might not be for you if...
You get claustrophobic – the small community can get too close for comfort

Queens' College

Founded – 1448

Size – Large (490 undergraduates, 450 postgraduates)

Academic Ranking – 2013 Tompkins Table = 7/29

Words that best describe it – Large, friendly, relaxed, sociable, extracurricular

Suitable for – Those that are outgoing and looking for a community feel

You'll write home about...
The famous Mathematical Bridge
Entertaining rumours about the history of said bridge
The sports facilities and societies
The Fitzpatrick Theatre

It might not be for you if...
You just want to relax – Queens' students can be a little boisterous at times

Robinson College

Founded – 1979

Size – Medium (386 undergraduates, 172 postgraduates)

Academic Ranking – 2013 Tompkins Table = 22/29

Words that best describe it – Unpretentious, open, diverse, supportive, modern

Suitable for – Those looking for a less traditional experience

You'll write home about...
The modern accommodation
The great food
The beautiful gardens and lake

It might not be for you if...
You want to be surrounded by classical buildings – the modern architecture is not to everyone's liking

St. Catharine's College

Founded – 1473

Size – Medium (436 undergraduates, 220 postgraduates)

Academic Ranking – 2013 Tompkins Table = 9/29

Words that best describe it – Open, social, inclusive, supportive, engaging, central

Suitable for – Those in search of a friendly, central experience

You'll write home about...
The central location
The accommodation
The brand new McGrath Centre, which houses the college bar, JCR and auditorium

It might not be for you if...
You like to cook – the self-catering facilities are poor

St. John's College

Founded – 1511

Size – Large (569 undergraduates, 337 postgraduates)

Academic Ranking – 2013 Tompkins Table = 13/29

Words that best describe it – Big, beautiful, fun, grand, sporty, cosmopolitan, rich

Suitable for – Those who want to be the centre of attention

You'll write home about...
The very large college grounds
The funding
The beautiful gardens
The May Ball
The sport, drama and music

It might not be for you if...
You're nervous about 'the Oxbridge thing' – it can get slightly overwhelming at times

Selwyn College

Founded – 1882

Size – Medium (400 undergraduates, 200 postgraduates)

Academic Ranking – 2013 Tompkins Table = 18/29

Words that best describe it – Sociable, close-knit, academic, supportive

Suitable for – Those looking for a close-knit community

You'll write home about...
Its proximity to many humanities departments
The fabulous new accommodation block
The friendly atmosphere
The space

It might not be for you if...
You want to be in the centre of town – it's a short walk away

Sidney Sussex College

Founded – 1596

Size – Small (350 undergraduates, 240 postgraduates)

Academic Ranking – 2013 Tompkins Table = 19/29

Words that best describe it – Central, friendly, cosy, close-knit

Suitable for – Those involved in university-level activities

You'll write home about...
The student-run bar
The location
Being housed with all the other first years

It might not be for you if...
You want a bit of space – Sidney is a small college located right in the centre of town

Trinity College

Founded – 1546

Size – Gigantic (695 undergraduates, 397 postgraduates)

Academic Ranking – 2013 Tompkins Table = 1/29

Words that best describe it – Grand, traditional, sociable, rich, impressive

Suitable for – Big Cheeses

You'll write home about...
The academic reputation par excellence
The huge library
Living in college for the duration of your course

It might not be for you if...
You like your colleges cosy – it can be a little too imposing for some

Trinity Hall

‒‒‒‒‒‒‒‒‒‒‒‒‒‒‒‒‒‒‒ \0/ ‒‒‒‒‒‒‒‒‒‒‒‒‒‒‒‒‒‒‒‒‒

Founded – 1350

Size – Medium (370 undergraduates, 270 postgraduates)

Academic Ranking – 2013 Tompkins Table = 3/29

Words that best describe it – Idyllic, small, central, sociable, sporty

Suitable for – Those looking for riverside calm

You'll write home about...
Being so central
The beautiful architecture and grounds
The lovely Jerwood Library on the river
The opportunities for musicians

It might not be for you if...
You want to be part of a big group – it can be a little too intimate at times

Balliol College

Founded – 1263

Size – Large (385 undergraduates, 340 postgraduates)

Academic Ranking – 2013 Norrington Table = 10/31

Words that best describe it – Unpretentious, liberal, energetic, high-achieving

Suitable for – Those who operate a little left-of-centre

You'll write home about...
The incredible selection of food available from the pantry
The grass you can sit on
The sports societies
The largest (and one of the last) student-run bars in Oxford

It might not be for you if...
You want all the Oxbridge trimmings – there is a lack of formal hall and formality in general

Brasenose College

Founded – 1509

Size – Medium (355 undergraduates, 220 postgraduates)

Academic Ranking – 2013 Norrington Table = 8/31

Words that best describe it – Old, stately, warm, easygoing

Suitable for – Relaxed sorts, traditionalists

You'll write home about...
Living in a castle
The extracurricular societies
The central location

It might not be for you if...
You are looking for a modern outlook

Christt Church College
—————————————— ⱳ ——————————————

Founded – 1524

Size – Large (440 undergraduates, 220 postgraduates)

Academic Ranking – 2013 Norrington Table = 17/31

Words that best describe it – Prestigious, grand, proud, beautiful, traditional

Suitable for – Those looking for the archetypal Oxbridge experience, future Prime Ministers

You'll write home about...
The accommodation
The funding and grants
Christ Church Meadows

It might not be for you if...
You don't like tourists or Harry Potter fans

Corpus Christi College
—————————————— ⱳ ——————————————

Founded – 1517

Size – Small (250 undergraduates, 110 postgraduates)

Academic Ranking – 2013 Norrington Table = 24/31

Words that best describe it – Friendly, supportive, intellectual, quaint, compact

Suitable for – Those who want to win University Challenge

You'll write home about...
The strong academic performance
The accommodation
The wonderful library – one of the wonders of the world according to Erasmus
The central location

It might not be for you if...
You want lots of space – the small size can get a bit claustrophobic

Exeter College

— 〰 —

Founded – 1314

Size – Small to medium (345 undergraduates, 235 postgraduates)

Academic Ranking – 2013 Norrington Table = 28/31

Words that best describe it – Central, open-minded, chilled, beautiful, close-knit, relaxed

Suitable for – Those looking for an idyllic central college

You'll write home about...
The central location
The strong musical tradition
WiFi in the college gardens

It might not be for you if...
You want to spread out – the college grounds are a bit cramped

Hertford College

— 〰 —

Founded – 1282 (achieving full college status in 1874)

Size – Medium (400 undergraduates, 190 postgraduates)

Academic Ranking – 2013 Norrington Table = 18/31

Words that best describe it – Democratic, unpretentious, central, social, relaxed

Suitable for – Progressive types

You'll write home about...
The relaxed environment
The Hertford Bridge (popularly known as the Bridge of Sighs)
The bar
The state-school-friendly attitude

It might not be for you if...
You're a foodie – the college meals are not amazing

Jesus College

—————————— ⟨σ⟩ ——————————

Founded – 1571

Size – Medium (350 undergraduates, 190 postgraduates)

Academic Ranking – 2013 Norrington Table = 14/31

Words that best describe it – Small, close-knit, welcoming, sleepy, central

Suitable for – Sports fans

You'll write home about...
The central location
The gentle atmosphere
The lovely buildings

It might not be for you if...
You want to live in college for the duration of your course – the external accommodation is quite far away from college

Keble College

—————————— ⟨σ⟩ ——————————

Founded – 1870

Size – Large (430 undergraduates, 220 postgraduates)

Academic Ranking – 2013 Norrington Table = 27/31

Words that best describe it – Friendly, buzzing, gothic, fun, traditional

Suitable for – Those looking for extracurricular experience

You'll write home about...
The proximity to the Science Area
The unique architecture
The lack of tourists
The O'Reilly Theatre

It might not be for you if...
You want to be in the middle of Oxford – it's a tad far from the city-centre bustle

Lady Margaret Hall

Founded – 1878

Size – Large (400 undergraduates, 205 postgraduates)

Academic Ranking – 2013 Norrington Table = 30/31

Words that best describe it – Pretty, friendly, scenic, relaxed, lively

Suitable for – Those looking to get away from it all

You'll write home about...
The accommodation
The gardens
The atmosphere

It might not be for you if...
You don't like cycling – the college is a 15-20 minute walk from the centre

Lincoln College

Founded – 1427

Size – Small (320 undergraduates, 290 postgraduates)

Academic Ranking – 2013 Norrington Table = 7/31

Words that best describe it – Friendly, small, busy, close-knit, high-achieving

Suitable for – Those looking for a sociable community

You'll write home about...
The accommodation
The food
The bar
The location

It might not be for you if...
You're looking for a big college – Lincoln is one of the smaller Oxford colleges

Magdalen College
—————————————— ☿ ——————————————

Founded – 1458

Size – Big (415 undergraduates, 195 postgraduates)

Academic Ranking – 2013 Norrington Table = 6/31

Words that best describe it – Big, inspiring, beautiful, surprising, challenging

Suitable for – Movers and shakers

You'll write home about...
Living in all three years
The space
The great music and drama scene
Having your own Deer Park

It might not be for you if...
You want friends outside college – they may all suffer from college envy!

Mansfield College
—————————————— ☿ ——————————————

Founded – 1886 (full college status granted in 1995)

Size – Small (210 undergraduates, 100 postgraduates)

Academic Ranking – 2013 Norrington Table = 15/31

Words that best describe it – Unpretentious, small, friendly, accommodating, relaxed

Suitable for – Humble types

You'll write home about...
The friendly community
The access-orientated approach to admissions
Being close to the Science Area and University Parks

It might not be for you if...
You want access to funds and bursaries – Mansfield is not the richest of colleges

Merton College

—————————————— ☙ ——————————————

Founded – 1264

Size – Small (315 undergraduates, 330 postgraduates)

Academic Ranking – 2013 Norrington Table = 4/31

Words that best describe it – Small, central, academic, pretty

Suitable for – Academics and extremely high-achievers

You'll write home about...
The great teaching and tutorial support
The cheap food and rent
The central location

It might not be for you if...
You don't really love your subject – too much focus on extracurricular activities is not encouraged

New College

—————————————— ☙ ——————————————

Founded – 1379

Size – Large (425 undergraduates, 245 postgraduates)

Academic Ranking – 2013 Norrington Table = 1/31

Words that best describe it – Social, big, active, academic, competitive, fun

Suitable for – Social types

You'll write home about...
The large student body
The beautiful and spacious surroundings
The celebrated musical tradition

It might not be for you if...
You're after a cosy college – new can be intimidating

Oriel College

——————————— ⚥ ———————————

Founded – 1326

Size – Small (305 undergraduates, 170 postgraduates)

Academic Ranking – 2013 Norrington Table = 9/31

Words that best describe it – Sporty, small, old, traditional, central, warm-hearted

Suitable for – Rowing and sports enthusiasts

You'll write home about...
The excellent facilities for sports
Being at one of the top rowing colleges
The central location

It might not be for you if...
You're a foodie – the college food is not that good

Pembroke College

——————————— ⚥ ———————————

Founded – 1624

Size – Medium (400 undergraduates, 170 postgraduates)

Academic Ranking – 2013 Norrington Table = 13/31

Words that best describe it – Inclusive, busy, sporty

Suitable for – Sporty types (especially those interested in rowing)

You'll write home about...
The location
The relaxed atmosphere
The distinguished alumni

It might not be for you if...
You want to live cheaply – the rent is more expensive than at other colleges

The Queen's College

Founded – 1341

Size – Medium (345 undergraduates, 145 postgraduates)

Academic Ranking – 2013 Norrington Table = 26/31

Words that best describe it – Cosy, friendly, down-to-earth, old-fashioned

Suitable for – Laid-back types

You'll write home about...
The beautiful architecture
The relaxed student body
The central location

It might not be for you if...
You want to get involved in university-wide societies – it can be quite insular

Regent's Park College (PPH)

Founded – 1752

Size – Small (120 undergraduates, 70 postgraduates)

Words that best describe it – friendly, familial, down-to-earth, busy, homely

Suitable for – those wanting to get involved in wider university life

You'll write home about...
Formal hall
The college tortoise, Emmanuelle
The JCR - one of the best in Oxford

It might not be for you if...
You're a big fish who needs a big pond

St. Anne's College
—————————————— \[0] ——————————————

Founded – 1879 (full college status granted in 1952)

Size – Large (425 undergraduates, 145 postgraduates)

Academic Ranking – 2013 Norrington Table = 12/31

Words that best describe it – Sociable, relaxed, down to earth, spacious

Suitable for – Chilled-out untraditional types

You'll write home about...
The large site
Good food
The lack of regimented traditions

It might not be for you if...
You want a picture-perfect college – it's not the prettiest

St Benet's Hall (PPH)
—————————————— \[0] ——————————————

Founded – 1897

Size – Small (54 undergraduates, 10 postgraduates)

Words that best describe it – familial, traditional, collegiate, pastoral

Suitable for – those who want a friendly, traditional and unstuffy college but want to throw themselves into the wider university

You'll write home about...
The monks
The social events
The camaraderie

It might not be for you if...
You are a woman (Benet's is an all-male college)

St. Catherine's College
——————————————— ∖☉∕ ———————————————

Founded – 1963

Size – Large (500 undergraduates, 255 postgraduates)

Academic Ranking – 2013 Norrington Table = 21/31

Words that best describe it – Social, friendly, sporty, vibrant, modern

Suitable for – Those looking for a modern touch

You'll write home about...
The excellent facilities for sports and the arts
Good food
The biggest college bar in Oxford

It might not be for you if...
You take an instant dislike to the architecture. It's a marmite affair –
you either love it or you hate it!

St. Edmund Hall
——————————————— ∖☉∕ ———————————————

Founded – c. 1371 (full college status granted in 1957)

Size – Large (405 undergraduates, 195 postgraduates)

Academic Ranking – 2013 Norrington Table = 16/31

Words that best describe it – Sociable, small, sporty, intimate,
relaxed, central

Suitable for – Sporty types

You'll write home about...
The sports
The location
The social life

It might not be for you if...
Food is very important to you – it's not great at Teddy Hall

St. Hilda's College

Founded – 1893

Size – Medium (405 undergraduates, 170 postgraduates)

Academic Ranking – 2013 Norrington Table = 20/31

Words that best describe it – Relaxed, friendly, spacious, inviting, fun, supportive

Suitable for – Those wanting a bit of riverside charm

You'll write home about...
The excellent music facilities
The spacious gardens
Being very close to the University sports complex

It might not be for you if...
You want the 'Brideshead' experience – it lacks the traditional Oxford trimmings (cloisters, quads, etc.)

St. Hugh's College

Founded – 1886

Size – Large (420 undergraduates, 225 postgraduates)

Academic Ranking – 2013 Norrington Table = 23/31

Words that best describe it – Spacious, unpretentious, chilled-out, friendly, calm

Suitable for – Those looking for a bit of tranquillity

You'll write home about...
The large grounds
The well-stocked library
The tranquil setting

It might not be for you if...
You want to live in the city centre – it's quite far out

St. John's College

— ☸ —

Founded – 1555

Size – Large (395 undergraduates, 225 postgraduates)

Academic Ranking – 2013 Norrington Table = 3/31

Words that best describe it – Friendly, rich, big, academic, diverse, high-achieving

Suitable for – Academic high-achievers

You'll write home about...
The location
The resources
The reputation

It might not be for you if...
You're looking for an undersubscribed college – entrance is usually competitive

St. Peter's College

— ☸ —

Founded – 1929 (full college status granted in 1961)

Size – Medium (340 undergraduates, 95 postgraduates)

Academic Ranking – 2013 Norrington Table = 22/30

Words that best describe it – Open, friendly, grounded, central, caring, cosy

Suitable for – Those looking for an alternative, light-hearted Oxford experience

You'll write home about...
The location
The cheap food
The friendly, unpretentious student body

It might not be for you if...
You're not a big fan of the Oxford Union – it's right next door

Somerville College

———————————————— ∅ ————————————————

Founded – 1879

Size – Medium (395 undergraduates, 90 postgraduates)

Academic Ranking – 2013 Norrington Table = 29/31

Words that best describe it – Friendly, open-minded, homely, supportive, untraditional

Suitable for – Those looking to avoid Oxford clichés

You'll write home about...
The library
The community spirit
Living in Jericho – a very trendy area

It might not be for you if...
You want the traditional Oxford experience

Trinity College

———————————————— ∅ ————————————————

Founded – 1554

Size – Small (310 undergraduates, 110 postgraduates)

Academic Ranking – 2013 Norrington Table = 2/31

Words that best describe it – Spacious, inclusive, friendly, warm, beautiful, open

Suitable for – Those looking for beautiful surroundings

You'll write home about...
The exquisite gardens
The central location
The high-quality food

It might not be for you if...
You want to cook for yourself – there are limited self-catering options on the main college site

University College

— ⚘ —

Founded – 1249

Size – Medium (365 undergraduates, 225 postgraduates)

Academic Ranking – 2013 Norrington Table = 25/31

Words that best describe it – Relaxed, fun, diverse, welcoming, cosy

Suitable for – Those looking for a close-knit community

You'll write home about...
The relaxed atmosphere
The central location
The distinguished history

It might not be for you if...
You want to stretch out – it's a bit of a squish

Wadham College

— ⚘ —

Founded – 1610

Size – Large (455 undergraduates, 155 postgraduates)

Academic Ranking – 2013 Norrington Table = 19/31

Words that best describe it – Alternative, open, political, sociable, friendly, unpretentious

Suitable for – Those looking for a diverse and progressive community

You'll write home about...
The relaxed atmosphere
The fantastic annual college events
The politically involved student body

It might not be for you if...
You want guaranteed college accommodation for the duration of your course

Worcester College

—————————————— ʘʃ ——————————————

Founded – 1714

Size – Large (430 undergraduates, 175 postgraduates)

Academic Ranking – 2013 Norrington Table = 11/31

Words that best describe it – Beautiful, friendly, relaxed, sociable, welcoming, sporty

Suitable for – Those looking for a sociable community

You'll write home about...
The accommodation
The food
The lake
The sports and music facilities

It might not be for you if...
You don't fancy competing against lots of other applicants – Worcester is fairly oversubscribed

What is a Permanent Private Hall or PPH?

PPHs are smaller than Oxford colleges and offer a more limited number of courses. Students at PPHs are still full members of the University, but studying at one of the Permanent Private Halls offers a unique Oxford experience. They were originally founded by different Christian denominations but, in most cases, students are not required to be of that denomination to apply (only sympathetic).

Students at PPHs have the same access to University and Faculty Libraries, they often share tutorials with students at other colleges, they sit the same exams and have the same degrees awarded by the University.

The following six PPHs accept undergraduate applications:

Regent's Park (founded 1752) is the largest PPH, with over 200 undergraduate, graduate and visiting international students. Slightly hidden away on Pusey Street (off St Giles) it has a small college feel and boasts a social life equal, if not superior, to most small colleges. It is definitely worth a look en route to all the bustle of Jericho. Regent's Park accepts undergraduate applications from both male and female students of any age, and offers the broadest range of subjects: CAAH (Classical Archaeology & Ancient History), Classics, Classics & English, English Language & Literature, Geography, History, History (Ancient & Modern), History & Politics, Law (Jurisprudence), PPE (Philosophy, Politics & Economics), Philosophy & Theology and Theology.

St Benet's Hall (1897) is, like Blackfriars, located fairly centrally on St Giles. It only admits a small handful of male students each year, and offers a wider range of subjects than most other PPHs: Classics, Classics & Oriental Studies, History, History & Politics, History & Economics, Oriental Studies, PPE (Philosophy, Politics & Economics), Philosophy & Theology, Theology and Theology & Oriental Studies. St Benet's is notorious for its Sunday lunches and termly parties, where friends (male and female) are invited into the large town house, garden and croquet lawn.

Mature PPHs:

Blackfriars (founded 1221) only accepts mature students (those over 21) and admits a large number of American students – usually 'Visiting Students' – which creates a diverse mixture of young people. It offers Theology, Theology & Oriental Studies, Theology & Philosophy and PPE (Philosophy, Politics & Economics). Blackfriars hosts the occasional party, and is located centrally on St Giles – the main street into North Oxford, near the popular Little Clarendon Street.

St Stephen's House (1876) offers only Theology to mature students (over 21s) who apply. It was founded in the fervour of the Oxford Movement, and is situated outside the town centre, on the main Iffley Road which heads east out of Oxford.

Wycliffe Hall (1877) only admits mature students (over 21s), and accepts applications for Theology and Theology & Philosophy. Wycliffe boasts one of the best Theology libraries in the University, and is situated towards North Oxford (a similar distance from the centre as St Anne's College).

3 PERSONAL STATEMENT

—— ❦ ——

A PRACTICAL GUIDE TO WRITING YOURS AND SOME INSPIRATION...

How important is the personal statement?

A strong application to Oxford or Cambridge, or indeed any top UK university, requires you to excel at every stage of the process – including your personal statement. However, when applying to Oxbridge, there are many points of contact between you and the university admissions tutors, meaning that a strong personal statement is not enough to secure you an offer. What it can do is give you a good start in your interview, demonstrating your interests and prompting interviewers to begin a discussion that will allow you to shine.

How is the statement used at interview?

You should view everything you say in your personal statement as a potential springboard for discussion at interview: you may be asked to elaborate on something you have written about, be it a book, work experience, particular areas of academic interest, or an extended project.

We surveyed thousands of students who applied to Oxbridge in 2013 to tell us what they discussed at interview. **64% were asked about their personal statement**. Below they describe some questions that came up…

- **Engineering** "I was only asked one question relating to my personal statement about some work experience I had done"

- **PPE** "I was asked about an idea on my personal statement. What ideas would you use as a basis for your moral theory? (I said equality) Where do you derive the idea of equality from? Moral? Theological? Is equality an intrinsic or extrinsic good? (I answered, with reference to Plato's Republic, both)"

- **Modern & Medieval Languages** "A lot of discussion on cultural things I had mentioned in my statement"

- **History** "Some broad and some specific questions about my personal statement… I wrote about gender history for example, and was asked very broadly, 'tell me about gender history'."

- **English** "The tutor primarily asked questions relating to my personal statement… for example, as I had noted that I had set various Blake poems to music, she asked how I thought poetry and song lyrics were similar or different from each other"

- **Geography** "I see you've written that you enjoy plate tectonics in your personal statement… talk to me about it"

- **History & Modern Languages** "You mentioned British Imperialism in your personal statement; do you think Spanish Imperialism differed?"

- **E&M** "Why do you question the basis of economics – rationality and the behaviour of firms – in your personal statement?"

- **Medicine** "We discussed action potentials, haemoglobin, cardiac output, respiratory systems, hormones, the liver, mental health… bear in mind nothing was asked out of the blue – it all led on from what I had said in my personal statement or stemmed from a graph"

- **History** "I was asked the same question about my personal statement in both interviews: I said I was fascinated by the link between history and literature, and so they asked me how literature can be useful in studying history"

- **PPE** "I didn't get asked at all about the books I had put on my personal statement"

Even if you're not asked about your personal statement at interview, the preparation that goes into researching and writing it will give you the knowledge and confidence to talk about and explore new ideas within your subject, which will only help to make your application stronger.

Who is your audience?

You can only submit one personal statement through UCAS, so it will be read by admissions tutors at all of the universities you apply to, although you may be applying to five universities with slightly different courses at each. This can be a particular problem if you are applying for one of Oxbridge's unique courses – such as Human Sciences (Oxford), or Land Economy (Cambridge) – and yet still trying to make your personal statement fit with the courses you are applying for at other universities.

The best advice here is to take a thematic approach: focus on the subject that is relevant to all your applications, but demonstrate through a piece of independent research – an EPQ or extended project – your particular interest in the area of that subject to show that you have looked at the topic from the perspective of the unique course.

Besides course differentiation, it is important to consider how much you include of non-subject-specific content. Oxford and Cambridge are not particularly interested in whether you are an Olympic rower or play five instruments to Grade 8 standard. They do, of course, recognise the scale of these accomplishments and they can indicate characteristics that will boost academic success. However, ultimately the tutors reading your statement care about one thing, and one thing only: how much potential do you have as a student in the subject you've applied for? Therefore, a strong personal statement for Oxbridge is consistently relevant to that subject. Other universities are often more interested in students as 'well-rounded' people, i.e. your extracurricular activities are of value, even if they don't directly relate to the subject. As such, it is a good idea to include these, but if you're applying to Oxbridge, you must strongly weight your statement towards subject-specific content. The following guide explains how you can do this.

A practical guide to turning a blank page into 4000 characters...

Staring at a blank page and no idea where to begin? Well this is your solution...

Step 1: Structure and planning

1) Take a piece of A4 paper, draw a line across it about 3 inches from the top. Do the same, 3 inches from the bottom.

Well done... you've just created your plan!

2) Start with the bottom third. Bullet-point all the extracurricular achievements you can think of. Good at piano? Put it in. Climbed Mount Kilimanjaro? Put it in. Played Polonius in the school play? DofE gold medal? Sure, why not? You don't need to hold back yet – this is just the plan!

3) Now the top third. The opening sentence is often the hardest, but this is a good way to get past that. Take 15-20 minutes to think seriously about the real reason you're choosing your degree. Try not to feel embarrassed about clichés and trite statements yet. This is your plan, so you can make it sound sophisticated later. Really strong personal statements begin with a real sentiment, rather than something you think the admissions tutors will want to hear.

The question 'Why do you want to study x?' is almost guaranteed at the beginning of the interview. Don't disregard it, however, as a warm up question. This is probably the single most important element of your application. A good answer demonstrates a real understanding of what the academic discipline of your subject is all about, as well as your motivation for pursuing it.

4) Now the middle. Your middle section is your content. Which novel did you read from your syllabus that really highlighted for you what it is you love about teasing out nuances in literature?

Which extra project did you do that best demonstrated what you love about problem solving? Which exhibition did you visit which highlighted to you what is fascinating to you about history? This has to be the academic section, and crucially it has to demonstrate work you've done outside of your A level (or IB or equivalent) syllabus.

To help focus your thoughts and ideas and get your creative juices flowing, try jotting down some answers to the following questions on a separate sheet.

Remember, this is all about your subject so keep it relevant!

- What have you read and/or done to help further your understanding of this chosen course?

- How do you think your current academic subjects support your chosen course and will help you to excel at university?

- What part of your current studies has most inspired you and why?

- What books or articles have you recently read?

- What did you enjoy about them? What do you feel you learnt from reading them? (Think about what challenged you or whether anything surprised you). Did you agree or disagree with the author/s? Did the particular book/article make you want to learn more about a certain subject? If so, what exactly?

- What work experience have you done that is relevant to your subject?

Once you've got these, select the strongest points and bullet them in your middle section.

Step 2: Refining and writing

1) Bottom third. Reassess your extracurriculars. Could any of them have furthered your understanding in your subject? Select two or three stand-out achievements and find elements of them that

would contribute to you being good in your subject. Perhaps you ran a marathon? Tenacity and mental stamina will be invaluable if you plan to pursue a career as a doctor etc. etc.

2) Look at your bulleted content for the middle section again. What was it about these experiences that highlighted to you what is so special about your subject? Once you have considered this for each one, look at how you might draw thematic links between them in order to lead comfortably from one idea to the next.

3) It's a good general rule of thumb to approach your subject and what interests you about it from three different angles across three paragraphs. If you are reading Chemistry, what interests you about Organic, Inorganic and Physical? Can you find an example of Organic that links closely with Inorganic? This would be a great transitional hinge to move from one point to the next.

Step 3: Checking your tone

When you are planning and eventually writing this, it is vital to be aware of the following distinction: bad personal statements try to make a mini essay out of each subject brought up in order to try to demonstrate knowledge of the text or idea. There is not enough space to develop a complex idea – save that for your interview! When you write your good personal statement, isolate a particular reason as to why you personally have engaged with your course, and then use specific examples to back this general idea up.

When writing, you can assume a certain level of knowledge in the reader: you wouldn't have to explain what the Duke of Edinburgh Award Scheme is, for example. This applies, more importantly, to books you are writing about. You don't need to describe what the books are about – rather what you think of them and what the argument means to you. Be specific and give examples to show that you have actually read the book and have formulated an opinion.

How to use your personal statement

Your personal statement should mention texts that you feel comfortable about. Everyone will tell you to be sure to read those texts – you've seen in the examples above, where many students were asked to expand on themes and ideas in their statement – but also it's vital to think of those texts or areas of study as doorways to a network of further wider reading that you've looked at.

"I was not asked about any of the books on my personal statement. However, I was asked if I'd read any books other than the books on my personal statement which related to its theme (i.e. what other books have you read that could relate to the slums of Mumbai?)"

Sara, 2013 Geography applicant

This is why it is so key to have more up your sleeve than is in your 4000 characters.

Check out the bibliographies or the journals and articles referenced in the book on your personal statement, and read some of those. This way, when you go into your interview, you have a wealth of material to draw from as a foundation so that you are not caught short when trying to answer a question using an example.

Some inspiration

Opener: Engineering at Cambridge

I find the built environment fascinating and perplexing, marvelling how engineers build such towering skyscrapers with complex designs that appear surprisingly simple. In reality it takes a vast amount of effort and skill to achieve the end result. This focused my desire to study engineering. I began to understand that it embraces not just bridges and buildings but water systems, nanotechnology and robotics. I like the idea of being involved in large-scale projects with tangible results and that each project could be different, each with a different set of problems to solve and requiring flexibility. Engineering is innovative and I am fascinated by the idea of developing new mechanisms that have never been attempted before and I am excited by the opportunity to apply the theory of physics and mathematics in a practical way.

Main content paragraph 1: Geography at Cambridge

I enjoyed the opportunity to pass on my knowledge of the formation of fold Mountains, U-shaped valleys and how the mountain has been shaped by human influences, such as tourism when I went walking with my brother in Wales. I read 'New Internationalist' and 'Geography Review', whose articles on climate change, multiculturalism, and globalisation have since complemented and expanded my academic studies of human Geography. I enjoyed "Development, Bottom Up or Top Down?", as this explored the nature and limitations of different development schemes, and "Climate Change and Crops", which advanced my knowledge of the impact of climate change, and how new crops could lead to further environmental damage.

Main content paragraph 2: Classics at Oxford

The critical examination of sources within History has augmented my analytical and evaluation skills, whilst the study of English has enhanced my ability to express ideas in a clear, coherent way. My initial love for language was triggered by French lessons and through this I have observed the value of reading literature in its original language and learnt to appreciate the subtleties which can so often be lost in translation. As my school does not offer Classical languages I decided to pursue them myself by attending JACT summer schools with the aim that I would be able to one day read the original works in Latin and Greek.

Main content paragraph 3: Law at Oxford

Undertaking work experience at Lincoln House Chambers allowed me to engage with a case and witness criminal proceedings at Manchester Magistrates' Court. A placement at the South Manchester Law Centre, where I actively assisted with an immigration case and attended tribunals, raised my awareness of the necessity of legal funding and pro bono work to attempt to make the law accessible for everyone. My appreciation for politics and international relations can also be seen through my involvement with Model United Nations, where I consistently received awards for debating and practised forming and justifying arguments, a skill which I believe stems from a history of dramatic arts with my local theatre company and LAMDA examinations.

The Ending: Medicine at Cambridge

Although aware of its negative aspects and limitations, I still believe medicine is the ideal career for me. Becoming a doctor would allow me to help others in a job combining my strong interest in science, enjoyment of communicating with others and working within a team as well as diverse future opportunities such as teaching and research. As a keen, diligent and determined individual capable of working well under pressure, I feel I will be prepared for the demands of the course and the career.

Ten golden rules for writing your personal statement from the personal statement gurus

We've asked personal statement experts Gavin and Guy Nobes, authors of *60 Successful Personal Statements*, who know the process from both the university and school perspectives (Gavin is a senior lecturer at the University of East Anglia, and Guy leads the Higher Education & Careers Department at Marlborough College) for their advice on how to structure your personal statement.

Here are their top tips:

1. Research the courses you are applying for thoroughly to show enthusiasm for and understanding of the subject

2. Be specific and display precise knowledge; never be vague

3. Be honest; only include what you know and are confident about discussing

4. Try to sound interesting and interested, but don't overdo it, gush or come across as arrogant

5. Express your information and ideas clearly

6. Don't be negative; try to see any failures as 'learning experiences'

7. Organise your material clearly and logically

8. Don't state the obvious or repeat yourself

9. Consider speeling, apostrophe's & grammer (mistakes are irritating and don't reflect well on you… !)

10. Don't misuse words in an attempt to look clever: your personal statement needs to be clear as well as reflecting the way you communicate

The platinum rule: show, don't tell

Rather than just claiming to be enthusiastic or informed about your subject, demonstrate your interest and understanding by describing:

- the background to your interest in the subject
- ways in which you are currently following up this enthusiasm
- what exactly you know about the subject

And remember, while the personal statement can take a good deal of your time, do keep reminding yourself that this is the chance to write about a very interesting subject that no one else will be writing about: you!

4 THE OXBRIDGE APPLICATION PROCESS

———————————— ▧ ————————————

A STEP-BY-STEP GUIDE TO THE
SPECIFICS OF SUBMITTING YOUR
APPLICATION

While Oxford and Cambridge share many steps in the application process, some aspects are dealt with differently. Our guide below runs through some specific details. For further information on any aspect of the application process, you can consult the Oxford or Cambridge website.

UCAS Form

Applicants to Oxford and Cambridge must submit their UCAS form by 15th October. On the form, you need to specify which college and course you wish to apply to. Universities will not be told where else you have applied. You can find the UCAS form on the website: www.ucas. ac.uk. If you're worried about the other universities you're applying to working out from your early application that you've applied to Oxbridge, you can submit your application to your other three or four choices later by logging back into your UCAS form and selecting your other choices (before the January deadline). You won't be able to edit your application - you will be submitting exactly the same application as you did to Oxbridge, just slightly later.

Offer

In the January following your interview, the college or department will send you a letter telling you the outcome of your application. If you have been successful, the letter will make you an offer and these usually have academic conditions attached e.g. A level results or STEP requirements. You'll receive your letter in the first two weeks of January.

Grades

You must achieve the grades set out in your conditional offer in order to secure your place. If you do miss your grades by a couple of marks, or if special circumstances affected your performance, get in contact with your college as soon as possible to see whether they might still be able to accept you. There's no set rule on this; it really depends on the college and the circumstances.

The Oxford application process

Organ Scholarship

The deadline for the Organ Scholarship Application Form is 1st September. Auditions usually take place in Oxford towards the end of September, and you'll have your academic interview at the same time. This means that you should be ready to submit your written work when you apply as it will be requested soon afterwards. Organ scholarship offers and academic places are then confirmed before the UCAS deadline. You must accept any scholarship offer you are made by a college, even if it wasn't your first choice. Offers will then be made formally through UCAS. Organ Scholars can apply to both Oxford and Cambridge and to more than one college, but must specify only one choice on their UCAS form.

Choral Scholarship

The deadline for the Choral Scholarship Application Form is early September and the choral trials usually take place in late September. You won't have an academic interview during this time; this takes place in December with all other applicants. Even if you're successful in your Choral Award application, you're not guaranteed an academic place – both successful and unsuccessful applicants should submit their UCAS application in the usual way before the 15th October, after the choral trials. Unsuccessful applicants for the choral scholarship may still gain an academic place. If you're unsuccessful with your application for a choral scholarship, but receive an academic offer, there may be an opportunity when you arrive to re-apply to a particular choir when you're at Oxford.

Written Work

You may have to submit written work as part of your application, depending on which course you're applying for. The deadline for Oxford is 10th November. Written work must be:

- No longer than 2,000 words
- Produced as part of normal school work and marked by your teacher
- Typed or (legibly) handwritten
- Submitted with a covering sheet which you download from the Oxford website

Your written work should be of a high standard and on a subject you're well informed on, as your essay may form the basis of your interview. Oxford is as interested in how you are taught and how you respond to feedback as in what you have written, so don't be too dismayed if you've made mistakes or have corrections from your teacher.

The Cambridge application process

Organ Scholarships

You will need to submit your Cambridge Online Preliminary Application form (COPA) by 1st September along with a draft of your personal statement. Auditions are held in Cambridge in mid to late September, and academic interviews happen at the same time, so you should be ready to submit your written work (if required) when you apply. Organ scholarship offers and academic places are then confirmed before the UCAS deadline. You must accept any scholarship offer you are made by a college, even if it wasn't your first choice. Offers will then be made formally through UCAS. In some cases, you may be asked to return in December for a further interview. Organ Scholars can apply to both Oxford and Cambridge and to more than one college, but must specify only one choice on their UCAS form. For more information on which colleges are offering scholarships and to download the application form, see the Cambridge website.

Choral Scholarships

The application process for Choral Scholarships changed in 2012. You now only apply for a Choral Scholarship once you have been offered an academic place at the university. You need to submit the Choral Award Application Form by 15th February of the year that you're planning to begin your course. You can apply for a Choral Scholarship at as many colleges as you wish (providing you're eligible) but your first choice must be the college that has offered you the academic place. If your application is successful you will be invited to a choral audition by the end of March. The audition will involve singing a prepared piece, sight-reading and ear tests. You can find out more on the Cambridge website, as well as have a go at some of their sample tests.

Extenuating Circumstances Form

This form is for applicants whose predicted grades are lower than Cambridge requirements due to personal or social disadvantages, but who have the potential and the motivation to follow a course at Cambridge successfully. Your school or college should submit this by the deadline of 15th October.

The Supplementary Application Questionnaire (SAQ)

The SAQ must be completed by all UK and EU applicants by the deadline of 22nd October (one week after the 15th October UCAS deadline). The form is designed to gather further information about your application, grades and subject motivation: for example, you'll have to submit your individual module marks in AS and/or A levels. You'll receive an email with the details you need to complete the SAQ form once you've submitted your UCAS form. If you're submitting a COPA, you don't need to submit an SAQ.

Written Work

Depending on the course you're applying for, you may be asked to submit written work. Written work must be produced as part of normal school work and marked by your teacher. You may need to submit one or two pieces and there's no official word count for the written work. It's best to contact the college you wish to apply to for their specific guidelines and deadline.

Your written work should be of a high standard and on a subject that you are reasonably well informed on, as your essay may form the basis of your interview. Cambridge has further information on their website.

STEP Requirements

Sixth Term Examination Papers in Mathematics consists of three papers, which give Cambridge additional information to A level grades. The questions test your insight, originality, grasp of broader issues in your subject and the ability to apply what you know to more complex or unusual situations. STEP is used by colleges as part of a conditional offer. Some colleges may require it for other courses in addition to Maths such as Economics, Engineering or Natural Sciences. Your application to take STEP should be organised through your school or college.

OXFORD
OXFORD UNIVERSITY
founded
c. 1096

APPLICANTS
from over
138
countries

72
UNDER-
GRADUATE
courses

A* A* A*
A* A* A* A* A*
**AVERAGE
GCSE GRADE**
*profile for successful
applicants*

5
APPLICANTS
*for every
place*

CAMBRIDGE

*in numbers**

CAMBRIDGE UNIVERSITY *founded* **c.1209**

11,723
OXFORD
undergraduates

12,077
CAMBRIDGE
undergraduates

11
MILLION SPENT
on outreach each year

41
BRITISH
Prime Ministers

11 **8**
Million
ITEMS

in the
OXFORD
Bodleian Library

in the
CAMBRIDGE
University Library

* Information gathered from the universities' own available statistics since 2011, or from the BBC.

My OXFORD APPLICATION

YOUR PLACE

Getting Your Grades
See p. 143

Language Requirements
See p. 157

(Conditional) Offer or Rejection
Early January. See p. 143

Interviews
Early December. See p.190–194

Written Work (if required)
Mid November. See p. 144

Admissions Tests (if required)
Early November. See p. 163–189

UCAS Form & Personal Statements
15th October. See our personal statement guide on p. 131–141

Choral & Organ Scholarships
Early September. See p. 144

College Choice
See our college profiles p. 113–128

Course Choice
Check out our bite-size profiles p. 43–88

YOUR PLACE

Getting Your Grades
See p. 143

STEP & Language Requirements
See p. 147 & p.157

Winter Pool
January. See p. 92

(Conditional) Offer or Rejection
Early January. See p. 143

Interviews
Early December. See p.190–194

Written Work (if required)
Mid November. See p. 146

Admissions Tests (if required)
Early November for BMAT, or at interview.
See p. 163–189

SAQ
22nd October. See p. 146

UCAS Form & Personal Statements
15th October. See our personal statement guide on p. 131–141

Choral & Organ Scholarships & Extenuating Circumstances
See p. 145–146

Overseas Applications
Earlier deadline may apply. See p. 160–161

College Choice
See our college profiles p. 100–112

Course Choice
Check out our bite-size profiles on p. 17–42

My
CAMBRIDGE
APPLICATION

5 INTERNATIONAL APPLICANTS

———— ·⟨♡⟩· ————

GUIDANCE ON NAVIGATING THE APPLICATION PROCESS AS AN OVERSEAS STUDENT

You're classed as an international applicant if you are domiciled outside of the UK or EU. It doesn't matter where you hold a passport as your status depends solely on your country of permanent residence.

Applying to Oxford or Cambridge as an international student can be very challenging. In 2013, international applications were up almost 10% on 2012. The success rate for international applicants applying to Cambridge for 2013 entry was 10.6% compared to 26.7% for UK applicants. These figures highlight the fact that if you are to gain a place, you must begin the process early and invest a lot of time and effort into achieving top grades and putting together a strong application.

Quotas for Medicine applicants

Prospective international Medicine candidates should note the following quotas:

- Oxford Medical School limits the number of international (non EU) medical students to a maximum of 14 each year across both the standard and Graduate Entry medicine courses.

- Cambridge limits its international places to 7.5% of its total intake, which equates to around 21 overseas places.

English language requirements

As all teaching at Oxford and Cambridge is done in English, all applicants must have a good verbal and written grasp of the language. If English is not your first language, but you have been in full-time education in the English language for the past two years you will not need to sit a test. Otherwise, you may be asked to complete a formal qualification, a list of which can be found on the respective university websites.

Country-specific qualifications

Many international qualifications are recognised by both Oxford and Cambridge. Both universities require the top grades in the highest level of qualifications available to students in your country. Make sure to check the universities' websites for country-specific entry requirements. There may also be specific entrance requirements for your chosen course.

UCAS (Universities & Colleges Admissions Service)

Every student applying to Oxford or Cambridge must submit their application through UCAS. From mid-September, you can apply to Oxford and Cambridge (and other UK universities) online. You can use UCAS anywhere in the world and can find out more information about it and applying online at www.ucas.com.

Your application does not have to be completed all at once; you can return to it later and change or add information before you submit it. However, you'll need to mark every section of the form as complete before you can send your application to UCAS. Please note the earlier deadline for Oxford, Cambridge and all UK Medical courses of 15th October. This may be even earlier if you're applying to Cambridge and would like to be interviewed overseas – read on for further details.

Academic reference

Along with your application you will need a reference highlighting your academic and personal suitability for your chosen course. This will usually be written by a teacher from your current school who knows you well and can give an accurate account of your abilities. A full written reference is required (name and address are not sufficient) and your reference must be written in English. Because applications to Oxford and Cambridge are earlier than other universities, you need to give your teacher enough time to complete your reference so it is worth asking for it before you break up for your school holiday.

If you are applying through a school, college or other organisation, you will not have access to your reference; it will be completed on your behalf by your centre.

If you are applying as an individual, you need to ensure that the reference section is completed in good time as you will not be able to send your application to UCAS without it. If you are applying independently but would like your reference to be written by a registered school, college or other organisation, you can request that the centre completes the reference for you in the 'Apply' section of the UCAS website.

For more information about the reference please refer to the UCAS website.

Admission tests and written work
For some courses you may be asked to sit an admissions test (see Chapter 6) or submit essays written in English (see Chapter 4). If you are applying for a course that requires you to sit an admissions test, you will need to register to sit the test.

This means that before 15th October (for most tests – be sure to double check for your particular course) you need to have found somewhere to sit your test and have been entered to take it. You cannot register yourself; you must find an approved test centre and they will do it for you.

If your school is not an approved test centre you can find a list of approved centres worldwide on the Admissions Testing Service's website. Alternatively, your school can apply to become a test centre (please note this may take some time so you need to look into it early).

Dates and costs for admission tests can be found on the Admissions Testing Service's website.

The Cambridge Online Preliminary Application (COPA)
The COPA is an online form you will need to complete if applying to Cambridge from overseas (this includes applicants from Iceland, Liechtenstein, Norway and Switzerland). It helps Cambridge to ensure they have complete information about all applicants and to make arrangements for overseas interviews.

A detailed guide to completing your COPA form can be found on the Cambridge website.

Supplementary Application Questionnaire (SAQ)

If you are applying to Cambridge you will also need to complete the SAQ online. However, as you have already completed the COPA form, the only information you will need to provide on the SAQ is your UCAS ID number and COPA Reference Number.

The Interview

As an international student, you may have different interview options available to you depending on your home country, university, college and course choice. If possible, we recommend that all students have a face-to-face interview and you should try (with an appropriate visa if necessary) to attend the interviews in the UK during December.

Alternatively, Cambridge conduct a number of interviews overseas in September and October. Please note that eligibility for these interviews is restricted and deadlines can be earlier.

In some cases, Oxford can arrange interviews over the telephone, video conference or Skype but this is not guaranteed. All short-listed applicants for Medicine at Oxford must attend interviews at Oxford in December to be considered.

Cambridge earlier deadlines for international applicants

If you are an international applicant who will be travelling to the UK for your interview in December, the usual Oxbridge deadline of 15th October will apply to you. However, if you would like to be interviewed in India, Malaysia, Singapore or China, please see the following table of deadlines.

Please note the following deadlines are for 2015 entry. They remain roughly the same each year, but for 2016 entry and beyond please refer to the Cambridge website:

9th September 2014	Students applying to Cambridge who would like to be interviewed in **India** must have submitted their UCAS application and COPA.
20th September 2014	Students applying to Cambridge who would like to be interviewed in **Malaysia, Singapore** or **China** must have submitted their UCAS application and COPA.
15th October 2014	Students applying to Cambridge who would like to be interviewed in **Cambridge, Australia, Canada, Hong Kong** or **Pakistan** must have submitted their UCAS application and COPA (restrictions apply to those wanting to be interviewed in Australia, Canada and Hong Kong). All students applying to Oxford must have submitted their UCAS application.

Cambridge international interviews take place:

Mid-September – India

Late October or early November – China, Malaysia, and Singapore

November or early December – Australia, Canada, Hong Kong, and Pakistan

Visas

Once you have been made an offer, if you are not a national from the European Economic Area or Switzerland, you will also need to apply for a Tier 4 student visa in your home country before you begin your studies.

The UK Border Agency requires you to be formally sponsored by a licensed UK higher education institution. Oxford or Cambridge will sponsor you but only once your offer becomes unconditional. This means when you have gained a place and met all the academic and financial conditions, therefore you will not be able to apply for a visa until you have an offer.

As circumstances for individuals vary, please visit the Oxford or Cambridge website in order to find out the requirements.

Visa details for interviews in the UK can be found on the universities' websites.

6 ADMISSIONS TESTS

HOW TO PREPARE FOR YOUR ADMISSIONS TEST WITH EXAMPLE QUESTIONS FOR YOU TO TRY YOUR HAND AT

Regardless of which test you have to take – you'll do much better if you're clued up before you sit it. Read our top tips for approaching the test and then get cracking on our practice questions. Your friends may tell you that they're not preparing, but if our research is anything to go on (96% of applicants we worked with told us they started preparing at least a month in advance) they're either in the minority or not telling you the whole truth…!

Know the structure, format and mark scheme

This will enable you to work on your examination technique. Think about your strengths and weaknesses in relation to the test and how you can improve upon these. Think about the timing of the test and how you usually react to time pressure. We surveyed applicants sitting an admissions test in 2013 and nearly half of these said the most difficult thing about the test was finishing it in time. Plan your approach. It is very important to know how you will navigate your way through the paper. Familiarity with the structure will help you to relax in the test itself. You should also work out how the test is marked, so that you can be sure you are allocating the right amount of time to each section of the test to help you get maximum marks and avoid running out of time on that big question at the end.

Practise the core skills required

Most of the tests are about analysis rather than factual knowledge. Think about this. Avoid doing reams of unstructured preparation because good sense and planning are more important – have a look at the past questions and try to analyse what kinds of thing students in your subject are being asked. 85% of 2013 applicants we surveyed said the most useful prep was practicing past papers. Think about how you would have approached the test if you had been faced with that particular question. Should you practise analysing language, identifying arguments in the newspaper, mental maths or applying what you have learnt in sixth form to complex new problems?

Our next section goes into detail on a number of the admissions tests, including advice from our graduate tutors on preparation that can really make a difference, and help with approaching example questions. Do always check the individual test and university websites for all the latest updates, including dates, timings, deadlines, marking and structure of the tests.

Good luck!

The Biomedical Admissions Test (BMAT)

The BMAT is a compulsory test for Medicine at Oxford and Cambridge, Biomedical Sciences at Oxford and Veterinary Sciences at Cambridge. It is also used for admissions at Imperial, The Royal Veterinary College and UCL.

To be successful in all three sections of the test you need to understand the skills examined and put in some efficient practice. Test your mettle with the examples below…

Section 1: Aptitude & Skills (marked out of 9) – 35 multiple choice questions with four possible answers testing numeracy, verbal reasoning, problem-solving and data analysis. You'll need to be able to do quick mental maths, interpret graphs and diagrams and think through a spatial, numerical or verbal reasoning problem logically. It's vital that you are able to work quickly and accurately and that you have a speedy way of checking your answers as you go along. Bear in mind that there is no negative marking (you won't be marked down for getting a question wrong) so if you're really stuck, just guess – and you have a 25% chance of getting it right!

Example question 1

'Increases in blood pressure associated with old age are common in developed countries, but are rare in underdeveloped countries where people of all ages remain physically active even into the later stages of life. In younger generations, obesity and diabetes are more common in developed countries, where physical activity is limited due to a largely sedentary lifestyle.'

Which one of the following can be drawn as a conclusion from the passage above?

A) Further gains in longevity in developed countries require a change in lifestyle.

B) People who are not physically active will suffer from obesity and diabetes.

C) Lifelong exercise is associated with maintaining good health.

D) A lack of exercise affects young people more than old people.

Section 2: Scientific Knowledge & Application (marked out of 9) – 27 multiple choice questions with five possible answers testing applied science and maths knowledge. This section will ask you to use the skills that have been tested in Section 1, and a level of scientific knowledge is required as well – from knowing how dominant and recessive genes work, to how the pH of blood changes whether it's arterial or venous. The BMAT isn't testing sophisticated knowledge – more whether you are able to apply what you've learnt to work your way through a problem logically.

Example question 2

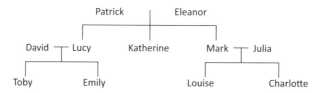

Patrick carries a recessive allele on his X chromosome. Which other members of his family could have inherited this allele?

A) David, Lucy, Katherine, Mark

B) David, Lucy, Katherine, Julia

C) Lucy, Katherine, Mark, Toby

D) Katherine, Lucy, Toby, Emily

E) Katherine, Toby, Emily, Louise

Section 3: Writing Task (marked on content 1-5 and quality of written English A-E) – a choice of four questions testing your ability to structure a logical argument and support your arguments with evidence. The essay questions are broad and don't require specific factual information. However, your answers should demonstrate your scientific knowledge: an average answer to an ethical question might address the moral and economic issues at stake, whereas a good answer would discuss specific medical cases and show a detailed scientific knowledge and understanding, supported by clear and pertinent examples. Our medics would also advise that you refer back to the question to ensure you don't stray from the topic. What's more, focus on the quality, not quantity in your writing: you will only be marked up to a certain word count – so make sure that you don't lose marks by bringing your conclusion in too late!

Example question 3

'Our genes evolved for a Stone Age lifestyle. Therefore, in order to be healthy, we should adopt Stone Age habits.' Discuss.

For the answers to all the above questions, as well as advice on how to approach them, visit **www.oxbridgeapplications.com**. We've also got up-to-date information on test dates and deadlines, as well as information on how your BMAT score will be used in your application.

The Cambridge Language Test

The Cambridge Language Test is one of the few tests at Cambridge which is sat at all the colleges (except the mature college Hughes Hall). The test is the same for all languages and candidates have 45 minutes to complete the test paper. You will be asked to read a brief passage in English (300–350 words) and then to answer a comprehension and free composition question in a single essay (200–250 words) in the language that you want to study. If you're applying to do two languages, you can pick which language you would like to answer in.

A key thing to remember is that the examiners marking the test will be looking at good grammar, accuracy and self-expression. The tutors aren't too interested in what you know, which is why you shouldn't worry if you're presented with is on a topic for which you don't have a strong vocabulary – what they want to see is how you use what you know. Illustrate your ability to use diverse sentence structures and interesting phrases and demonstrate how you can manipulate the language you know to fulfil your needs. Brush up on your verb endings, agreements and tenses. This is a much better way to prepare than trying to learn reams of specialist vocabulary you may never need to use.

Have a go at our practice question at
www.oxbridgeapplications.com

Oxford Modern Languages & Linguistics Admissions Tests

Students applying to study a course involving a modern language and/or linguistics at Oxford are required to sit the Modern Languages and Linguistics Admissions Test. You will take the test at the start of November. This test includes the following papers, of which you shall have to sit one or two, depending on the course for which you're applying:

- Language Test (for Czech, French, German, Modern Greek, Italian, Portuguese, Russian, Spanish, if taken to A level)
- Language Aptitude Test (for courses involving Celtic, Italian and Russian ab initio)
- Linguistics Test (for all courses involving Linguistics, single language courses (except French and German) and all joint courses with Polish (except French and German))

The **Language Test** tests your vocabulary, writing, comprehension and translating skills and certain parts of the target language's grammar. Brush up on your A level (or equivalent) grammar and try to go a bit further by asking your teachers what the next stage of grammar learning is. You should be able to recognise new grammatical forms, even if you can't yet use them. Practise manipulating your language so you can deal with any gaps in your vocabulary when you come to translate.

The **Language Aptitude Test** tests you with grammatical and comprehension questions on a language which has been invented for the test. Revise the terms used to describe parts of language, for example suffix, pronoun, preposition so you understand what the question is asking you. Think about how the languages you know are constructed – how do French and English differ in the way they express doubt? Try to spot patterns in different languages and practise applying grammatical rules to explain them.

The **Linguistics Test** tests how you tackle unfamiliar linguistic data and your awareness of subtleties in language and meaning. Tutors will look at your reasoning behind how you solve the questions – not necessarily at whether you got the answer correct or not. It can be helpful to do some research into how different languages are constructed. You should also practise analysing graphs and tables of data as this is something that often comes up in the test.

Oxford Classics Admissions Tests

If you are applying for Classics, you will take one or two sections of the Classics Admissions Test, depending on whether you have studied a classical language to A level or equivalent before:

- Latin translation
- Greek translation
- The Classics Language Aptitude Test

If you wont have Latin or Greek to A level or equivalent (Course I) you will take a translation test in the language(s) that you are studying. If you will not have either Latin or Greek to A level or equivalent (Course II) you must sit the Classics Language Aptitude Test.

For the Latin and Greek translations, revise the points of grammar you need to construct accurate sentences. It is also worth reading through some of the translations you have done before to refresh your vocabulary, but it is not worth learning reams of new words.

The Classics Language Apitude Test (CLAT) tests your ability to pick up language skills. The best preparation is to think about the languages that you know and how they are constructed. It can also be useful to go over the way that Latin and Greek function so you can practise thinking logically about language.

The Cambridge Law Test

The Cambridge Law Test is a one-hour admissions test required for the undergraduate Law course by most colleges at the University of Cambridge. It is an essay-based exam consisting of three questions, of which you will have to answer one.

It was introduced by Cambridge to replace the LNAT (National Admissions Test for Law), which you are required to sit when applying for many other undergraduate Law courses. It's a paper-based test and you will answer one question in the hour. The questions are selected by the individual colleges from a question bank, and come in three types. Most colleges will use only one of the three types so it is wise to check your college website in case this information is shared prior to the interview period.

There is no factual preparation necessary for the CLT as no legal knowledge is required. The test is designed to test your logic and reason and your ability to transfer this into writing. That being said, an awareness of current events would be an asset as these can be used as examples in answers. This is also true for your interview. Make sure that you keep up to date with newspapers and endeavour to read more in-depth legal analysis where possible.

Additionally, learning to identify exactly what each question is asking (i.e. determining what the implications of each question are) is very important and will go towards demonstrating that you have considered each possible argument or viewpoint.

Although you only have one hour, it is important that you plan your essay first. It is therefore advisable to split your time into 15 minutes planning and 45 minutes writing. Writing essay plans to time in order to practise structuring answers fully and successfully is very good preparation. Make sure you also give yourself time to check through your answer so you can correct any spelling or grammar mistakes and plug any logical gaps.

Question type 1: Problem

- You will be given a statement of law which you will have to apply to different situations

- This question assesses your ability to understand and apply the statement and explain you reasoning

Example question 1

'Frustration occurs whenever the law recognises that without default of either party a contractual obligation has become incapable of being performed because the circumstances in which performance is called for would render it radically different from that which was undertaken by the contract'. – Davis Contractors v Fareham

When a contract is frustrated, it is brought to an end with neither party being held blameworthy for not performing their side of the contract. A is a jockey and B is the owner of 'Flash' a prizewinning racehorse. B has contracted A to ride Flash in an upcoming race. Has frustration occurred in any of the following situations?

A) The day before the race, A is involved in a car crash and breaks both his legs leaving him unable to race.

B) The race rules are changed the week before the race to say that only novice racehorses may run.

C) A gets a phone call that a friend has been taken into hospital while on holiday in France and flies out to see them. A's flight back that night is cancelled and he is unable to get back in time for the race.

Question type 2: Comprehension

- You will be given a passage of text which you will have to summarise and on which you will answer a series of questions

- This question assesses your ability to understand the text and present balanced, structured arguments

Visit **www.oxbridgeapplications.com** for a practice comprehension question and advice on approaching a question like this.

Question type 3: Essay

- You will be given a statement of opinion which you will have to discuss

- This question assesses your ability to give opinions in a coherent, structured and balanced way

Example question 3

"To question the validity of the trial process is to weaken the one

protective safeguard that stands between us and arbitrary state power".
How far do you agree with the statement? Give reasons for your answer.

For the answers to all the above questions – as well as advice on how
to approach them, visit **www.oxbridgeapplications.com**. We've
also got up-to-date information on test dates and deadlines, as well
as information on how your test score will be used as part of your
application.

English Literature Aptitude Test (ELAT)

You'll need to sit the ELAT if you are applying for English Language
& Literature and English & Joint Schools at Oxford. You will be given
six unseen literary texts – prose, drama and poetry, either full texts or
extracts – of which you must choose two or three to compare and
contrast in any way you find interesting.

To excel in the ELAT you need to focus on close critical analysis,
while keeping a firm hand on the argument you decide to explore.
Ensure you understand the purpose of the test and then have a go at
our example question…

Choosing your texts

It's wise to dedicate some time to choosing which texts you want to
compare and contrast – this will after all dictate your essay content
and the direction you take. Don't be afraid to choose two texts to
compare rather than three. You won't lose marks for looking at fewer
texts; remember that with all things Oxbridge, it's quality not quantity
that counts! When choosing your texts, try to identify the overarching
theme. Then think about how you can approach your essay – either
by looking at texts which explore it in a similar way, or which take a
very different angle. Think about different forms, periods and styles and
consider how you could marry this with your analysis of the themes
within your essay.

Planning your essay

You have 90 minutes in total and it's worth using 15-20 minutes to plan your essay. Consider how you're going to structure the essay, what each paragraph will address and which aspects of the text you are going to focus on. You should also consider how you're going to carry out your comparison. Will you compare the two texts alongside each other, or focus on one text and draw your comparisons from a second (and possibly third) text? Make sure your essay isn't just pointing out literary techniques – you should always be explaining and relating how particular sounds and structures contribute to the poem's overall treatment of the theme. Finally, be sure to plan a strong conclusion – the admissions tutors are looking to see how you structure arguments when writing a critical analysis.

Writing your essay

Once you've chosen your texts and planned your essay structure, the writing is the easy bit. Try to keep your writing clear and focused – don't be tempted to pepper your essay with long words for the sake of it. Clarity of communication is really vital and is what the admissions tutors are looking for. You should quote from the texts that you are examining. Keep the quotations short and quote the line number as a reference. Never leave a quote standing on its own: quotations should build your argument, not just illustrate it, so you should always comment on what you have quoted. Finally, make sure you give yourself 5-10 minutes at the end of the test to read over your essay and check for any spelling, grammar or punctuation mistakes.

Compare and contrast these two extracts

'Tell me more about Mr Dorian Gray. How often do you see him?'

'Every day. I couldn't be happy if I didn't see him every day. He is absolutely necessary to me.'

'How extraordinary! I thought you would never care for anything but your art.'

'He is all my art to me now,' said the painter gravely. 'I sometimes think, Harry, that there are only two eras of any importance in the world's history. The first is the appearance of a new medium for art, and the second is the appearance of a new personality for art also. What the invention of oil-painting was to the Venetians, the face of Antinous was to late Greek sculpture, and the face of Dorian Gray will someday be to me.'

Extract from The Picture of Dorian Gray, *Oscar Wilde (1891)*

My mistress' eyes are nothing like the sun;
Coral is far more red than her lips' red;
If snow be white, why then her breasts are dun;
If hairs be wires, black wires grow on her head.
I have seen roses damask, red and white,
But no such roses see I in her cheeks;
And in some perfumes is there more delight
Than in the breath that from my mistress reeks.
I love to hear her speak, yet well I know
That music hath a far more pleasing sound;
I grant I never saw a goddess go;
My mistress, when she walks, treads on the ground:
And yet, by heaven, I think my love as rare
As any she belied with false compare.

'Sonnet 130', *William Shakespeare (1609)*

For our English graduate's approach to the above texts – visit **www.oxbridgeapplications.com**. We've also got up-to-date information on test dates and deadlines and information on how your ELAT score will be used in your application.

History Aptitude Test (HAT)

You'll need to sit the HAT if you are applying for History or History & joint schools at Oxford.

To write a successful answer paper you need to be confident in analysing and constructing arguments, happy to pull apart a source and to use logic to summarise your thoughts efficiently. Practice and enthusiasm for historical skills will help you.

Question 1a & 1b (10 and 20 marks)

You'll be asked to read a source and summarise a particular point in one sentence. You'll then be asked to explain one of the arguments in the source briefly, from the perspective of the author. Both questions ask you to answer in your own words; you need to be able to show that you have understood what you're reading and can pick out the important points. 1a and 1b both specify that your answers should be short – aim to be clear and concise and get straight to the point.

Example questions 1a & 1b

1a) Using your own words, write a single sentence explaining how 'Rule! Britannia' is commonly understood, as identified by the author.
1b) Explain what the author means when he suggests the song has 'hitherto neglected meanings'. Use your own words and do not use more than fifteen lines.

To read the full source, visit our free online resources for the HAT at **www.oxbridgeapplications.com**

Question 1c (40 marks)

This question takes the theme of the source and asks you to apply it to a period of history with which you're familiar. It's quite a different approach to A level History, and tests whether or not you can think laterally about causes and consequences beyond what you've studied.

It also separates those who stick to their syllabus and those who try to explore ideas further – another excellent reason to start reading around your subject early! Your essay should be a clear argument, which you can strengthen with clear and pertinent examples. Try to use your examples to build your argument, rather than just as illustrations. This will give you a much clearer direction and a more sophisticated essay.

Example question 1c

'In history, long-term causes are everything; short-term events only determine when they bear their fruit.'

Discuss the accuracy of this statement with reference to a particular historical period or topic with which you are familiar.

Question 2 (30 marks)

You have to analyse an unseen source. Don't worry that if it's on a subject you've never studied before and that you're being asked to talk in depth about ideas and ideologies you're unfamiliar with – all the answers are in the source and this is your chance to go right back to the fundamental skills required to be a good historian. You should dedicate some time to planning your answer: how are you going to approach each section? What examples from the text can you use to back up your reasoning and how will you bring your argument together to finish with a strong conclusion?

Example question 2

The following extract is taken from an account by an African American remembering his childhood in the American South in the early twentieth century:

❝I heard another story in my family. On my daddy's side, they all from Mississippi. But, they was from mixed types, too. They came to Louisiana with a little bit of money. They claimed that they lost their records when they moved here from up there. So, all their new records: white. Then, they put their kids in white schools, and that was it. I even heard they voted all those years when colored couldn't. They did, my daddy and his brothers. They looked white. And, they had the papers to back it up. What difference did it make that they had some black blood? It wasn't visible! And, every now and then, here in Louisiana, somebody gets it in their head to burn down the courthouse. It's terrible, but for us, that works out fine. We get new records, and we become white. **"**

What can the extract tell us about racial attitudes in the Southern United States in the early twentieth century?

For answers to all the above questions and to read the rest of the extract, visit **www.oxbridgeapplications.com**. We've also got up-to-date information on test dates and deadlines and information on how your HAT score will be used in your application.

The National Admissions Test for Law (LNAT)

You'll need to sit the LNAT if you're applying for Law at Birmingham, Bristol, Durham, Glasgow, King's College, Manchester, Nottingham, Oxford or UCL. The first section is multiple choice, where you'll be asked to analyse 12 passages and answer three or four questions on each. You also need to write an analytical essay from a choice of three titles.

Put your logical thinking cap on and try your hand at the questions below…

Identifying assumptions

An assumption is something which is not stated in the argument, but taken for granted in order to draw the conclusion. So, first of all you should work out what the conclusion of the argument is. Then look for the reasoning the author gives to support this conclusion, and think about any important point which is not actually stated. You are trying to spot the missing link, the reason that should be stated but has been left out.

Example question

"The symptoms of mental disorders are behavioural, cognitive, or emotional problems. Some patients with mental disorders can be effectively treated with psychotherapy, but it is now known that, in some patients, mental disorders result from chemical imbalances affecting the brain. Thus, these patients can be effectively treated only with medication that will reduce or correct the imbalance."

Which of the following is an underlying assumption of the above argument?

A) Treatment by psychotherapy can produce no effective reduction in or correction of chemical imbalances that cause mental disorders.

B) Treatment with medication is superior to treatment with psychotherapy.

C) Most mental disorders are not the result of chemical imbalances affecting the brain.

D) Some patients with mental disorders can be effectively treated with psychotherapy, others need medication.

E) Treatment with psychotherapy has no effect on mental disorders other than a reduction of the symptoms.

Tackling inferring questions

An inference is something that the reader can conclude based on the information given in the passage. In order to answer this you need to evaluate which of the five statements could legitimately be a conclusion following on from the information given. If one of these statements relies on some other information then it is less likely to be an inference directly from the information given.

Example question

"Partly because of bad weather, but also partly because some major pepper growers have switched to high-priced cocoa, world production of pepper has been running well below worldwide sales for three years. Pepper is consequently in relatively short supply. The price of pepper has soared in response: it now equals that of cocoa."

Which of the following can be inferred from the above statement?

A) Pepper is a profitable crop only if it is grown on a large scale.

B) World consumption of pepper has been unusually high for three years.

C) World pepper production will return to previous levels once normal weather returns.

D) Surplus stocks of pepper have been reduced in the past three years.

E) Pepper growing profits over the last 3 years have been unsustainable.

Writing your essay

Structure is very important in the LNAT. Have a clear introduction which tells the reader where you're going, sets any parameters that you'd like to impose on the essay and defines any ambiguous terms used in the question. The body of the essay should contain your argument and, if possible, you should try to deal with one or two counter arguments. Using a real-world example makes your argument more concrete and shows the reader that you have an awareness of the world around you. It's important to keep up to date with current affairs so you have a ready supply of pertinent examples. Make sure your conclusion reiterates the main thrust of your argument without simply repeating itself.

Example question

"Women now have the chance to achieve anything they want."
How do you respond to this statement?

For the answers to all the above questions visit **www.oxbridgeapplications.com**. We've also got up-to-date information on test dates and deadlines and information on how your LNAT score will be used in your application.

Mathematics Aptitude Test (MAT)

You'll need to sit the MAT if you are applying for Mathematics, Mathematics & joint schools, Computer Science or Computer Science & joint schools at Oxford. The test is the same for the different courses, but there are particular sections to answer depending on which subject you're applying for. We recommend checking which questions you need to answer beforehand so that you're clear before you go into the test as the division of questions can be quite complex.

Multiple Choice Questions (40 marks)

The questions are simple and solving the problem will normally only require one stage of mathematics. All the questions draw on the mathematics you've been taught in C1 and C2 modules of A level maths, but the questions might not be as straightforward – they require you to apply your mathematical knowledge to new problems. You should have enough time to check through your answers when you've finished and you should do so, as no marks are awarded for correct workings but an incorrect answer. If you're really stuck on a question, just guess – you have a 25% chance of getting it right and you won't be marked down if you're wrong.

Example question 1

Which of the following is a factor of the polynomial $x^5 + 6x^3 + x^2 + 8x + 4$?

A) $x + 4$

B) $x^3 + x + 2$

C) $x^3 + 2x + 1$

D) $x + 4$ & $x^3 + x + 2$

Example question 2

Which of the following is the graph of

$$f(x) = \frac{x \sin^2 x}{\cos x} \text{ between } -2\pi \text{ and } +2\pi?$$

A)

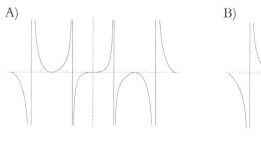

B)

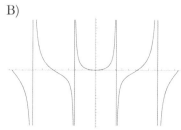

C)

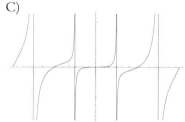

D)

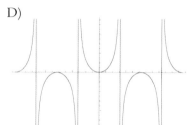

Tackling longer questions (60 marks)

In the second section of the test, which you should spend about 90 minutes on, you need to answer longer questions. These questions are dependent on the course that you're applying to. These questions usually require more than one stage, so you might need to take different aspects of your Maths course and combine them to reach the right answer. The questions have been designed so that you can still approach them, even if you're not doing the A level syllabus, but it would be wise to check through what C1 and C2 cover if you haven't done them, so you don't get caught out. There really is no substitute in your preparation for doing practice questions. Even if you don't answer the questions, being able to quickly identify the right method to solve the problem will be very useful when you come to take the test.

Example question

A) A glass has a circular base of radius r_1 and a circular top of radius r_2. If the height of the glass is H, find an expression for the volume.

B) If you half fill the glass with juice, up to $\frac{H}{2}$, and put a straw, length l, diameter d to the base of the glass and suck the drink up until it reaches your mouth (i.e. it fills the whole straw), find a polynomial equation for H_n, the new height of juice in the glass.

For the answers to all the above questions visit **www.oxbridgeapplications.com**. We've also got up-to-date information on test dates and deadlines and information on how your MAT score will be used in your application.

The Cambridge Thinking Skills Assessment (TSA Cambridge)

You'll need to sit the TSA Cambridge if you are applying for Computer Science, Economics, Engineering, Land Economy and Physical or Biological Sciences at certain Cambridge colleges. You'll sit the test when you go up to interview and you'll have to answer 50 multiple choice questions in 90 minutes. Have a read of our advice on how you can excel in the different types of question in the TSA Cambridge multiple choice questions in our TSA Oxford section. Then come back to have a go at these practice questions:

Example Question 1

Person A: 'I would never go white water rafting since it essentially involves being carried along a dangerous current in a rubber dingy.'

Person B: 'But the guides are well trained and there is very little risk of getting hurt.'

Person A: 'But it could still go wrong and the consequences could be disastrous.'

Person B: 'Lots of people go white water rafting when they are on holiday and there are very few accidents in spite of this.'

Which of the following conclusions can be reliably drawn from the above argument?

A) The white water rafting guides prevent any accidents from occurring.

B) White water rafting accidents are always fatal when they happen.

C) It is safer to white water raft in the UK than elsewhere in the world.

D) Many white water rafting accidents are not reported in the press.

E) White water rafting seems to be a safe hobby

Example Question 2

More cinemas should start showing live theatre performances on their screens to increase their profits. There is demand as many people can't get to the theatre or cannot buy tickets for productions as they have sold out. Cinemas would be able to sell more tickets and therefore increase their revenue.

Which of the following, if true, would most strengthen the argument?

A) Cinemas would need to invest in expensive equipment in order to screen performances.

B) Seeing a play at the cinema is not the same as seeing it live on the stage.

C) Cinemas can charge more for tickets to see theatre performances than regular films.

D) There are more cinemas than theatres in the UK.

E) Cinemas must pay a substantial fee to the theatres to screen their shows.

Example Question 3

It is currently 10:00 in Existan and 14:00 in Fediland. James posted a parcel to Sam from Existan at 16:00 yesterday and it arrived with Sam in Fediland at 07:30 today. How long did the parcel take to be delivered from the moment James posted it to the moment it arrived with Sam?

A) 9 hours 30 mins

B) 11 hours

C) 11 hours 30 minutes

D) 10 hours 30 minutes

E) 12 hours 30 mins

Example Question 4

Lucy is an author. She receives a royalty fee of 40% of profits of each of her books that is sold by Aquarocks. In 2011 Aquarocks sold 1,400 of her books, with a total revenue of £56,000 and a profit of half this sum. In 2012, it is expected that 20% more books will be sold and Lucy has negotiated a new royalty fee of 50% of the profit, plus £5 for each extra book sold compared to 2011.

If the expectations turn out to be true, and, as in 2011, profit is half of revenue, how much money will Lucy receive in 2011 if the price of the books stays the same?

A) £16,800

B) £25,200

C) £35, 000

D) £68,600

E) £18,200

For the answers to all the above questions visit **www.oxbridgeapplications.com**. We've also got up-to-date information on test dates and deadlines and information on how your TSA Cambridge score will be used in your application. You can also try your hand the questions in the LNAT and TSA Oxford section for further practice.

The Oxford Thinking Skills Assessment (TSA Oxford)

You'll need to sit the TSA Oxford if you're applying for PPE, Economics & Management, Philosophy, Psychology & Linguistics, Experimental Psychology or Geography at Oxford. You have to answer 50 multiple choice questions in 90 minutes and then write an answer to an essay question.

To ace the test, be cool and logical throughout and practise as much as you can, as there's definitely a style of thinking that you need to adopt to do well.

Numerical Reasoning Questions

These multiple choice questions often boil down to a mathematical equation, either presented in a simple or more complex format. You need to be able to identify the key elements of the equation in order to attempt the answer and have the mental maths knowledge and speed to be able to work quickly through the problem. Make sure you have revised percentages, fractions and key formulae (eg. speed) before you take the test. It's worth devising your own quick checking method for your answers so you don't lose marks through silly mistakes.

Example question 1

Lauren has gone to the sweet shop to buy sour fizzballs for her friends. She knows that yesterday they were 5p each and has brought enough money to buy a certain number to share amongst her friends. When she arrives at the sweet shop there is a special offer on sour fizzballs: if you buy 10 or more the price of all fizzballs is reduced by 1p each. She finds that she can now buy 3 more than she had initially planned to, spending the exact amount she brought.

How many can she buy today?

A) 12   **B)** 15   **C)** 10   **D)** 17   **E)** 20

Verbal Reasoning Questions

In the TSA Oxford, you may be asked to identify or draw a conclusion from a passage, identify an assumption, identify an argument with the same structure or principle as the passage or identify one key piece of information that will weaken or strengthen the argument in the passage. You should try to break down the passage so that you can identify what the argument is and an example that could strengthen the argument. Think carefully about the wording being used — it can be very easy to skim over a word, especially when you're under time pressure, and miss a fundamental flaw in the argument.

Example question 2

In England there is an average of 8,500 instances of domestic carbon monoxide leaks a year, yet only 1.8% of houses have a carbon monoxide detector fitted. If more home owners could be encouraged to fit carbon monoxide detectors then the number of carbon monoxide leaks could be substantially reduced.

Which of the following is the best statement of the flaw in the above argument?

A) It assumes that the detectors are completely accurate.

B) It ignores the fact that carbon monoxide leaks are very rare and detectors are relatively expensive.

C) It implies that when a leak is detected it is prevented, but just because the leaks are detected does not mean they don't happen.

D) It ignores that there may be other gases which leak into a property.

E) It assumes that all houses are exposed to the same risk of carbon monoxide leaks.

Writing your essay

Oxford TSA essay questions are usually quite broad, so think carefully about what the most important points are, which you would like to include in your answer, and how they link together. If you're making an argument for one point of view ensure you give a reasoned explanation and consider alternative arguments. Ensure this plan is clear in your introduction. It shows you're aware as to how you will proceed, rather than simply rambling through the arguments. If the question asks you to form an opinion, you should always come to a conclusion in order to show your thoughts are fully developed.

Example question 3
Should fines be based on the individual's income?

For the answers to all the above questions visit **www.oxbridgeapplications.com**. We've also got up-to-date information on test dates and deadlines and information on how your TSA Oxford score will be used in your application. You can also try your hand at the questions in the LNAT and TSA Cambridge section for further practice.

The Physics Aptitude Test (PAT)

The Physics Aptitude Test is a two-hour test required for all undergraduate Physics, Engineering or Materials Science courses at Oxford. This is sat in November prio to interview.

The mathematical and physics knowledge you will need to answer the questions corresponds roughly to the GCSE and AS level Maths and Physics syllabus. Therefore, to be successful in both sections of the test you need to revise these. Calculators are not allowed. Test your mettle with the examples below…

Section A: Mathematics for Physics (50 marks)
– This section consists of 12 mathematical problems

Example question 1

Find the set of real numbers λ for which the following quadratic equation holds:

$$x2 + (\lambda - 5)x + 4\lambda = 0$$

Section B: Physics (50 marks)

- Part 1 (10 marks): 10 multiple choice questions each with a choice of four answers
- Part 2 (20 marks): 3 short questions
- Part 3 (20 marks): 1 longer question with three parts

Example question 2

What would the minimum length of a plane mirror need to be in order for you to see a full view of yourself?

A) ½ your height

B) ¼ your height

C) ¾ your height

D) Your full height

For the answers to all the above questions visit **www.oxbridgeapplications.com**. We've also got up-to-date information on test dates and deadlines, as well as information on how your PAT score will be used in your application.

7 THE INTERVIEW

WHAT TO EXPECT AND HOW TO
KEEP YOUR COOL

Why do Oxford and Cambridge interview?

To excel in the Oxbridge undergraduate teaching system you must be able to listen, converse confidently, engage academically, absorb information about your subject and develop your own informed opinion on the topics you are studying. In essence, the interview acts as a mini tutorial or supervision to assess, along with all the other aspects of the application, whether you will enjoy learning in this environment and whether the tutors will in turn like teaching you.

The majority of Cambridge applicants are invited to attend an interview in December. A greater percentage of applicants to Oxford than at Cambridge are not invited, and in most cases these decisions are based on scores in admissions tests. Interviews are the final piece of the application jigsaw, and it is from there that the university makes its ultimate decision.

Interviews allow admissions tutors to explore exactly how you think, how you adapt to new concepts and ideas and how you handle the pressure of reaching conclusions aloud. For example, if an admissions tutor gives you a physics formula to solve that you have not previously encountered, how do you react? Do you attempt to work through it or do you freeze with terror at the thought of making a mistake in front of your interviewer? If the first scenario sounds more like you, it's a good indication that you might be an interesting student to teach; you are showing that you're responsive to new ideas and can apply your existing knowledge to problems you have not seen before, a skill you will have to exercise in a real tutorial/supervision.

So, what are admissions tutors looking for?

They are looking for genuine motivation and enthusiasm for the chosen subject, logical, critical and lateral-thinking and an ability to think flexibly and independently. This might seem a daunting list but, in reality, many bright applicants will already have these qualities.

Like the personal statement, the interview gives you the chance to demonstrate your interest in your chosen subject. It's easy to say that you've understood a philosophical concept in your personal statement, but can you summarise the point in a sentence and then explore its application to a situation you haven't previously considered? Genuinely passionate individuals will tend to be those who have really thought about why they want to read their chosen course at university, and have a stock of solid examples to back up their points.

Approaching the unknown

Admissions tutors may also use the interview to discuss how to approach material that has not yet been looked at in the application process. In an interview for Music, you may be given a score and asked to break it down to demonstrate your theoretical and critical appreciation of compositions. In a language interview, you may be asked questions in the language you wish to study, to assess oral ability and, crucially, whether you enjoy speaking, testing new constructions and learning from your mistakes. You may be able to talk confidently about topics you have covered at school or in your own time but can you apply the logic you have to situations beyond your experience?

What to expect

Many successful applicants are surprised to find the interview an enjoyable experience and, we promise you, that's not as crazy as it sounds! Over 70% of the applicants we worked with in 2013 enjoyed at least one of their interviews. Think of the interview as a two-way conversation, not as an interrogation. If you find yourself enjoying the experience, the chances are your tutor will be too.

When it comes to preparing for your interview, the general rule is to be ready for anything. You may be interviewed by one person or two, or even three or four. When there is more than one person in the room, a good tip is to address your answers to the interviewer who asked the question, with regular glances to include the rest of the interview team. It may be the case that one party leads the interview, whilst another observes and takes notes. It can be off-putting to have a silent presence in the room, especially if the observer begins to scribble furiously halfway through your answer.

You may have one general interview and one subject interview (more likely at Cambridge) or two or more subject interviews. You may be interviewed at a college to which you have not applied (more likely at Oxford) or you might be interviewed at the college to which you applied, as well as one or two others.

Be prepared to stand your ground

One thing you can't control in the interview is how the interviewer reacts to you. You may be faced with an aggressive or tough interviewer, who launches an intellectual assault at you. The interviewer isn't trying to make you crumble but to see whether you can stand your ground in a heated academic debate. They want to see whether you can strike a balance between listening to your interviewer and taking their views into account, whilst also defending and maintaining your own viewpoint.

If you find yourself in this situation, a key thing to remember is that you must remain respectful and rational. Be prepared for 'such as?' and 'for example?' type questions, but don't let them put you off or force you into making a foolish point. Every time you make a case, ensure you have an example to hand to support and strengthen your point.

Be receptive to prompts from your interviewer

Whilst you may wish to argue your point to its logical end, don't be afraid to adjust your argument in light of new material or prompts offered to you by your interviewer. This isn't necessarily a sign of weakness, and often your interviewer will want to see how you assimilate new information. The interview isn't the place for stubbornness or pride. Remember that your interviewers have studied the topic under discussion for a lot longer than you and they might decide to play devil's advocate in the interview to see how you react under pressure.

Be ready to explain and explore

Friendly, arguably passive interviewers may appear laid-back and open, however they are perhaps the toughest to read. With a passive interviewer, you don't have a ferociously aggressive combatant pushing you forward, challenging you and forcing you to perform to the best of your ability. The onus, in this situation, is on you to turn what feels like a casual conversation into an intellectual discussion in which you demonstrate your academic potential.

If you find your interviewer uttering 'And?...', remember that you are being invited to explore your ideas in further detail or from a different angle. There are two good tips when tackling this situation: you could either try to develop your initial answer further or, alternatively, pause and reconsider the implications of the question. Never be afraid to give yourself a couple of seconds to think. It's much better to give a considered answer after a few moments than to plough on without much direction.

If you have tried both these responses and you are still met with 'And...?' it may mean that the interviewer has a specific response in mind that you cannot fathom. If you have explored your answers as far as you can take them, gracefully disengage yourself by asking them either to re-phrase the problem for you, or admit that you don't know the answer that they're looking for and ask them to help you. The humble admission, 'I'm afraid I don't know but I'd like to find out,' turns the problem into a virtue, as you seem (and we hope you are!) thirsty for new knowledge.

8 APPROACHING QUESTIONS

OUR TEAM OF OXBRIDGE GRADUATES EXPLORES POSSIBLE ANSWERS TO INTERVIEW QUESTIONS

Working with a team of Oxbridge graduates from different subject disciplines, in this section we look at how you might approach sample interview questions. Some of the questions discussed here are real and have been put to applicants at their interviews, others are based on past questions and have been carefully created by our team to ensure they give an insight into subject-specific interviews.

The key thing to remember is that there is seldom a right answer, unless it is a specific mathematical problem you are asked to solve or a fact-based question. Our graduates have made suggestions as to how you might approach a question, but their answers are by no means to be interpreted as a set 'model answer' or indeed suggest that there is a standardised approach to both generating or answering such questions. The points made are to serve as a guide as to how you might go about tackling them. You do not need an encyclopaedic memory to answer Oxbridge interview questions successfully. Nor do you have to be a genius in the making. Each year, interviewers come up with a host of new and appropriately challenging questions and problems to see how aspiring Oxbridge applicants go about tackling them. Therefore, please do not expect that just because we've concentrated on a question, that you will be asked this in your interview – the chances of this are exceedingly slim – it's much better to get to grips with the logical and creative thinking that these questions require rather than trying to revise specific answers.

Humanities & the Arts

Archaeology & Anthropology

Questions to get you thinking...

How would you carry out the ethnography of a curry?

How would you describe the role of the media within American politics?

If you were shown the jawbone of an animal, how would you identify which animal it belongs to?

Describe your school in anthropological terms. (past question)

This question aims to encourage the consideration of the cultural make-up of your school and moves into wider discussion on issues such as multiculturalism, gender and class. It would be easy to meander and go off point. Be conscious of what you are saying and support your points with examples and evidence.

Anthropology is concerned with people and cultures, so the interviewer will be expecting you to be able to analyse your school as an anthropological field site. In anthropology, this kind of focused study (i.e. site-specific) is termed as an ethnographic investigation. The notion of an 'anthropological perspective' is very broad and encompassing, and this can be demonstrated even within the site of the school. For example, within a single site, an anthropologist could examine a number of topics, including cross-cultural, gendered, socio-economic status, and age interactions between people.

You could expand your argument to compare your own schooling system to another cross-culturally. A provocative current example is the expression of religious freedom, as exemplified in how lenient the schooling system should be in permitting religious symbols (such as the headscarf) to be on 'display' in so-called secular sites such as the school. You could link in issues of multiculturalism and secularism, and how this has been tackled in the educational system in different ways in different countries, comparing, for example, Britain's lenient approach to headscarves in schools in contrast to the French government's 2004 ban on headscarves in schools. Other possible issues you might consider: Is your school single-sex or mixed; How does gender impact on education? Is it a state school or private; Should education be free? Are school uniform regulations a breach of human rights?

You may also be asked how you would carry out this investigation. This relates to methodology, and you would be expected to demonstrate a range of approaches in your answer (conducting interviews, questionnaires, doing cross-cultural comparisons, utilising archival resources), including offering a realistic timeframe for such an investigation.

Would you agree that tourism, if it is led by indigenous people, will lead to a more positive result for the culture of the country? (past question)

In answering this question, avoid jumping straight in. Don't go for a wild stab and avoid a dogmatic 'yes/no' response. The interviewer will be looking for how you can engage intuitively and contemplatively with a complex current issue in anthropology.

A good place to start is to identify the key themes in the question. Here, for example, the question relates to cultural representation, identity, multiculturalism, and globalism. You could ask what defines the 'tourist'? Does the fieldwork ethnographer count as a tourist? What about the gap-year student? Note the problems in terminologies: 'tourist', 'indigenous', 'primitive', 'authentic' – such words are inherently ideologically fuelled and there is a risk that we are dividing them into two simplified categories, 'Us/Them'. Is there a need to distinguish between the categories of tourist and indigenous in this way? (especially in this time of so-called global cosmopolitanism).

You could argue that these categories – born specifically from a Western social setting – are ultimately deeply ingrained in a set of persistent and preconceived ideas – West/rest, primitive/modern, old/new.

Yet with such cultural multiplicity, and in a time of increasing social change, such static constructions simply cannot hold force. By paying respect to the dynamics and differences of cultural situations, the task of anthropology is to re-contextualise the pervasive us/them polarities in favour of a more processual, scientific approach.

James Clifford argues in his book *The Predicament of Culture*, that one ought to hold all such dichotomising concepts in suspicion, attempting instead to replace their essentialising modes of thought by thinking of cultures 'not as organically unified or traditionally continuous but rather as negotiated, present processes'.

Top tips
If you are interested in studying Archaeology & Anthropology and want to find out more about the types of issues raised by these questions, you might want to dip into J. R. Bowen, *Why The French Don't Like Headscarves: Islam, The State, and Public Space;* Joy Hendry, *Reclaiming Culture: Indigenous People and Self-Representation.*

Architecture

Questions to get you thinking...

Does visiting a historical site give you a better appreciation of the architecture than you can grasp from a picture/photo?

What issues that were important in building Ancient Greek temples are still relevant today?

Why do we need architects?

Do you think architecture changes views of society?

What is your favourite building and why? (past question)

A handy hint with this sort of question is to try and think about specific details of why you like a building. Is it the building type, location, integration of sustainable/eco-friendly systems, material, shape, façade, interior, exterior that you appreciate? Remember that architecture is more than just 'buildings' as such. It is about design with certain proportional qualities, or design order with a conscious spatial awareness.

One Architecture graduate we spoke to said that her favourite building is the Dutch Embassy in Berlin by OMA. It is a good example of a modern building which uses interesting (and inexpensive) materials. The programme is expressed on the façade through the building's materiality (cantilevered green glass) which gives it a subtly iconic look. When inside the building, the processional circulation allows one to experience the building from the outside in, which makes it an interesting building to visit. The details of the different working areas from an interior perspective make the place feel special and the employees take pride in working there. The building also responds well to its context on the Berlin urban block next to the river.

With a question like this, do try and choose a building you have visited. Remember that it is ok to pick a well-known, iconic building but make sure you are very specific as to why it is your favourite. It may be more interesting to choose something that is perhaps more unusual and less likely to be chosen by another applicant. This is typical of the types of questions that have been asked in previous interviews and therefore it is good to have a few examples of different buildings that you like and that you feel confident to talk about. You should also know which architect (if relevant) designed the building, and a bit about some of their other work, which you might like to refer to.

Do architects need to consider light within buildings differently in different countries? (past question)

This question tests how much you have thought about the specifics of design with respect to context and location, as well as testing your environmental knowledge. It is asking you to identify that different countries have different climates and seasons which need to be examined with regards to construction and design in order to help maintain a comfortable microclimate within a building.

You could tackle the question by thinking of examples of why light may be considered differently. What is the building's function? Who are the end users? Where is the building located? Think about what other factors are dependent on light – heat (solar gain) and thus ventilation, and how these might be manipulated for different climates. Diagrams are always a good idea to help illustrate your answer. For example, you might want to show how light changes seasonally (low light in winter verses a higher sun in summer).

If 'yes' is your answer, you can support your point by stating that tropical countries around the equator have similar daylight hours all year round, compared with more northern and southern countries that have a large seasonal flux of sunlight. In order to prevent too much solar gain from direct sunlight, it would be preferable to use shading devices and materials with a high thermal mass to keep a building cool in hot weather. In countries where solar gain needs to be maximised to help heat a building, lots of glass might be used to let in large amounts of light (like a conservatory).

A poor attempt at the question would avoid the environmental issues related to light (i.e. for aesthetic purposes) and also one where the applicant simply stated a 'yes' or 'no' response, without elaborating further.

Top tips
Your portfolio is a key part of the application process. Do think really carefully about how to organise this. What is special about your portfolio and what are your individual strengths? Think about the order of your work, how you can explain why you have chosen the pieces that you have and the links between them. What skills can you show? Can you produce work in different media? Does your work illustrate what inspires you and your technique? It is a skill to be able to combine and present a multiple medium portfolio effectively and quickly. It is usually more convenient to have the pages free and not contained within plastic sheets so that interviewers can see the quality

of the work better, and where possible original drawings (as opposed to scans/copies/prints) should be used. If models or art works are too big to carry then try and make sure they are well documented with photos.

Before the interview, think about architecture in respect of the profession. As one graduate stated, a great architect is, 'for me, a professional who understands the requirements and aspirations of a client (budget, aesthetics, functionality), with respect to designing a practical and buildable structure, and with the capability to respond sensitively to its context and potential environmental impact.' Take the time to think about what it really means to be an architect.

Fine Art

Questions to get you thinking...

Can you use a variety of media to communicate your ideas?

Would you like to be treated as an artist from the word go?

Do you think artistically and does your work exist in its own right?

Interviews for Fine Art tend to be a mix of testing artistic awareness, perception and skill. Our Fine Artists have offered the advice below, based on their own interview experiences, which they believe would be helpful to any aspiring Fine Art applicant to think about in advance of their interview, with its focus on both the theoretical and the practical. Fine Art at Oxford is an extremely competitive course (with only 25 students each year). The Ruskin School is world renowned, and applicants have usually completed an art foundation course before applying. Our Fine Art graduate explains elements of the application process.

Art tutors tend to be quite different animals from other academics. They can be very inviting and hospitable, incredibly patient, and somewhat laid-back. It is true to say that they are like practising artists (as most of them are) and that they are intensively interested in what you make or more importantly what are you are going to make in the future, and they are there to help you achieve it. The more personal your artwork, and the greater relevance it has to you and your view of the world, the more likely it is that the tutors will believe your passion and sincerity.

Portfolio (go for quality not quantity):

Your portfolio should weigh no more than 10 kg, and should be submitted to the Ruskin School. The deadline is in mid November, but make sure you check the Oxford website for the exact day. You should demonstrate development and diversity in your ongoing approach to art by including:

Types of art

Drawing should be central to your portfolio
Preliminary studies with final work
(Good quality) photographs of 2D and 3D work
BIG work is beautiful (it tends to hit home!)
Black and white drawings, not only colour
Art in a mixture of media
Work that isn't 'perfect' or 'finished'

Features of art work

Make it recent and exciting
Produce a spread of ideas and subject matter
Demonstrate your ability and potential
An evident commitment to art and design
Inventiveness and originality
Experimentation with materials and sources
Logical presentation

Sketchbooks

Sketchbooks and personal notebooks are paramount to your application. They are of great value in recording images and exploring ideas, and should not be too contrived. They should also show your artistic thought processes and on-going development. Limit the number of sketchbooks you submit by providing those that show the greatest variety.

The Interview

One of our tutors had a panel of five artists (four tutors and a current student) firing questions at them. Their advice is: 'Do not be afraid to argue and create a heated debate. I enjoyed bearing witness to the tutors' passionate and emotional debate about art, and to suddenly realise that I was contributing to it! In interviews, tutors tend to look through and pick out pieces of your art work, complimenting and questioning your work, in an attempt to locate your driving force and reason for creation. They may help you to see the relevance of your work to the greater art world and also suggest peripheral artists who are dealing with similar problems or issues. Taking new work to the interview is crucial. The tutors need to see that you are artistically inquisitive and continually researching and expanding on ideas. This will provide further fuel for the interview, and you must demonstrate a deeply informed awareness of contemporary art.'

Practical Test

One full day is spent on a practical test. The aim is to take you out of your comfort zone, but also to allow you to be in your element while at interview. You should remember that they will probably compare your portfolio work with what you produce on the test, so try to approach the topic they give you with fresh ideas, while maintaining your usual thought processes or means of engaging with a topic. The work you produce in the practical test should not seem incongruous. Use the materials provided creatively and you may wish to bring your favourite charcoal or paints.

History

Questions to get you thinking...

What is a historical source?

If you are closer to an event, will you record it more accurately?

How do historians obtain evidence?

What is the position of the individual in history?

Should history aim to please the public? (past question)

In this question you are being asked to comment on the subject as a concept. Your judgement is also being assessed. What is history? Who does it serve? And what is it for? These are all crucial questions that form the subtext. Your ability to define, conceptualise, and think deeply about your subject is what lies at the heart of this question. You have the opportunity to show here that you have thought long and hard about history – what it means to you and what it means to others. Remember that your interviewer will have, in all probability, some very fixed views on what his/her subject is about. You must, therefore, be prepared to defend anything you say. There is nothing wrong with disagreeing, arguing, or debating with your interviewer – in fact it can be a good thing – but you must have a well constructed argument to do so. As one Oxford History graduate commented, 'If I were an interviewer, I would expect candidates with views differing from my own to be able to engage in debate and to take the conversation somewhere interesting and new for me.'

There are three elements to tackling this question. Firstly, your definitions, both of history and what it means to 'please the public'. Secondly, your argument based on these definitions. Thirdly, your conclusion, following on from your chosen approach.

A good way to answer this question is to state your conclusion to the question – 'yes' or 'no' – and then go on to explain your answer. If it is 'no,' you might argue 'I do not think that history should aim to please the public. For me, history is about – or is at least aiming to be about – objective truth, and 'pleasing the public' should never be a factor in a historian's judgement.' History that is guided by what the public or certain people want to hear is nothing less than propaganda. It is subjective and therefore, in all likelihood, ignores counter arguments and facts that would lead towards a more accurate understanding. Most historians accept that it is impossible to be entirely objective in their work, but equally most – unless they are postmodernists – recognise objective history as the goal of their research.

Can you give me an example of where Historians may be looking into the past for patterns that are not there? (past question)

In this question your knowledge of historiography, independent reading, and understanding of historical methodology are being assessed. You could perhaps give an example of a Historian and then explain the nature of his/her work and the conclusions that he/she has drawn. You could then apply your analytical judgement to assess whether or not the Historian was justified in looking for patterns. The obvious answer/example in my mind is Marxist Historians such as Christopher Hill, E. P. Thompson and Eric Hobsbawm.

Another Oxford Historian we spoke to said, 'As I understand it, Marxist Historians – at least in their pure form (there are very few left) approach History from a unique perspective fostered by the political and economic ideology – Marxism. They believe, following on from Marx, that the "history of all hitherto existing societies" has been the history of "class struggle" [The Communist Manifesto]. In its simplest and crudest form, Marxists believe that the social hierarchy is divided into three – the aristocracy, the bourgeoisie, and the proletariat – and that there is a permanent antagonism between them. Based on their rather more complicated theory of the laws of production, Marxists believe that the history of modern Europe (indeed of all societies) sees, or will see, the overthrow of the aristocracy by the bourgeoisie and then the overthrow of the bourgeoisie by the proletariat. This is not an objective conclusion, (although the Marxists try to prove their theory by facts), but an ideological conviction that has as much significance for contemporary politics as it did for History'. Therefore, Marxists Historians have searched, within their individual areas of research, for social and economic patterns that point towards the proof of this theory. Such is a bare-bones answer to the question, but a strong candidate would develop his/her answer further to involve a commentary on the pros and cons of Marxist History.

Top tips

Try and tackle questions head on. Pick a position and argue your case, showing an awareness of the complexities of the question. Definitely try and take a position rather than faffing in the middle, although 'not necessarily' is always a valid answer.

Do keep up your source work as this is likely to be tested at interview as well as through the HAT (History Aptitude Test) at Oxford University. You may be presented with a source at interview and asked to talk around it or to answer a specific question. Ensure that you work with what you are given. Do not underestimate the amount of information you can draw from the text. Try to leave your ethical and moral positions aside and look at the piece in the context of its style, its purpose and its meaning.

You should always be prepared to bow to the superior knowledge of your interviewer, if indeed he or she is right. (The likelihood is that they are!) There is no point in maintaining stubbornly that the battle of Trafalgar was fought in 1804 when it clearly wasn't. When you do give ground, however, (accepting a point of view is obviously a key part of education) you should do so in a way that shows your willingness to learn and grasp new ideas. Therefore try and take what you have just learned and run with it.

You may be asked factual questions, although this is not particularly common. Make sure you are hot on the work you have done at school, the arguments you have picked up from your reading outside school and be aware of what is going on in the press, particularly with regard to politics and economics. Try and demonstrate interest in societies and the way in which they interact.

Try and ensure that you show chronological breadth in terms of your reading and understanding of History. Many students come into the interview room with lots of information on modern History: Stalin, Hitler, Weimar Germany and Russia in the 19th century. Can you compare different periods and/or show understanding of ancient, medieval, early modern and modern History?

Although it is important to have facts at your fingertips in historical research, how you organise and draw conclusions from information is the toughest skill. When you are confronted with difficult questions, on paper or in an interview, remember that focusing on human motivation behind actions can be a good place to start and that, pulling apart a question or logically breaking down your approach to it can take you somewhere exciting.

History of Art

Questions to get you thinking...

What is art?

Have you ever thought about why a building was constructed?

Are you interested in art created in a particular medium?

Do you enjoy art galleries and exhibitions?

These are some questions you should think about if you are considering History of Art. With so few places on the courses at both Oxford and Cambridge, our History of Art graduate suggests some ways in which you can successfully prepare for the interview...

What is the value of art?

What monetary value can art have? You should demonstrate an awareness of the modern art industry and how it works, such as who owns the art, who decides the price (for example, auction houses like Sotheby's), and the process by which it is commissioned, distributed and sold. Be aware, too, that the motivations behind selling art are sometimes different from those behind making art.

Who decided the canon of art and what is it? The responsibility lies with critics and Art Historians (such as E.H. Gombrich). Be aware of prejudices in their selection of artists (for example, Giorgio Vasari's *Lives of the Artists*, published in 1556, selected the 'best' artists. They were all

Italian, and the emphasis was on his great friend, Michelangelo). Why do Western universities still focus on the Western canon when teaching their students? Does this propagate a one-sided approach to art? Have Art Historians attempted to look elsewhere?

What is the emotional value of art? An individual can connect with a visual stimulus in a unique way. Additionally, in the Middle Ages, the majority of people were illiterate and visual images of biblical stories allowed them to connect with their faith. Today, we can still connect with figures in art through powerful facial expressions.

What cultural significance can art have? How does art reflect culture and what role does it play? What can we find out about past cultures through art? To an Art Historian, art is a valuable source with which to research costumes, relationships, the role of women, and the role of foreigners.

Your response to a piece of art

Oxford requires you to submit a 750 word response to a piece of art or design before you come for interview. Both universities may use images you have never seen before at interview. Here are some points to consider:

General

Your initial response
Purpose and provenance
Material
Texture
Colour
Size and scale
Location
Style and period
Subject matter
Sculpture

Production method (carving or lost wax?)
Form (open or closed?)
Presentation (is it mounted?)

Top tips
With your submitted written work, demonstrate that you can describe
and analyse an image in words. Avoid simply dropping names of artists
in your personal statement. Try to engage with some of their art too!

Music

Questions to get you thinking...
Is music useful within society?
Why are musical events written about?
Is the study of an instrument a valuable pursuit?
How is music related to free will?

The following questions highlight some of the issues within the study
of academic music today. Our Musicians have shed some light on all
the components of their interview process, and the differences between
Cambridge and Oxford, to help a potential Music applicant jumpstart
their interview preparation.

Is some music more important than others?
With a question like this, take time to consider the parameters. Are
there different ways in which music is important? Is music more
important if it is performed and heard, talked and written about, or
if we can see its impact on our past, present or future? Has it started a
revolution or served as an anthem for an army or a nation?

How do we measure importance? Why are certain composers perceived
as geniuses? Why does our regard for Bach, Mozart and Beethoven
cause debate today? Should we use the term 'musical canon'? Are

certain composers or pieces of music important because of their effect on a genre? Perhaps you could think about Wagner and opera or Beethoven and the string quartet. Is society aware that we marginalise certain musical styles? The study of ethnomusicology (music of non-Western cultures) is a hot topic in the academic study of music.

Use musical examples you feel comfortable with in tackling this question. This approach will allow you to support your arguments and speak with assurance.

Musical Analysis and 'Preparatory Study'

You may be asked to look at a score shortly before your interview, or in the interview itself. Without hearing the piece of music, you should be able to identify some of the following features: The form: is it in binary, ternary or sonata form? How do the instrumental or vocal lines interact? Are the cadences perfect, imperfect or interrupted? What do you notice about the phrase lengths, climaxes, keys and modulations.

You can have a go at some musical analysis on our website **www.oxbridgeapplications.com**

You may be asked to analyse a piece of prose, such as an account of an opera performance. Once again, remember to think critically about what the writer is saying and why they are saying it.

Performance: Oxford asks you to perform, on your principle instrument, a piece of music no more than five minutes in length. Choose a piece that suits you and is perhaps by a composer you mentioned in your personal statement. Tutors may enjoy something they do not hear regularly.

Harmony: Cambridge may ask you to harmonise a soprano line and/ or transcribe a phrase of a four-part Bach Chorale (which will test both your harmony and aural skills).

Top tips for written work

You need to be able to write clearly about music – demonstrate this!
Go beyond your school reading and demonstrate mature research skills.

Philosophy

Questions to get you thinking

Discuss Plato's theory of knowledge.

What is a lie?

Is death rational?

What's the difference between intelligent, wise and clever?

Oxford and Cambridge Philosophy interviews test your logical and lateral thought and require a critical and rational response to challenging philosophical questions. Our team of Philosophy graduates have put together some example questions, based on real ones, to help you to explore philosophical ideas and concepts, and give you a taster as to how you might approach potential interview questions such as these.

If a person is teleported by being destroyed and re-created exactly, is this the same person?

This question tests your ability to recognise issues of personal identity within this thought experiment.

That the person is destroyed might suggest that they no longer exist, but in their being re-created exactly, we are tempted to say that the re-created being is the same person. The bundle theory claims that if there is psychological continuity, where the re-created being has the same memories and personality as the destroyed being, then the recreated person is the same person. But what if two copies are made of the destroyed being? Surely they cannot both be you?

At this stage you could draw the distinction between numerical and qualitative identity. You are numerically identical to the person you were 15 years ago in that you are still the same person, but you are not qualitatively identical as you do not have the same qualitative properties, for example, you may have a different set of teeth.

For this thought experiment, you therefore might conclude that the person who is re-created could be the same person as the person who was destroyed, in the sense that they are qualitatively identical. This would also be the case if there were two copies of the re-created person. They are not, however, numerically identical.

If I am young today then I will be young tomorrow; if I am young tomorrow I will be young the day after that...so I will be young in 80 years' time. Discuss.

This question tests your ability to see past the tricks of language to detect the logic underneath, and your ability to argue rationally in the form of: premise one, premise two, conclusion. We can show that premise one is invalid by comparing, 'if I am young today then I will be young tomorrow' with 'if I am wearing red today then I will be wearing red tomorrow'. The structure 'if x today, then x tomorrow' is not logically sound.

Premise one would be true if it followed that, if you were young on day A, you would be young on day B. If we accept premise one, then premise two, 'if I am young tomorrow I will be young the day after that' logically follows, because what is true on day A would be true on day B (it would be a transitive property). Thus the conclusion 'so I will be young in 80 years' time' holds.

As we have pointed out, premise one is incorrect. The quality of youth is affected by the progress of time. A person becomes progressively older each day. Therefore age, or 'youngness', is not a static quality, it is incremental.

With these types of question, admissions tutors are looking for you to demonstrate logical thought and reasoned opinions. Above all, they want to see how you a build and structure a coherent argument. Think aloud and be sure to work steadily through the question so that you come to a sound conclusion. And if you get stuck at any stage, do not be afraid to ask the interviewer. They want to see how you think and if you need to ask a relevant, intelligent question, this shows you are capable of thinking independently and willing to explore the subject.

Top tips for Philosophy interviews
In Philosophy interviews, students can all too easily rely on their intuition. Avoid this as much as possible. Think through your answers and support your arguments with evidence of logical thinking. Read books to help you to develop a genuine interest and understanding of the subject (not just A level material) such as Wilfrid Hodges, Logic and Edward Craig, *The Shorter Routledge Encyclopaedia of Philosophy.*

Literature & Languages

Classics

Questions to get you thinking...
What role did the chorus have in Greek plays and how well does it translate into a modern context?

What would happen if the Classics department burnt down?

What parallels can be drawn between East-West cultures today and the gap between classical civilisation and now?

Classics interviews often ask you to analyse a classical text. For the purposes of this exercise, we have chosen a particular poem.

Comment on this poem by Catullus.

odi et amo. quare id faciam, fortasse requiris?
nescio, sed fieri sentio et excrucior.

The interviewer will not expect you to offer a complete translation into English and you do not need to understand every word. An unseen commentary allows you to apply your existing knowledge of vocabulary, grammar and context intelligently and gives you the opportunity to offer insightful and analytical suggestions as to why Catullus chose that word, that image, that syntax etc. in his poem. Be instinctive and concentrate on your impressions of the poem – look, understand, evaluate, and respond.

You might start by commenting on the form of the poem – it is a couplet. You could point out that Catullus expresses paradoxical, conflicting feelings: 'Odi et amo' – 'I hate' and 'I love'. You could then highlight the fact that he exploits this couplet form well by asking a question in the first line and then answering it in the second line. What might strike you next as you look closer at the poem is the use of verbs – 'odi... amo... faciam... nescio... sentio... excrucrior' – six verbs all in the first person, which focus the reader's attention on the author's intense feelings and actions, which are contradictory and successfully communicate the push–pull of emotions. He hates, he loves, he does, he does not know, he feels and he is in torment. Look at the first three words and the last three words, which mirror the same construction – verb – conjunction – verb. If you analyse the four verbs used – 'odi...amo...sentio...excrucior', you might notice that the two outer verbs indicate a negative feel and the two inner words are generally positive, producing an ABBA chiasmus in the poem. It can even be said that positioning the first word and the last word – 'I hate' and 'I am in torment' at the very beginning and at the very end of the poem suggests that the overriding feelings are negative, and renders the overall tone of the poem gloomy. You could also suggest that his tight structuring is an attempt to organise and comprehend his conflicting emotions.

You might also know that Catullus was a member of the Neotericoi – the 'new poets', who were experimenting with a shorter form of poem, which they called an epigram and which aimed at brevity, succinct phrasing and intense emotion contained in few words. You might comment on how successful you feel he has been to this end. It is the structure of this poem, the syntax and the word choice which are the most notable features – the analysis of which can lead to the most thorough understanding of the state of mind of the author. Commenting on how and where certain words are used allows you, the reader, to understand the author's intentions and to impress the interviewer with your analytical ability.

For more tips on analysing an unseen extract, see the approaching questions section for English.

Would ancient history be different if it were written by slaves? (past question)

A question like this calls on your on-the-spot intuition and it allows you to draw on your knowledge of any texts you have studied. The interviewer is looking for you to demonstrate an ability and a willingness to think for yourself and to develop an argument that cannot have been simply digested and regurgitated from another source. As an interviewer, you are looking for someone who has read enough ancient history to have sufficient knowledge of the subject matter to express an informed opinion, coupled with an ability to analyse the subject matter interestingly and originally enough to come up with a stimulating and persuasive argument.

Firstly, you might like to stress that there were many different types of slave, and many different possible experiences of history in the Ancient World. A Greek private tutor, a paedogogus, might have had very different ideas from a gladiator. Some household slaves, particularly those with an ability to educate Roman youth or with knowledge of medicine, would have had very different ideas from a German slave, prized for his physical strength, used in an auxilia army role. Secondly, you could mention how slavery in Greece varied from city state to city state: a helot would view things very differently from a slave in Athens (where striking a slave was forbidden and masters apparently tolerated back-chat from slaves). Here you could refer to the comedies of Menander, Plautus and Terence, where the slaves have a relatively jolly time of it. Thirdly, it might be a good idea to comment on how treatment of slaves changed over time and how the law evolved. A slave in the Roman Republic would have had fewer rights than a slave of the Imperial period (when the right to kill a slave at a whim was removed).

You could mention that it helps, when you are writing history, to have taken part in it. The majority of ancient Historians were wealthy men with leisure and contacts. Herodotus travelled through many lands at a time when this was unusual. This required a private income (a big one) and free time (lots of it). Livy was a provincial of Plebeian origin, but he was educated in oratory and Greek, indicating rank. The educational level required to write history, the leisure time, the breadth of experience, would have been so far removed from the experience of most slaves that an answer to this question is, at best, highly speculative.

That said, one of Claudius' freedmen (ex-slaves) would have had the ear of the emperor and would have had much to say about foreign policy – and would have been in favour of the Imperial system, as opposed to the romantic Republican (and Historian) Claudius, or Livy, who wanted to abolish the system of emperors (where slaves favoured by the emperor could wield real influence) and bring back the old Republic (where masters had the right to maim or kill their slaves). We can speculate that an Athenian slave would have written favourably of the legislator Draco, who made the murder of a slave punishable by death, despite his prevailing reputation for severity. He might have had less rosy an opinion of Aristotle, for whom slaves were 'living tools' fit only for physical labour, or Homer, who wrote that 'Jove takes half the goodness out of a man when he makes a slave of him'.

Top Tips

In Classics interviews, you might be asked about overarching topics of Classical literature and your interviewer might touch on philosophy, history, archaeology, art, philology or linguistics. It is highly beneficial to develop in-depth knowledge of at least one of these topics, in order to enter into a discussion with your interviewer.

Developing a special interest can help. Soak up a particular author (e.g. one of the great Greek Tragedians Aeschylus, Sophocles or Euripides or study Ovid's use of myth), a genre (e.g. Latin love elegy, Ancient Greek political comedy etc.), a historical period (e.g. Peloponnesian War or the final days of the Roman Republic) architectural style or period of art. Do not be afraid to have strong or even controversial opinions and reactions to ancient authors or historical events. The interviewer is looking for someone who has passionate reactions to the Ancient World; just ensure you use examples to support your argument. Show initiative and be proactive in your search for new knowledge. Visiting museums (for example, the Parthenon friezes at the British Museum), Ancient Roman and Greek archaeological sites, going to the theatre to watch an Ancient Greek play, or simply watching a suitable documentary on the BBC or History Channel can show you are a motivated student, capable of going one step further to research your subject away from the classroom.

It's always good to brush up on grammar and your vocabularly to prepare for unseen passages you might be presented with in the interview, but do not spend hours revising. You may be asked about the essays or commentaries you have submitted as well as what you are studying at A level, what you enjoy about Classics and what you look forward to studying on the course. Re-read any submitted essays/commentaries and develop new arguments and points in case you are questioned on them in the interview.

It's good to develop your critical thinking skills. Train your analytical responses to the literature you have already studied by reading scholars' critical responses (secondary literature) and deciding whether you agree with their views. You are entitled to have an opinion, you just need to have evidence to support your case.

Top tips for studying Classics ab initio

The interviewer may want to test your ability to react critically and analytically to a literary text, as this exercise makes up a large part of the course. Delve into a literary genre or start reading a particular author in any language and assess your reactions to the text in terms of style, language, context, themes, imagery, tone, register etc. Why did you like/not like it? Read a selection of plays/prose/poetry in translation to help you develop an understanding of the genres and periods and to get you excited about them. One possibility is to choose an author, for example Ovid or Aristophanes, who has left us a large legacy of work and track their literary development to gain a better understanding of the historical context.

It can be helpful to familiarise yourself with terminology used in literary criticism such as anaphora, pathetic fallacy, soliloquy, oxymoron and onomatopoeia, but do not get too caught up revising every single critical word and its meaning. Start familiarising yourself with the epic poets Homer and Virgil. Begin to learn the Greek alphabet and try translating some passages of Greek and Latin into English with the help of a dictionary and grammar guide to get to grips with basic language structures.

English

Questions to get you thinking…

Do you think that the director of a play should have absolute power, or should he/she be flexible?

Why study English at university rather than read in your spare time?

How is poetry linked to music and the other arts?

Is a protagonist's gender important?

The big picture

The biggest difference between studying literature at Oxbridge and studying it at school is that tutors are looking for students who can be independent thinkers. At Oxbridge, you are much more likely to have your accepted notions challenged with questions like, 'Why do you think that?' You must therefore be prepared to justify all your opinions. You'll be expected to be familiar with what critics, past and present, have had to say about particular works and to position your own responses in relation to theirs. Because the Oxbridge courses are structured chronologically, going from Old and Middle English texts all the way to contemporary works, you'll be expected to start making links between works from different periods and genres and show your understanding of how English literature has developed over the centuries.

Be prepared

Come into your interview knowing which works of literature you can discuss most thoroughly and passionately. Tutors will be looking for students who have not just dutifully read the set texts for their A levels, but who are excited about literature and have gone on to do outside reading. That doesn't mean you should try to read everything under the sun: you can't do that, but the works you do know should be diverse. Think about which texts and authors you know best. Are they all from the same period? Are they all novels? Perhaps explore some older works or read some poetry. If you enjoyed the books by a particular author, read some of his other works, or read what the critics have to say. In short, if, in the months leading up to the interview you are always reading some challenging, literary work and you are thinking about it critically, making connections with other works you've read, then you'll be in good shape. Look at the reading lists for the Oxbridge courses online to see what kinds of works you'd be reading there. This should give you some ideas for new things to dip into.

The interview

Be prepared to speak about any work that you've mentioned on your personal statement. The tutor may spend most of the interview talking about that, or they may not mention it. Make sure you spend time carefully choosing what to say in your personal statement. Tutors will pick up on statements that read like laundry lists, i.e. 'I read this book, this book, and this book.' Frankly, it doesn't matter that you have read the book – what's important is that you have something significant to say about it! Avoid generalisations and do not drop in comments or opinions you've heard about the books, which aren't really your own. These are things tutors may challenge you on. One applicant was asked whether they thought David Tennant made a good Hamlet, having mentioned they had seen the production in their personal statement.

Writing the personal statement is good preparation for the interview. If you devote time to asking yourself questions like, 'Which works interest me most? What do I think literature's purpose in the world is?' and refine your answers so that they are strong and specific, then you will not only have a good personal statement, you will also have done a necessary self-evaluation which will make you more confident in discussing your opinions.

Your tutor may be interested in getting into some of the biggest debates from the history of literature, such as 'Does literature have a moral purpose?', 'Should a work be judged based on an author's intentions or by some other criterion?' If you find a useful introductory anthology to literary criticism and browse through it, you can familiarise yourself with these questions and start to develop your own opinions. Remember, the big questions don't necessarily have a right answer: the key is to make a claim and be able to justify it, especially when the tutor challenges you by offering a conflicting opinion.

Don't forget to think about more personal questions, such as 'Why do you want to study literature?' or 'Why do you want to study at Oxbridge?' These are often the sorts of questions that students forget to ask themselves, but it is crucially important that you have good answers to them. This will demonstrate that you're excited about this field of study and that you've put some thought into the application process.

Tackling the unknown

An important part of many interviews is analysing an unseen text. This can be a bit nerve wracking – but don't panic! The interviewer is not testing you on whether you know the text, but rather on how you approach it and what you can draw from it. Don't be afraid to acknowledge something that you don't know – if you've got a poem by W. H. Auden and you're not sure whether Auden is a man or a woman, ask! It's much better than struggling on and referring to Auden as she all the way through your interview. A good approach is to start off with the basics – who is speaking? What is going on in the piece? Is there a story? – and move on to explore the nuances in greater detail as your confidence grows. The aim of analysing an unseen text is not to reach an answer, but to show the interviewers your ideas and your interpretation of the piece. As one of our English graduate tutors said, 'lots of students try to get to grips with an unseen passage by simplifying it – but they then lose all the nuances and ambiguities that made it interesting in the first place. The great thing about literature, is that the more you examine it, the more complex it becomes.'

Get the technique right

Young literature students often focus too much on content and theme in a literary work and forget to make links with form and technique – a common pitfall too when it comes to Oxford's English admissions test – the ELAT (English Literature Admissions Test). Remember that poems and novels are different from essays: writers may have an intention or a theme that they have set out to explore but they're doing it through literary techniques. That's what makes literature different from, say, a philosophical essay or an opinion piece in The Guardian. Always try to identify the techniques that are at play in the text. Try to link form to content: often the way that a writer has chosen to express himself has a strong connection to the ideas that he is trying to convey.

Analyse this poem by Philip Sydney

Having to analyse a poem on the spot might sound terrifying, and many Oxbridge applicants consider it by far the most intimidating part of the interview process. However, if you go in armed with some simple but useful analytical techniques, you'll have nothing to fear.

Your interviewer is not expecting you to have prepared an exhaustive discussion of, for instance, Renaissance sonnets and their Italianate influences in the 20 minutes or so you've had to look at the unseen poem before your interview; rather, the idea is that you can put forward your own ideas and claims about the way the poem works, and the effects it achieves.

XIX

On Cupid's bow, how are my heart-strings bent,
That see my wrack, and yet embrace the same!
When most I glory, then I feel most shame;
I willing run, yet while I run repent;
My best wits still their own disgrace invent:
My very ink turns straight to Stella's name;
And yet my words, as them my pen doth frame,
Advise themselves that they are vainely spent:
For though she pass all things, yet what is all
That unto me, who fare like him that both
Looks to the skies and in a ditch doth fall?
O let me prop my mind, yet in his growth,
And not in nature for best fruits unfit.
Scholar, saith Love, bend hitherward your wit.

Sir Philip Sidney, from Astrophel and Stella (1591)

The first thing to do is to ensure that you understand the literal sense of the poem: what is happening, who is speaking, what does he/she want, are there any narrative twists etc.? For this poem, you should first establish that the speaker is experiencing the agony of love as he attempts to write a poem for his beautiful beloved, Stella. Without a basic knowledge of what's going on, you won't be able to explore the poetic techniques the writer is using to express it.

Next, think about the form the poem is taking. This will help you to compare your expectations of the genre with how the poet is using that genre. Here, we have a Petrarchan sonnet (abba, abba, cdcd, ee), which, as is traditional with Petrarchan sonnets, has the torments of love as a theme. Knowing whether the poem is working with or against tradition will also help you to talk about its effect.

You should pay close attention to the words and groups of words used (the language or diction). This will lead us to consider imagery, mood and to develop our ideas on the theme. In this sonnet, the poet frequently creates pairs of contrasting words or ideas ('glory' and 'shame'; 'I willing run, yet while I run repent'; 'him that both/Looks to the skies and in a ditch doth fall'). The poet uses these contrasts to express the conflicting impulses and feelings involved in being in love – a mixture of joy and pain – and to put them across vividly to the reader. Be thorough with what you notice here – and back it up with examples from the poem – the more evidence you have, the more convincing your points will be.

All of this should lead you to your conclusion: a brief summary of your argument about what you think the poet is trying to achieve. Think of all the details you've picked up as weight for your argument. It's important that you conclude your argument, as it will prove that you're able to link textual details with the poet's intention in using them.

Top tips
Try to ground your impressions about what the poem means by pointing to the places in the text where you can find evidence for your assertions. If you see evidence of poetic techniques such as those mentioned above, use the technical terms, but make sure you're using them correctly. Perhaps study the definitions of frequently used literary terms like irony or satire before the interview. If you do use them, be prepared to say what they mean. And, finally, it's almost never valuable

to say that a literary work is interesting. The natural response to that is, 'Why? What's so interesting about it?' Skip that step and get into the meat of what the poem or text is doing. The more specific you are, the more substantive things you'll have to say and the more you'll impress the tutor.

Modern & Medieval Languages

Questions to get you thinking...

Could you say that an author is actually just another character in their novel or their play?

Do you notice any differences between English and European literature? If so, why might these be?

What do you think Voltaire meant by 'Il faut cultiver notre jardin'?

What is meant by subject and object?

Literary analysis

Literary analysis is usually an important part of a languages interview at Oxford and Cambridge, as literature is a large part of the course. You don't need to worry if you have not studied literature as part of your AS or A level course.

You will, however, need to show an interest in literature and an ability to analyse and think critically about literary ideas, language and styles. A good approach can be to read the work of a few authors or periods of literature which genuinely interests you. Find one or two authors you really like and read a selection of their works across their career with the aim of building up an understanding of the key ideas which preoccupied them.

Alternatively, you could pick a period or a theme (for instance, German literature about the Holocaust or 20th century East German literature) and read books by different authors (such as Christa Wolf, W. G. Sebald or Günter Grass) and appreciate concepts relevant at the time and their expression in the literature. Adopting one of these strategies should give you enough material to use in the interview as well as help you to explore your chosen subject in greater depth. You don't need to be an encyclopaedia of literature, but you do need to feel confident discussing literature intelligently with your interviewer. Remember too, that you could be asked to comment on any text you have mentioned in your personal statement. Be sure to prepare these texts thoroughly before the interview.

Speaking in your chosen language/s

You may be asked to speak in your chosen language in the interview. The first rule is, don't panic! This is a chance to demonstrate your ability. Arm yourself and prepare for this possibility by speaking the language as much as you can with friends, teachers or family members. It can be helpful to pick a topic to discuss and then practise defending an argument. You could put together a list of 'starter' phrases, or come up with and memorise a few useful phrases. While there are no guarantees that you will need to draw on them in the real interview, this exercise can give you confidence when answering an off-the-cuff question in the interview itself. Try to be as accurate as you can, but don't shy away from experimenting with more complex sentence structures: Admissions tutors are looking for students who want to speak the language to a high level and aren't afraid to make mistakes as they learn.

Analysing an unseen text

You may be given a text to read (normally but not exclusively a poem or a piece of prose) on which to comment and discuss. At first, this can seem a rather daunting task, especially if you are unfamiliar with some of the vocabulary, the style or the context. There are two key techniques you can apply to help you with such a task. Firstly, the 'analytical' approach: going through the text in a systematic and structured way may help you dissect and identify important points. Secondly, the 'building block' approach: start with something you definitely understand, however minor it seems. Building upon the word or sentence you know may allow you to deduce meaning and context in the piece accurately.

We've also put together some further guidelines that may also help you:

Getting started

Although there is no way of knowing which text you will be faced with, there are certainly things you can do to prepare. It is always a good idea to read as widely as possible to build up your vocabulary. You might consider making a vocabulary list which you carry with you on the train, on the bus or even into the bathroom!

While a broad vocabulary will help you, remember that literature goes beyond words and reflects historical, philosophical, scientific and emotional ideas. Therefore, you may want to consider the key literary developments in the country(ies) of the language(s) you want to read. This sounds grander than it is. In practice it simply means having an overview of the historical, political and social developments reflected in the literature of particular periods in history and how they interlink. For instance, if we were to isolate the French literature of the 18th century, we would see that some of the key ideas that influenced writers during this period were the (non-)existence of God, the dominance of reason over religion and the relationship between the state, the government and the people. Try and see the wider picture and ask yourself why authors wrote what they wrote. It may be helpful to make a timeline to illustrate the key developments and themes in history and literature and the authors associated with each period and theme.

You need to train yourself to think critically about language and ideas. Practise this by picking articles from newspapers, magazines or books, reading them carefully and thinking about how it makes you feel. Consider your instant reaction to the style, the content and the overall ideas expressed. In short, push yourself to have an opinion. The interview will test what you know and how you apply this knowledge to what you don't. You need to show you can think on your feet and respond critically to unfamiliar ideas.

In the interview

When given the text, read it through several times and try to get a feeling for what it is about. Try and identify the key themes and the context. Perhaps try reading it aloud. This can be helpful if you are given a poem, as this tactic will help you identify some of the points mentioned below, such as the rhyme scheme. Take as many notes as will be helpful. Don't overdo it because if you write too much on the page you might end up confusing yourself and losing your key points. In short, jot down the most important points and highlight any sections you think are particularly useful.

If you come across words/a word you don't know, don't worry, this is perfectly normal and you will not be the only one! Really try and understand the overall sense of the text, concentrate on the words you do understand and take time to get to grips with the ideas expressed. Once you have understood the themes, you should be able to interpret the words you didn't understand. You may even find that they are not as important as you previously thought. If you do get really stuck, break the word down and try to decipher the meaning from the root. Call on all your powers of lateral thought here!

The basics

Start by assessing what kind of text you are dealing with. This usually boils down to one key question: is it a poem or a piece of prose? This should be clear from the form and structure of the text and once you have identified the form, there are a few basic technical points to consider.

If you are dealing with a poem, consider:

- The form and the structure: How has the poet arranged the lines and the stanzas of the poem? Certain forms and structures marry certain themes: the sonnet is often employed when love is the key theme, the ballad often lends itself to narrative poetry.
- The rhyme scheme: How does the pattern of rhyme contribute to the meaning of the poem? An inconsistent rhyme scheme can

suggest conflict (possibly the poet's own, possibly external). How many syllables are there in each line? Which syllables are emphasised and why?

- The syntax: How are the lines broken up? Is it logical or disjointed? Does it serve to highlight a theme or an idea?
- The punctuation: Often used to emphasise an idea or a theme, how does it influence the reading of the poem? Be sensitive to the poet's use of punctuation and highlight particularly interesting constructions.
- The language: Examine carefully the poet's choice of words. Why has the poet chosen a particular word: to convey an idea or to create an aesthetic effect?
- Imagery: Think about whether the imagery used is abstract, literal or figurative. How does the imagery affect you?

If you are dealing with a piece of prose, you should consider:

The location of the extract in the text: Is the text taken from the beginning, the middle or the end of the work? How do you think the story will/has develop(ed)?

The characters: Who are they? What is their relationship to each other? How will their relationship impact the rest of the story?

The tone: The tone may be bound up with the narrator (see below). How is the story narrated? Is the narrator involved, detached, ironic or satirical? What effect does the tone have on your reading of the passage? Did the writer intend this?

The above points in relation to language, punctuation and imagery also apply and should be considered.

Poets and authors employ a tool kit in terms of language, rhythm, syntax, etc, which always serve a purpose. Techniques might be used to emphasise a key theme, for aesthetic reasons, to conjure a certain image or idea or to affect the reader.

Be sensitive to how you feel as you read and share your ideas in the interview. The best answers are often the most honest, so be aware of your own responses to the text.

If you are unfamiliar with certain poetic forms or patterns of rhyme scheme, try and familiarise yourself with the most common (e.g. the sonnet, the Petrarchan sonnet etc) but don't worry too much about this. You aren't expected to be familiar with every form of poetry ever written! Dip into different styles in English and your chosen language and familiarise yourself with how poetry works and, in particular, how poetry in a foreign language works.

The context

The style in which the text is written, the language employed and the main ideas expressed often shed light on when the text was written. This may not be obvious on a first reading and you may, therefore, have to dig deep into the piece. Reading widely across different periods can help you to develop sensitivity to context, (and should be enjoyable!) but this is by no means essential.

The historical context of a piece can be an interesting talking point in the interview. If you are able to deduce that the text is a product of the Spanish Civil War, for example, maybe you could use your knowledge of this turbulent period to comment on the poignancy of the writer's words. Do try not to go off on a tangent to show how much you know about 20th century Spanish history. Relevance and answering the interviewer's questions is key!

Do remember not to confuse context with the content of the story or the poem. This is easily done. Context relates to the surrounding circumstances in which the text was written. For example, the 18th century French thinker Voltaire wrote many short stories (known as 'contes') which are set in ancient Babylonia, in outer space, or in the Old Testament. However, the context remains 18th century France and the social, political and philosophical ideas of the day (see above).

The key themes

Identifying the main themes of the extract is important and usually fascinating! If the language or vocabulary is difficult, why not try employing the 'building blocks' technique explained earlier?

Once you have identified a few themes, look for links across the text. These links might be found in relation to one individual theme (i.e. look for the different ways in which the same theme is expressed) or to several themes (i.e. the way in which different themes are linked across the piece).

Remember to try and consider the points mentioned above in relation to style, language, punctuation, rhyme scheme, and how they add to our understanding of the theme (positively or negatively). This allows you to come across as a student aware of languages as an academic discipline.

Identifying the key themes of the piece (and considering the language used) can help you with the context. For example, if the text is littered with different ideas and images and the language is rich and textured it could be a Surrealist work and thus date from 1920s.

The narrator

Do bear in mind that the author/poet of the piece is not the same as the narrator and that the author/poet may have created a specific persona to narrate the piece. Examining the tenses employed will help you identify whether there is a first person narrator or a third person narrator. If the author or poet has created a narrator, it is important to be sensitive to how this figure is involved in the piece and how his narration of the story or poem affects your interpretation of it. For example, you could consider whether the narrator is trustworthy. Does his tone suggest he is treating the subject-matter ironically and thus not necessarily fairly?

The development of the piece

It is a good idea to think about how the text develops. Consider whether it starts and ends with the same theme, idea or style or whether it begins with one theme and progresses to another, and ends in a completely different place. How does this development bear on the overall theme of the poem? Does it convey a positive or a negative image of the over-riding theme?

Useful phrases

While it is important to be honest and genuine in answering the interviewer's questions, the delivery of your answer can be improved by beginning with 'smart starters'. Below is a short list of phrases that can be used to help you to introduce your arguments. Bear in mind that this list is neither exclusive nor exhaustive and is not a guaranteed recipe for success. It is merely there as a guide to delivering pertinent answers. More than anything else, having a phrase ready to use can increase your confidence and buy you a bit of extra 'thinking' time as you consider your response.

My first reaction was ... /A first reading of the text suggested to me ...
A closer reading revealed that ... /Scrutinising the text in more detail shows that ...
If we were to isolate the theme of ...
If we narrow the text down to the following themes ...

Summary

The above points can help you tackle any unseen text. The most important thing is to work through what you are given in a structured way. You won't have that much time to prepare so the better prepared you are to deal with an unseen piece of text, the more you will get out of your preparation time.

Above all, try to remember that exercises like this are designed to see how you react to unfamiliar concepts and how well you express your own ideas. The task is not designed to catch you out, this is why it is important not to worry too much about vocabulary you don't know. Focus your time and energy on identifying the key themes, examining the language critically and showing sensitivity to style. It is far more important to demonstrate a few insightful reactions to the text than to know all the words.

Bear in mind that there isn't necessarily a 'right' answer to some of the questions you are asked (for instance, there can never be a 'right' answer to the question 'what do you think of the poem?', since this question asks for your opinion). Most of the time the tutor will want to see what you think about a particular point – so don't get yourself worked up in the interview by trying to work out the answer the tutor wants to hear. Be as honest as possible, although admitting you don't have a clue is never advisable! If you really are unsure, ask the tutor to clarify areas of uncertainty, but show a willingness to find out the answer yourself by asking intelligent and probing questions.

A note on joint schools

If you are applying to read Modern Languages and another subject, the above still applies to the Modern Languages side. However, it might be a good idea to think about the links between your other subject and your chosen language. For example, if you are applying to read English & Spanish, you could consider the influence writers such as James Joyce, William Faulkner and John Dos Passos have had on Latin American authors, especially Mario Vargas Llosa and Gabriel García Márquez. Similarly, for History & French, you could think about the impact of French colonisation on writers such as Aimé Césaire and Patrick Chamoiseau. You will be interviewed in both subjects, but one of your interviewers may be interested to hear about the connections you have made between your two subjects and how you think the social, political and cultural developments of a country influence its literature.

A note on studying a language ab initio

If you are applying to read a language ab initio you need to demonstrate a natural aptitude for languages and an ability to pick up languages and linguistic concepts quickly. To test your ability, you may be given something to read and comment upon in the language. You might prepare for this by engaging with the language as much as possible. Further reading can help: study the grammar and try to build up your vocabulary, perhaps by making a vocabulary list. It is a good idea to show that you have dipped into the literature and begun to develop an interest in a few authors or periods. You could apply the same strategy as described earlier: pick an author, a theme or a period, look at the literature and start forming your own opinion about your chosen area.

Top Tips

Prepare thoroughly for the literature aspect but don't go overboard, even if you can swim! Focus on a few authors, themes or periods. Be aware of the wider context in which the literature you have read operates. Brush up on the grammar of your chosen language before the interview and make sure you are comfortable conversing on a range of different subjects. Reread your personal statement and be prepared to answer questions on anything mentioned. Train yourself to respond instantly to ideas and arguments by reading passages from newspapers, novels or collections of poetry.

Social & Political Sciences

Economics/Economics & Management/PPE

Questions to get you thinking...

Who do you think is the greatest economist?

What do we mean when we say someone deserves a reward?

Would you support the privatisation of the NHS?

What is the biggest economic problem facing Britain today?

Economics interviews often test your understanding of economic theory and current affairs. For the purposes of this exercise we have created four example questions, based on similar ones that have been asked in the past. The first is an example of a microeconomics question, the second a macroeconomics question, the third an example of a logical thinking question and finally a mathematics question.

What factors could be expected to affect the price of houses in a free market?

At the core of this question is the interaction of supply and demand for houses. Given this, a logical way to answer the question, could be to work out the factors affecting supply and demand and then go on to explain how their interaction results in a final equilibrium price. To make your answer even stronger, it would also be good to consider what might affect the price of an individual house as opposed to what affects the price of houses in general in a free market.

Major factors affecting demand for housing include: the incomes of households in the economy, which affects the amount they are able to spend on housing in general, mortgage interest rates are key, as lower rates make houses in general more affordable and vice versa, likewise expectations of future house prices and future mortgage interest rates affect what householders might be willing to pay for housing.

The demand for a house rather than houses in general could be affected by: the preferences of householders in the economy, for example, are Georgian houses in fashion or is there a fad for the clean lines of modern architecture? This factor might also apply to houses generally, for example, if owning your own home is a sign of status in a society this may increase willingness to pay across the economy, the size and nature of the house, e.g. is it a cottage, flat, bungalow, mansion, and so on, the location of the house, for example is it located in a densely populated urban centre where there are many jobs or in a rural area; is it near good schools and local amenities?

Meanwhile, housing supply is determined by the existing stock of houses, and the building of new houses.

The next step in answering this question is to draw a graph of supply and demand and illustrate the equilibrium price. One thing to note is that because a new building contributes only about 1.1 per cent to the existing stock each year, the supply of houses is relatively inelastic even over long periods. This means that the supply curve will be steep. In contrast, demand is relatively elastic because consumers are highly sensitive to house prices. This means the demand curve will be relatively shallow.

You could also demonstrate how changing demand or supply conditions would affect the equilibrium. For example, during the mid to late 1980s incomes grew rapidly, while financial deregulation in 1987 made mortgages cheaper and easier to obtain. This led to a rise in demand, shifting the demand curve up and right and causing a housing market boom.

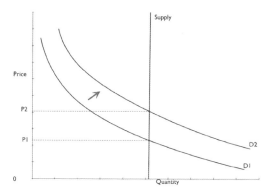

What effect would a tightening of monetary policy have on the value of government bonds in the bond markets?

The first step in answering this question is to define the various terms: 'monetary tightening' is a constriction of the supply of money by the central bank. 'Government bonds' are assets sold by the government to investors as a way of borrowing money. Investors hand over cash for the bonds to the government, in exchange for a promise by the government to repay this money at a specified future date. In the meantime, the investors receive interest payments from the government to compensate them for the amount of money they could have made by investing this cash elsewhere, and also for the risk that the government will go bankrupt and not repay the debt.

Next, a good answer would go on to explain how a central bank tightens monetary policy. It does this through 'open market operations' which work as follows: the central bank sells government bonds to investors from its own portfolio in exchange for cash. This reduces the supply of money the public holds. As we know from the law of supply and demand (see previous question), an increase in the supply of bonds in the market for a given demand will cause the price of the bonds to fall. One thing to note here is that this is equivalent to a rise in the interest rate because less money is needed today for a given value in the future. Bond prices, therefore, are inversely related to interest rates.

At this stage, a strong applicant would look to expand further on the results of this action on aggregate demand in the economy. The rate of interest on savings in the economy has increased so consumers may be encouraged to save rather than spend. If foreigners want to buy debt then they must first buy domestic currency: an increase in the interest rate will increase their demand for domestic currency which, as we know from the question above, will make domestic currency relatively more expensive. Exports become more expensive and imports cheaper. You will add another layer of dynamism to your answer if you show knowledge of the current interest rate set by the central bank, the Bank of England, and recent changes in interest rates.

What is the angle between the hands on a clock at quarter past three?

This is a simple case of mental arithmetic. The best way to answer this question is to create a mental picture of a clock. Do NOT fall into the trap of thinking the angle is zero! There are 360 degrees in a circle and 12 hours on a clock face, so the angle between each hour is 360/12 = 30 degrees. The minute hand is directly over the '3' marking. However, the hour hand will be a quarter of the way between the '3' and '4' markings. Therefore, the angle between the hands is 30/4 = 7.5 degrees.

Draw a graph of y = sin(x²)

As you will know from A level maths, the graph of y = sin(x) looks like this:

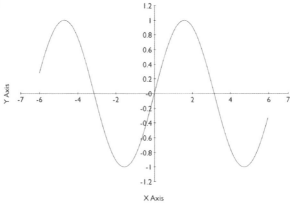

When working out how to draw $\sin(x^2)$, think about the fundamentals of the graph, rather than trying to plot specific points: first, evaluate what the maximum and minimum values for y will be. Since the maximum value of y for $\sin(x)$ is 1, no matter how large x, the maximum value of $\sin(x^2)$ will also be 1. Likewise the minimum value will also be -1, as this is the minimum for any value of x and thus x^2. Next, think about the frequency of oscillations. As x increases, x^2 increases exponentially, the rate at which y oscillates between 1 and -1 will increase. This will mean the gap between maxima and minima will decrease as x gets larger than zero or less than zero.

Finally, note that the graph of $y = x^2$ is symmetrical about the y axis, and thus so will the graph of $y = \sin(x^2)$. Hence the graph will look as follows:

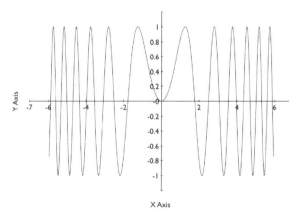

Top tips
Have a glance through our glossary. Economics is full of jargon. This can seem tricky at first, but as your understanding of the subject develops it will become clear how useful it is to have words for very specific concepts. Here are some examples of vocabulary that an Oxbridge interviewer may use:

Budget deficit/surplus – the excess/shortfall of government spending over government receipts from taxation.

Business cycle – the short-term fluctuations in the economy's output around its trend path.

Central bank – the institution responsible for implementing monetary policy (e.g. the Bank of England in the UK and the Federal Reserve in the USA).

Consumption – goods and services purchased by consumers.

Econometrics – the use of statistical techniques to quantify relationships in economic data.

Economics – the study of how individuals and societies allocate scarce resources.

Endogenous variable – one explained by the model.

Equilibrium – a state of balance between opposing forces, such as supply and demand in the market.

Exogenous variable – one taken as given; assumed rather than explained in the model.

Fiscal policy – policy on government spending and taxation.

GDP (Gross Domestic Product) – the total income/production of the economy earned/produced domestically.

Inflation – the rate of increase in the level of overall prices.

Investment – goods purchased by firms to increase their stock of capital.

Macroeconomics – the study of the economy as a whole; typical variables of interest include inflation, interest rates and exchange rates.

Microeconomics – the study of individual behaviour with respect to consumers' and firms' decisions about the allocation of resources.

Monetary policy – policy on the money supply and interest rates.

Monopoly – a market in which there is only one producer.

Profit – revenue minus costs.

Real variable – a variable which has been adjusted for inflation (as opposed to a nominal variable).

Unemployment rate – the percentage of the labour force without jobs.

You may be asked questions to test your comprehension of an article relevant to an economic topic. You may also be asked to talk about a couple of areas of the subject that especially interest you (such as economic growth in the third world), or an economist you admire (for instance John Maynard Keynes) and therefore it is helpful to think about how you might approach such questions. It is a good idea, if you can, to talk about one or two books or articles you have read in your interview, particularly if they are mentioned in your personal statement. If you bring up a book, though, make sure you are able to talk in some detail about its ideas!

An understanding of mathematics is fundamental to economics and that is why Oxbridge Economics tutors deem Mathematics an important subject to have studied at A level or equivalent. If you are new to the subject, your interviewers will naturally not expect you to know as much as your peers who have done Economics before and in this instance your interviewer will likely ask you more logic or maths-based questions. However, you should be able to show an initial understanding of key principles, to show you are committed and motivated to study the subject.

Geography

Questions to get you thinking...

What is the role of the media in Geography?

Describe a problem in your area which a geographer could solve.

What can we do to stop global warming?

How would you persuade an 11-year old to pursue Geography through GCSEs and beyond?

Geography is a multidisciplinary subject and the breadth of questions that applicants have been asked in past interviews reflects this. For the purposes of this exercise, our geographers have created some sample questions, based on similar ones that have been asked in previous years, to help you think about the subject a little bit differently.

Should Physical and Human Geography be taught together and why?
This question tests your grasp of the purpose and scope of geography in an academic context. A good answer to this question may begin by breaking the question down, in other words, explaining what is meant by the terms Physical and Human Geography. You might say Physical Geography investigates how the environment and natural habitats of earth operate. In contrast, Human Geography explores the spatial and temporal differences between human societies. The key point is that our physical and human worlds are mutually dependant and both Physical and Human Geography focus on exploring the links. You could then choose examples either from school work or wider reading e.g. volcanic eruptions to explain why such phenomena benefit from analysis of both the human and physical impact.

This would naturally lead to a conclusion (and it is important that you do reach one) that Physical and Human Geography must be taught together. You might then wish to elaborate, suggesting that one of Geography's greatest strength is its ability to bridge the arts, social and natural sciences. Geography enables us to consider and analyse complex problems using a broad lens.

At school, modules on Physical and Human Geography tend to be taught separately. At university the boundaries are more blurred, with topics such as climate change discussed from a human and a physical perspective. In fact, at Oxford and Cambridge, undergraduate courses contain compulsory modules of Human and Physical Geography, while at other universities there is often a very real division between the two. If you choose to argue in favour of an integrated approach then it is useful to mention that this element of the course particularly appealed to you. This shows you have done your research and are up to date with contemporary teaching debates. Interviews may focus on Human or

Physical Geography, or you may be tested on both.

What is more important, the economy or the environment?

This question tests your skills and how well you can structure a logical argument. A definitive answer would require subjectivity, however, before you reach your conclusion, the interviewer is testing your ability to think objectively and to use examples and your existing knowledge to support your points.

Firstly, break down the two terms – the economy and the environment. The first refers to relations of production, exchange and consumption of goods and services. It is regulated by human structures. Issues of scale are important. National economies now operate globally and are increasingly interconnected. The environment refers broadly to the natural habitats of earth: the landforms and processes that operate to renew our eco-systems and provide the tools necessary for human existence.

Once you have defined these terms, you then need to consider the value of each concept. But how can you measure this? The environment and the economy are integral to our lives, and are extremely complex concepts. In evaluating the importance of each we are ultimately asking: Which do humans rely on more? Could we exist without one? Ultimately both are fundamental to our existence. With a question such as this, is it possible to reach an unbiased conclusion? Admissions tutors want to see evidence of your ability to interact with such a complex, macro idea and to have the confidence and intellect to ask these sorts of questions. This shows you have that ability to be flexible with your existing knowledge and are open to thinking and talking independently – exactly the qualities admissions tutors look for in successful applicants.

Top tips

At the core of Geography are questions about place and space. Keep interested in these concepts and think about how they relate to you in terms of your reading, your studies and your daily life. One applicant was asked to talk about what they found interesting about their local area, another about what they thought made for an interesting geographic article in a magazine. You need to be interested and engaged with your subject, and in turn that will make you interesting.

In an interview you may be asked to analyse the key skills you have developed through fieldwork. The basis of your fieldwork investigation may be Human or Physical. Make sure, with this sort of question, you evaluate activities that you undertook during fieldwork, i.e. why something was particularly useful or why something was not. You may be asked factual questions. This is more likely to occur if you have mentioned a particular topic on your personal statement or have been given source material for the interview. Interviewers do not expect you to possess detailed knowledge on every geographic topic. Ensure you stay calm and use all the reading you have done before the interview to apply your knowledge to the question before you. Remain logical, think laterally and support your arguments.

Law

Questions to get you thinking...

How important are jury trials?

When it comes to IVF treatment, should a male have rights equal to those of a female?

Do you think that anyone should be able to serve on a jury?

If A gave B £100 thinking it was a loan and B accepted the money thinking it was a gift, should he give it back?

At interview and throughout their degree, Law students are challenged to think analytically and this is reflected in the questions posed in interviews. For the purpose of this exercise, our legal minds got together and came up with this meaty law question, based on real past interview questions. The second question in this section is a real past question.

Are judges really necessary since they don't always make the law certain?

This question does require you to understand the basics behind judge-made law. While Oxbridge interviews do not strictly require prior knowledge of the law, you should have a grip on the basics here, from your awareness of legal cases in the news.

In summary, law in England and Wales comes primarily from two sources – statutes that are passed by Parliament and from judges (common law). Unlike other regimes (notably, civil law systems), common law allows that judges not only interpret and apply the law but that they contribute to the evolution of the law by laying down precedent. Essentially, a ruling by a higher court on a point of law, as long as it does not run in the face of a statute, is binding on lower courts and they must follow that ruling. For example, if the Supreme Court rules that a 'mobile phone' includes a hands-free kit, then a lower court cannot overrule this and rule that a mobile phone does not include a hands-free kit.

An initial reaction to this question could, and should, be questioning that perhaps judges are necessary for other reasons anyway so that even if they don't make the law certain, they are still necessary. You may argue that judges are necessary in order to apply the law, to be neutral arbiters in disputes and to sanction appropriately those who act contrary to the law. Question what the state of a regime would be if judges didn't exist – who would decide who was right or wrong if there was a dispute?

Next, you should go on to assess the claim that judges don't always make the law certain. First, try to understand why the claim would be made. It could perhaps be because judges are allowed this law-making power and so they are able to make rulings that change the law. Secondly, assess the claim. You may agree that judges don't always make the law certain – for example, if a judge ruled that 'driving' includes sitting at traffic lights, questions would still emerge such as 'does it matter if the engine is on or off?' or 'does it matter how long you expect to be stationary?'

So the judge would not have made the law certain here, but perhaps you should question the state of the certainty of the law without this intervention. The law would be a lot less certain without a judge clarifying, to some extent, what 'driving' meant. So even though the judge did not make the law certain, s/he certainly went some way towards helping clarify the law and this may support the argument that judges are still necessary.

Smith sees Jones walking towards the edge of a cliff. Smith knows Jones is blind but does not like him, so allows him to walk off the edge of the cliff. Is this murder? (past question)

Obviously, murder has a legal definition. However, this question is not designed to test your understanding of the application of the law of murder to this situation (unless you have been given the law of murder and are expected to do this!). What it is really asking is whether Smith should be treated by the law in the same way as someone who commits a paradigmatic instance of murder, for example, a pre-meditated killing. Again, it is a normative evaluation testing your arguments justifying (or not) Smith's punishment. So your arguments should be on the issue of the moral blameworthiness of Smith and whether this blameworthiness is equal to that of a murderer.

In moral terms, it could quite simply be argued that if you know that somebody is going to die for certain, then you should stop them and prevent their death. However, this is obviously subject to various caveats which you should mention (or allow the interviewer to mention and respond to accordingly).

Is it certain that the person is going to die? In this case it seems from the facts that Jones is going to die for certain (especially bearing in mind that he is blind). This probably adds to the moral culpability of Smith since surely there is not much of a burden on Smith to warn Jones bearing in mind the certainty of his death. Perhaps if the risk of death is not high, then there should not be this corresponding culpability e.g. if Jones was not walking towards the edge and only near the edge but aware of the drop.

How much do you need to do to prevent this death? In this case, if Smith is close enough to Jones that he could simply shout out to Jones to warn him then this is hugely morally blameworthy. Contrast this with the position whereby somebody is drowning in dangerous water – you should probably not be as morally culpable for failing to jump in to save that person as in Smith's case here. The fact that Smith knows that Jones is blind perhaps makes this even worse since he knows that Jones is less able to look after himself walking near a cliff. Although you could say that perhaps Jones is also not free of blame since should a blind person be walking near the edge of a cliff? Should anyone be walking that close to a cliff edge?!

So you could conclude that Smith is extremely morally culpable if he could easily have prevented this death without much burden on himself. In addition, the fact that Smith does not like Jones perhaps makes this worse since it may imply that Smith consciously did not take any steps to warn Jones and so Smith somehow wanted his death to arise as opposed to just realising that it would be a consequence.

However, you should go the full stretch with this question and compare this moral culpability to that of a 'murderer'. Take the example of a pre-meditated shooting in the head. Is somebody who omits to warn someone of their death, no matter how certain it is, as morally culpable as someone who takes the active step of getting a gun, pointing at somebody's head and pulling the trigger?

You could argue that they are just as morally culpable or you could say that they are not – this is subjective. However, you could allude to distinctions such as omitting to do something versus taking practical steps or pre-meditation versus a sudden situation.

Top tips

Even if you do believe that you have some knowledge of the law in a certain area, ensure that you apply it with hesitance. Remember who you are conveying this knowledge to! Much of what is being asked is inherently subjective and there is no correct answer. Therefore, don't think that you may be 'wrong'. If you have a thought that sounds sensible then state it. The interviewers are looking to see your thought process so don't be afraid to think aloud and go through your thoughts step by step. Be receptive to contributions from the interviewers – they will help you formulate your views and your arguments but may also challenge any propositions. Take these on board and deal with them and remember that this doesn't necessarily mean accepting them. You are encouraged to think about what is said to you and challenge it if you feel that you can sensibly do so.

Politics (for PPE and HSPS)

Questions to get you thinking...

Is democracy the best system?

What would you say to someone who claims women have equal opportunities already?

Why do we need government?

Does the welfare state trap people into poverty?

Do you think political groups can have political legitimacy? (past question)

To answer this question, you need to ensure that you are clear about what a political group is, what political legitimacy is and then how (if at all) this political legitimacy can be obtained by these groups.

When we think of a political group, the most obvious type of group is a political party, but there are also other groups which could be classed as political groups. For example, there are groups which exert political pressure such as trade unions and lobby groups such as Greenpeace.

Political legitimacy is the acceptance of a group as an authority, which has a right to rule. It is a basic condition for governing or exercising power as without it the exercise of power will struggle and collapse.

Political legitimacy can be created through the consent of those subjected to it, and the belief both by those exercising the power and by those subjected to it that the institutions and methods of ruling are the most appropriate ones for the society.

In your wider reading you may have come across two political thinkers – John Locke and Max Weber. Locke (regarded as one of the most influential Enlightenment thinkers) believed that political legitimacy is derived from general explicit and implicit consent. Max Weber (German sociologist and political economist) identified three sources of political legitimacy: charismatic authority, traditional authority and rational–legal authority. It is suggested that people may have faith in a particular rule because they have faith in the individual rulers (charisma), because it has been there for a long time (tradition), or because they trust its legality, this is the rationality of the rule of law (rational–legal).

If we use Weber's three descriptive sources of legitimacy, you can see how a group may be able to obtain political legitimacy.

A group could have charismatic authority if people have faith in the individual leaders of a group. Traditional authority could stem from people simply accepting the authority of a group as it has always exercised power over them, for example a trade union. A group may gain legitimacy from rational–legal authority because people trust its legality, perhaps because it has been appointed by the rule of law they support.

People do not agree on how political groups can have authority. While someone may give authority to a group because it has been there for a long time this may not make it legitimate for others. This benchmark of legitimacy may vary from person to person. Some may believe in democratic authority, where a group is legitimate if it is supported by the majority of people, while others might claim that authority could come from religion, such as a group that believe they are appointed by God to rule. Others may suggest that even usual democratic authority is not enough for political legitimacy as the tyranny of the majority is not a legitimate way for a group to rule over everyone, for example, minority groups.

Are there always winners and losers in politics? (past question) To answer this question we must look at what the different actors in politics are hoping to achieve, we can then see how they can win and lose.

For politicians in elections, it could be said that there is always a winner and a loser, lasting for the length of a political term. However counter arguments to this could be that the politicians are not actually winners or losers in an election but it is the will of the people which is expressed through the election which is always the winner.

A politician who is placed second or third in an election, although not entering office, then has won if they believe in the democratic system. Furthermore, even from a selfish political point of view it may be beneficial to have not entered office in that election (due to political or economic turbulence) but to have participated in the democratic system with the possibility of entering in office after the turbulence.

In many political systems they also result in differing political parties having to work together, at both a local and national level. Whilst coalitions are common in more proportional electoral systems such as Germany and Italy they are not unknown (such as the current Conservative-Liberal coalition in the UK).

In such a coalition system it may be possible for the politics of compromise and consensus to overcome the partisan nature. It may be difficult however to avoid having winners and losers – it is unlikely that a coalition will include all parties and therefore there will still be losers, even if it could be argued that there are no winners, due to the members of the coalition compromising.

Aside from the politicians, ordinary individuals in the distribution of public funds or taxation may be seen to be winners and losers, with some individuals paying higher taxes than others whilst receiving lower benefits and vice versa. It is difficult to see how there could be winners without losers.

With a question like this, draw on any extra reading you may have done and dip into your current affairs knowledge for pertinent examples to back up your arguments.

Top tips
Come prepared with opinions but remain respectful to established political theorists' views to avoid seeming dogmatic and arrogant.

Theology

Questions to get you thinking...
Are we in a position to judge God?
Is Britain a secular society?
Is it morally wrong to attempt to climb a mountain?

Can you think of any circumstances in which murder would be justifiable?
A question like this tests your knowledge of applied ethics. It might work well to answer this with reference to Christian philosophers or theologians, such as Kant.

Kant was a deontologist (someone who considers the morality of an action to be intrinsically linked to its adherence to certain rules). It is likely that someone following Kant's ethical approach would take a firm view against murder.

A Kantian position would adopt the categorical imperative, which states that an act should only be pursued if you would want it to become a universal law.

In the case of justifying murder, take a situation where we will gain a huge amount of money if the person is killed. In this instance, we could not reasonably wish this maxim to be universalised and therefore, following Kant's logic, we would judge the murder as unjustifiable.

Another example could be killing one person to save the lives of twenty others, for example, Bernard Williams' 'Jim and the Indians' thought experiment. Kant would respond, given that the other part of his categorical imperative demands that you treat people as ends rather than means, that killing one person as a means to save twenty is never acceptable.

You can conclude that murder, from a deontological Christian standpoint at least, would never be justifiable. From this point, the discussion would develop with your tutor, who may want to examine different sides of the problem.

Should the church compromise?

This type of question focuses on current and historical issues that face and have faced the church. A good way to approach this question is to start by breaking the question down and analysing the language used: 'Should the church' is a difficult start to the question. A good answer may make the point that there is no discrete entity called 'the church', so remember to make appropriate distinctions where possible between different churches. What does the question mean by 'compromise'?

The word compromise suggests forsaking or adjusting one's own position in order to accommodate another view.

Here is one possible approach: there are many different churches, for the purposes of this example, let's take the Church of England. The issue here is whether the C of E should stick resolutely to its position on a particular issue or whether it should be prepared to adapt and change with society. If the Church is not open to compromise or change this would suggest the 'truth' resides solely within the Church. However, from a Christian perspective, the Word has been created by God and the Holy Spirit can operate and inspire individuals, independent of the Church. It is possible, then, for individuals or groups outside the Church to discover truths that the Church should accept. History provides numerous examples of this happening. The Church has compromised in the past and modified its views on a whole range of issues such as slavery, its relationship with other religions, and women priests.

You could then qualify this by saying that the Church should compromise on an issue for the right reasons – that is, because the compromise represents a more authentic witness to the life and vision of Christ than the previous position. For example, you could suggest that the Church should allow certain sexual relationships outside marriage, provided they are a genuine expression of love between two consenting adults. An act of compromise, such as this, does not undermine fundamental Christian values, such as self-sacrificial love (agape). It is possible to justify a compromise theologically, with reference to scripture and other parts of the Christian tradition. Jesus, for example, privileges the commandment to love others, and was himself prepared to break the established laws on occasion e .g. Matthew 5:38.

Top tips

At your interview you may be asked a variety of questions. Generally speaking, our graduates said that it is unlikely you will be asked about any specific theologians unless you have mentioned them in your personal statement. Moreover, you are more likely to be asked questions either pertaining to ethical and philosophical issues within theology or a critical evaluation of modern theology.

Physical, Chemical & Mathematical Sciences

Chemistry / Natural Sciences (Bio. & Phys.)

Questions to get you thinking...

What makes a material hard?

Explain how catalysts work.

How many atoms are there in a brussel sprout?

Name a reaction in which a bond is made.

Do you think O-H and O-D (deuterium) bonds differ in strength? (past question)
At any stage of the interview, do not be afraid to ask for help as you work through the questions. This is a purely theorising question. You are not really expected to know the answer but the interviewer will want to see how you approach it.

Start by thinking about what you know about deuterium, i.e. the fact that it has a significantly greater atomic weight to hydrogen. It is twice as heavy so you should be able to theorise that the bonds will be very different.

Assuming the bonds do have different strengths, how will this affect the rate of exchange of hydrogen or deuterium ions in an aqueous solution? For example in a carboxylic acid? (past question)
Begin by thinking about what you already understand about dynamic equilibriums and how activation energy affects reaction rate. Based on

this you can draw a reaction diagram of each dynamic equilibrium (one being the O-H equilibrium, the other being the O-D). Consider the reaction speed in both directions as well as how this affects the rate of exchange.

Don't be afraid to ask if you can draw diagrams as it will help you think clearly and follow through with your ideas. Drawing diagrams is also an essential part of the chemistry tutorials and supervisions you will be having in the future.

Given different rates of exchange, how will this affect the equilibrium point and therefore the acidity of the non-deuteriated and deuteriated forms? (past question)

You could start by explaining the formula for an equilibrium point based on reaction rates:

$$K_p = k_1 / k_2$$

where K_p is the equilibrium at constant pressure. Based on what you know about the different reaction rates for the hydrogen and deuterium exchange you can predict the different equilibrium points. This will then allow you to go on to explain the different concentrations of H^+ and D^+ and how this affects acidity.

If this interests you, you can go further by reading about the Kinetic Isotope Effect.

a. How does the radius of an ion affect the strength of its interaction with water? (past question)

You may already know that small ions are strongly polarising and will therefore have a strong interaction with water because their charge is more densely concentrated.

b. How do cation and anion radii affect the ionic bond strength in an ionic lattice? For example NaCl. (past question)

You may know from your school work that ionic lattice bond strength is affected by ionic radius and ionic charge. Greater ionic radii increase the distance between the ions in the lattice, and the strength of interaction is a function of $1/r$.

c. What does the graph of $1/r^2$ (r squared) look like? (past question)

You are being asked this as a precursor to the next question. You will be able to use this graph to show that as the ionic radii increase there is a sharp drop off in the strength of the interactions.

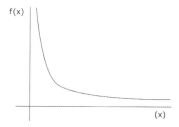

Given the answers to a, b, c how would you explain solubility trends in the series NaF -> NaCI and AgF -> AgCl?

This is the culmination of the answers you have given in the first three parts. You know the factors affecting the bond strength in the ionic lattice, and the strength of the cation and anion interactions with water. Using your knowledge that Na^+ is a relatively small anion and Ag^+ is a relatively large anion, you need to theorise about how the solubility trends down the halide group will differ. Drawing a Hess's Law diagram for this reaction would be a useful way of working through this analysis. You can use all of the knowledge and skills from your schoolwork and apply them to the question.

Hopefully you've seen from this that you can work through what seems like a complex problem by building on what you already know. If at any point you get stuck in your interview, you can ask for help. Even if you do end up with the wrong answer or make mistakes along the way, it doesn't matter too much as long as you've been thinking intelligently as you work through the problem.

Budding Chemists should also check out the questions in both the Maths and Physics section.

Computer Science

Questions to get you thinking…

Tell me about binary searches. What about their efficiency?

What are the possible ways of making a secure transfer?

How do you understand Newton's Laws?

'The game of chess will be played perfectly by the computers of 2016.' What is the meaning of this statement and is it likely to be true?

We spoke to a number of Oxbridge Computer Scientists, who experienced a range of interview questions, some mathematical or logic-based, while others tended to focus on the science of computers. We take a look at these types of questions.

If you have a sorted array of numbers, how would you find number n? (past question)

In other words, if you have a random array of 100 numbers, in ascending order, how would you find the number 38? The challenge is to answer this question out loud using logic. You might initially think to look at each number sequentially, but that would be inefficient. The tutor might suggest other starting points. What about the middle number? What if the middle number is bigger than n? What if the middle number is smaller? In these cases, which portions of the array might be sensible to focus on? What the tutor is looking for is for you to work with them. So really take on board their advice, articulate what you are thinking and why. They are there to help you get to the right answer (as they might do in the future with a successful candidate during their time at the University).

What is the one fundamental difference between a spreadsheet and a database, as surely both hold information? Perhaps there is no fundamental difference? (past question)
A good place to start here would be to acknowledge that both a spreadsheet and database hold information, but the way in which they hold information differs. A spreadsheet is a flat file document that stores each line of information in serial. There is a list of attributes, or columns that each record has a piece of information in. The spreadsheet can be searched for values and calculations can be made using information in certain columns, or fields, but without the use of macros and higher order coding, not much else can be done. In contrast, a database is more intelligent in the way it stores information. Moreover, the user must be more aware of the relationships between the data they are to store. Rather than just simply listing records, in a database there are different entities which each contain their own kind of record. There are relationships defined between these entities that ensure that data stored is correct – referential integrity ensures that related data is consistent e.g. 'John Smith' is always referred to as 'John Smith' and there is never the opportunity for 'John Smiht' to be confused with 'John Smith'.

In addition, you might add here that within the infrastructure of the database, inferences (otherwise known as queries) can be generated. These are smart, modifiable views of the data created by the user. In this way, a database can address a more complex requirement than a spreadsheet can.

A good conclusion will then come back to the initial question, stating that therefore, as illustrated, there is a fundamental difference between a spreadsheet and a database.

What is the structure of URLs? (past question)
Firstly, when answering a question such as this, it is always good to demonstrate that you understand the concepts to which the question

is referring. In this instance, you should define a URL. URLs of the form http://my.example.com/page.html are pointers to a particular page on a website. They are unique, case insensitive and should make more sense to the user than the corresponding IP address.

You can then explain in detail, the major parts of the URL structure. URL's have five major parts as follows:

- The first http:// is the protocol being used to access the page. This may be https:// or even ftp:// if a file transfer is being done.

- Next is the subdomain. This is an optional part and is defined by the owner of the domain. It may signify a different section of the same site or simply forward to another URL.

- Then it is is the top level domain including the country code and/or organisation code. The suffix signifies the location of the organisation and its type. Options include .com, .co.uk, .org or even .edu.

- Next is the directory under the main domain. A homepage URL would not normally feature anything from this point onwards.

- Finally, consider the format of the file. Previously, this always featured html or .htm. Nowadays, it is optional.

Top tips

All aspiring Computer Scientists should brush up on their Mathematics and Physics as they often ask technical questions. Practise answering and articulating answers to maths and logic questions out loud. The interviewer needs to be able to understand and follow your train of thought and you need to be able to justify your problem-solving logic verbally. Don't fret about not getting an answer right in the interview – this will probably happen and it does not matter. Be aware that the interviewer is there to support you and help guide you to your answer – be responsive to their suggestions and interact with them.

Mathematics

Questions to get you thinking...

Can you prove that any natural number consists of prime factors or is a prime number?

You are given an infinite square grid where each square contains a natural number and is at least the mean of the four neighbouring squares. Prove that each square contains the same number.

A body with mass m is falling towards earth with speed v. It has a drag force equal to kv. Set up a differential equation and solve it for v. (past question)

To answer this question, you need to be comfortable with the integration and differentiation you have studied at A level.

Try to work out which forces are involved, and draw a simple diagram to aid your understanding.

By Newton's Second Law of Motion we know that $F = m\dfrac{dv}{dt}$. This must be equal to the balance between the weight pulling downwards and the drag force against the motion.

Make sure you get the correct signs in the equation. The weight acts in the negative direction, and the drag force against it. Therefore, remembering that velocity is negative, $mdv/dt = -mg - kv$, where g is the acceleration due to gravity.

Dividing through by m we get $\dfrac{dv}{dt} = -g - \left(\dfrac{k}{m}\right)v$. For clarity let z=k/m.

By separating the variables we find that $\int \dfrac{\delta v}{g+zv} = -\int \delta t$

At this point it is helpful to make the substitution u = g + zv, and so du = zdv.

Therefore $\left(\frac{1}{z}\right) \int \frac{\delta u}{u} = - \int \delta t$ which gives us $\ln\frac{|u|}{z} = -t + C$, and so $\ln|u| = -zt + C$

Remembering log rules gives us $|u| = e^{-zt} + C = Ke^{-zt}$.

Substituting back in we get $|g + zv| = Ke^{-zt}$, and so $v = - g/z + Ke^{-zt}$

Don't worry if you make a calculation error, it is your general approach to the problem that is more important. A tutor will want to see if you can think carefully about the maths involved.

If you pick 51 of the numbers 1-100, will you have: An even number? A multiple of 3? A square number? A square number plus a cube number? Two numbers, one of which is a multiple of the other? Co-primes? (past question)

This question builds upon easier problems to reach more complicated ones, to help you settle into the interview. Don't be surprised if you get something quite simple earlier on, the harder parts will come later!

There are 50 even numbers in the integers from 1-100, and therefore if you pick 51 numbers you will definitely have an even number.

Comparatively there are only 33 multiples of 3, and so a multiple of 3 is not guaranteed.

Simply list the square numbers – 1, 4, 9, 16, 25, 36, 49, 64, 81, 100. It is possible to choose 51 numbers not containing these numbers.

There are 5 cube numbers to consider, namely 0, 1, 8, 27, 64. Since there are 11 square numbers in consideration (including 0), there are at most 55 numbers equal to a square number plus a cube number from 1-100. However more than 6 of these numbers are over 100, and so it is possible to pick 51 numbers from 1-100 without picking a square number plus a cube number.

The question now becomes considerably tougher, and it might be tempting to look to the earlier parts for a solution. However instead partition the numbers from 1-100 into different sets generated by the formula $k \times 2^n$ where k is an odd number (for instance $\{1,2,4,8,16,\ldots\}$). There are 50 such sets, and all numbers from 1-100 are in one of these sets. Therefore if we choose 51 numbers between 1-100, one must be the multiple of another.

Co-primes must not share common factors. If no two numbers amongst our 51 are to be co-prime, it is clear they cannot simply all be multiples of a single number. Instead the most efficient way to make such a set would be for all members to have precisely two prime factors from $\{2, 3, 5\}$. However this set is smaller than necessary, and so we must have co-prime numbers.

There are a variety of ways to tackle this problem. Even if you cannot give a well-formulated solution, explain your intuitions to the tutor.

Sketch the graph of: $y = \sin x$, $y = \sin(x^{-1})$, $y = x^2 \times \sin(x^{-1})$ (past question)

This is an interesting question and one that builds on school work. The interviewer will want to see you being as thorough as possible, thinking about the notable points on a graph.

It is possible to tackle the question in a systematic way – work out what happens as x approaches 0 or x approaches infinity.

- Draw the graph of $y = \sin x$ that you have studied at A level, marking where some of the turning points are.

- The graph $y = \sin(x^{-1})$ oscillates rapidly between 1 and –1 as x approaches 0, and is undefined when $x = 0$. y is greater than 0 when $x > \frac{1}{\pi}$, and reaches 1 when $x = \frac{2}{\pi}$. From this point x converges to 0 as it approaches infinity. The graph can be rotated around the origin.

- Again the graph of $y = x^2 \times \sin(x^{-1})$ oscillates rapidly as x approaches 0. However it does not oscillate between 1 and –1, but instead is bounded above by the graph $y = x^2$ and below by $y = x^{-2}$. As x approaches infinity, $y = x^2 \times \sin(x^{-1})$ diverges to infinity. This can be seen by the fact that sin x is approximately equal to x when x is small. Hence sin(x-1) is roughly equal to $1/x$ when x is large, and so $y = x^2 \times \sin(x^{-1})$ is large. Bonus points for a good explanation of why $\sin(x^{-1})$ is roughly equal to x^{-1}, using the expansion of sin x.

Top tips for Mathematics interviews
Make sure you are completely on top of all AS and A level work. It may be an idea to move ahead of the syllabus, if you have the inclination, as this may give you more confidence.

Make sure you are comfortable with applying proofs and formulae to questions you haven't met before and be prepared to stand and write on a white board from the beginning of the interview. You may be asked to do this!

If you have forgotten a proof or a formula, do ask. Tutors are there to help you in tutorials and tend to be more excited by a mind that can apply information than a mathematician who can repeat rules they have learnt. That being said, do still revise so that you feel prepared and confident.

Remember not to neglect mathematics studied early in your AS level course and be prepared to answer logic questions using estimation and logic. In these cases, keep thinking about how numbers work. How can you show you think logically and how can you use numbers to illustrate your point? To be successful as a mathematician, you have to prove you can think with numbers.

Physics / Engineering /Natural Sciences (Phys.)

Questions to get you thinking...

Explain how an aircraft flies.

What is time?

Why do sausages split lengthways rather than around the circumference?

If you are on a boat with a hairdryer and a sail, and you blow the hairdryer into the sail what are the forces acting on the boat?

Our team of Engineers and Physicists have put together questions for this section, based on the types of questions they and other applicants had to answer at their interview. All the questions are suitable for the above subjects, and some will be also be suitable for Mathematics.

Sketch the graph of $y = \frac{A}{x^4} - \frac{B}{x^2}$ **, where A and B are constants.** This is a fairly straightforward question that tests a range of A level techniques. The only real subtleties lie firstly in identifying those techniques and how they are useful in graph sketching, and secondly in noticing that the nature of the constants A and B affects the shape of the graph.

Make sure you understand what you need to draw by calculating intersections, for example, before drawing your graph.

A suggested approach to the problem

– Think about symmetries first. Is the function odd or even?

As all the powers of x involved in this curve are even (–4 and –2), the curve must be symmetric about the y axis.

– Then consider the x-intercept

The x-intercept occurs when y = 0, and can be found by solving the equation $\frac{A}{x^4} - \frac{B}{x^2} = 0$ for x (in terms of A and B). This gives $x = \pm \sqrt{\frac{A}{B}}$ at y = 0.

Notice that these intercepts conform to the symmetry deduced above.

– Now consider the y-intercept

Similarly, the y-intercept occurs when x = 0. We cannot substitute this into the given expression as that would involve dividing by zero, so we know that there must be an asymptote. Instead we can consider the behaviour as x → 0 (x tends to 0), for example by trying small values of x, by taking limits, or by considering an expansion.

Trying x = 0.1 and x = -0.1 both give a value of y = 10000A − 100B, which is clearly large and dominated by the sign of the first term. Thus if A is positive (negative), y will go to positive (negative) infinity as x → 0, from either direction. This is symmetric about the y axis, as required.

By limits, which may not be covered in the Mathematics A level course (although keen students, or ones taking Further Mathematics, may well be familiar with their use!), the derivation proceeds as:

$$\lim_{x \to 0} y = \lim_{x \to 0} \left(\frac{A}{x^4} - \frac{B}{x^2} \right) = \lim_{x \to 0} \left(\left(\frac{1}{x^4} \right) (A - Bx^2) \right)$$
$$= +\infty \ if \ A > 0, -\infty \ if \ A < 0$$

and we see that the same result is recovered. Notice that this limit depends on the sin of the constant A.

– Look at the behaviour at large x

The technique of taking limits is also useful here. However, we are now considering the different limit:

x → ±∞

Trying x=10 and x=-10 both give a value of y = 0.0001A − 0.01B, which is small and dominated by the sign of the second term. When B is positive, y will approach 0 from below, likewise when B is negative, y will approach 0 from above as x → ∞.

Formally taking limits:

$$\lim_{x \to \pm\infty} y = \lim_{x \to \pm\infty} \left(\frac{A}{x^4} - \frac{B}{x^2}\right) = \lim_{x \to \pm\infty} \left(\left(\frac{1}{x^4}\right)(A - Bx^2)\right)$$

$$= -0 \; if \; B > 0, +0 \; if \; B < 0$$

where '+/− 0' means '0 approached from above/below', and we see that the same result is recovered.

We now know enough to sketch the form of the graph:

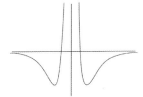

This is the form for positive A and B.

Note that we have not yet deduced that there are turning points. However, we know that this curve is symmetric, tends towards positive infinity as x tends to 0, and has only two x-intercepts, but the curve approaches 0 from below as x tends to either positive or negative infinity.

A complete sketch will have all the relevant points labelled, which we have not done here, so the final thing to do is to calculate the coordinates of these turning points. See if you can do this now.

− Turning points

We find the turning points by the usual A level method: setting the differential to 0 and solving for x, then substituting these x values into the original expression to find the values of y at these points, thus finding the coordinates of any and all turning points. A common, although minor, mistake here is to forget to find the y values.

Performing the differentiation gives $\frac{dy}{dx} = -4Ax^{-5} + 2Bx^{-3}$. Setting this equal to 0 and solving for x gives:

$$-4Ax^{-5} + 2Bx^{-3} = 0$$

$$\Rightarrow \left(-\frac{2}{x^5}\right)(2A - Bx^2) = 0$$

$$\Rightarrow 2A = Bx^2$$

$$\Rightarrow x = \pm\sqrt{\frac{2A}{B}}$$

and our two values for x. Note that these two values of x obey the symmetry we discovered previously.

– Conclusion

Now we find the value for y at these x values. By the symmetry, the value for y will be the same for both values of x, so we only need to perform one calculation. For simplicity, we will take the positive root:

$$y = \frac{A}{\sqrt{\frac{2A}{B}}^4} - \frac{B}{\sqrt{\frac{2A}{B}}^2} = \frac{A}{\frac{4A^2}{B^2}} - \frac{B}{\frac{2A}{B}} = \frac{B^2}{4A} - \frac{B^2}{2A} = -\frac{B^2}{4A}$$

Notice that the negative root would be either squared or raised to the power of 4, and thus give the same value as the positive root – this justifies our statement that we only need to calculate the positive root.

Thus we have found the symmetries of the curve, the coordinates of the x-intercepts and the turning points, and deduced its behaviour as $x \to 0$ and $x \to \pm\infty$ and thus sketched the graph.

Why do wind turbines have three blades?

A question that asks for why something is a certain size or shape, or as in this case has a certain number of something, is almost always the result of a compromise.

If asked a question like this, a good strategy is to look for two (or more) competing factors in the design, driving to opposite extremes. The model solution below provides a good example.

This style of question is popular because it requires interviewees to consider a problem from a number of different viewpoints and identify the important factors.

It also allows the interviewer to offer counter arguments to the 'correct' solutions, thus testing the student's scientific debating skills: whether they can defend a position and how they adapt to new ideas. Examples of this are given in the model answer below.

A suggested approach to the question

There are a number of elements that influence wind turbine design, such as theoretically-tricky aerodynamics and practical considerations, for example cost. We can immediately see that there cannot be one dominating factor. If there were, this would drive the optimum number of blades to either a minimum (one) or a maximum (a fan-like structure).

A common early idea is to consider practical limitations, such as cost, availability of materials and so on. Whilst these are relevant issues, and mentioning them displays an awareness of the reality of commercial engineering projects (thus demonstrating that you have enough of an interest in the subject to know something about its practice), they do not display any scientific knowledge on the part of the applicant, and so should only be mentioned in passing. A student who focuses on these issues may, in the eyes of an interviewer, be doing so (either consciously or unconsciously) because they do not understand, or even recognise, the more fundamental physical issues.

For a wind turbine, the 'maximising' effect is a simple one – indeed, almost too simple, and could easily be overlooked: as the turbine wishes to extract as much energy from the wind as possible, it will be more effective if it can capture more wind. Thus, a high number of blades is preferable, to increase the surface area of the turbine.

A possible counter argument here would be to point out that adding more blades also adds more weight, and (assuming the blade design doesn't change) does not alter the surface area per mass. While more blades would capture more wind, the turbine would also now be heavier and require more force to move, negating the effect of the extra captured wind. While this sounds reasonable, a simple line of reasoning would deduce that each blade adds a given driving force to the turbine (in fact, the driving force will not be the same per blade, as discussed in the 'slipstream' argument below, but that is a different issue) otherwise the turbine would never move – each blade must capture enough energy from the wind to move, even with its weight taken into account, or the turbine would not work at all. Thus since each blade produces more than enough force to account for its own weight, adding blades adds to the total force produced.

This requirement is missed by a lot of students, and thus interviewers can use it to identify the applicants who are able to consider the 'big picture' and understand the question being asked, rather than diving straight into physics or maths without pausing to think carefully about the problem.

The 'minimising' effect is more subtle, and is a more straightforward test of the student's knowledge of physics. By the nature of a turbine, each blade follows the same path, and thus moves in the slipstream of preceding blades. At first this may appear to be a good thing – for example, in many racing sports (from speed skating to Formula 1) competitors prefer to race in the slipstream of their rivals, taking advantage of the reduced wind resistance, and thus move faster while using less energy. One may think that a blade moving in the slipstream of previous ones could move faster for less input energy, as with the racers, and thus turn the turbine more quickly and generate more energy. However, this approach shows some muddled thinking, and the analogy is not accurate. The turbine is not being powered from within with the aim of reaching a high speed, as with the racers. It is trying to extract energy from the air, so blades moving in slipstream (by definition, an area where there is little wind to affect the motion of the blade) will not be very effective at doing so. Each additional blade added to the turbine is less efficient at extracting energy than previous ones, so the most efficient option would be just one blade.

The above 'racing' analogy would be a good potential counter argument for an interviewer to use: it sounds plausible, and has a basis in physics that a student would recognise and is easy to explain and understand. However, it has flaws as explained above. A good student will examine the analogy carefully and spot not only that it is inappropriate for this situation, but also why, and use this to enhance their own understanding of the physics in the actual problem. Thus, we have two factors, one favouring a small number of blades, one a large. Balancing these two factors gives three as the optimum number of blades. However, deriving this quantitatively requires physical and engineering ideas and mathematics well beyond the scope of A level students and possibly even undergraduates, and would not be expected. The point of this question is to explore qualitative arguments, and to test applicants' ability to consider and balance opposing viewpoints without recourse to explicit mathematical formulae.

Integrate $\dfrac{1}{1+\left(\frac{sin2x}{(1+cos\,2x)}\right)^2}$ **with respect to x.**

This is a straightforward question that shouldn't pose much of a problem to a serious candidate. Nevertheless, there are a couple of subtleties to mention. A level students are taught a few methods of performing complicated-looking integrals, such as by parts or by substitution, and the interviewee will have to select the best option.

In fact, the best option here is not one of these integration techniques, but just to simplify the integrand before performing the integral. After the student has realised that this is the best method, the manipulation is simply a test of A level ability. Some interviewers may also insist upon the inclusion of the integration constant (usually denoted c). This manipulation uses trigonometric identities with which the student should be familiar from A level:

$\cos2x + \sin2x = 1$ the double angle formulae: $\sin2x = 2\sin x \cos x$ and $\cos2x = \cos2x - \sin2x = 1 - 2\sin2x = 2\cos2x - 1$.

The manipulation of the integrand, using these, is thus:

$$\frac{1}{1 + \left(\dfrac{sin2x}{(1+cos\,2x)}\right)^2} \equiv \frac{1}{1 + \left(\dfrac{2\sin x \cos x}{(\cos^2 x + \sin^2 x) + (\cos^2 x - \sin^2 x)}\right)^2}$$

$$\frac{1}{1 + \left(\dfrac{2\sin x \cos x}{2\cos^2 x}\right)^2} \equiv \frac{1}{1 + \tan^2 x} \equiv \frac{1}{\left(\dfrac{1}{\cos^2 x}\right)(\cos^2 x + \sin^2 x)} \equiv \cos^2 x$$

$$\equiv \frac{1}{2}(1 + \cos 2x)$$

and the integral is now easy to perform:

$$\int \frac{1}{1 + \left(\dfrac{sin2x}{(1+cos\,2x)}\right)^2}\, dx = \int \left(\frac{1}{2} + \frac{1}{2}\cos 2x\right) dx = \frac{1}{2}x + \frac{1}{4}\sin 2x + c$$

Top tips

Ensure that you make your assumptions explicit to the interviewer at all times. What is constant? What is changing? What simple concepts and formulae can be applied to the problem in front of you? (While the problem may look difficult, if you break it down into simple chunks, it should be possible for you to make sense of it, if not reach a firm conclusion). Ask questions! Many interviewees are wary of asking questions of the interviewer and remember that Physics is a discourse, it is not just questions and answers. It is about ideas and communicating these ideas clearly. Make sure that you clarify terms of the question if they confuse you. And finally, think before you speak, especially with regard to mathematics problems and sketching graphs. Do not sketch prematurely!

Medical & Biological Sciences

Biological Sciences / Natural Sciences (Biological)

Questions to get you thinking...

How does insulin function?

What is a mitochondrion? Why do you only inherit mitochondrion genes from your mother?

Why may a drug not have the same effect on a human as on a dog?

How do we know that species become extinct if we don't know that they exist?

What happens during PCR? (past question)

A good way to approach this question is to first state what PCR stands for – Polymerase Chain Reaction. Of course, if you do not know what PCR stands for, ask the interviewer to clarify. If you know what PCR is, a good next step would be to summarise it clearly: PCR is a technique used to amplify a single or few copies of a piece of DNA to generate thousands to millions of copies.

After summarising, a good approach would be to highlight the details of the technique: PCR is used to amplify a specific region of a DNA strand. PCR uses two primers which are complementary to the '3' (3 prime) ends of the sense and anti-sense DNA strands. A DNA polymerase (enzyme) is used to replicate the DNA between the two primers. The PCR mixture is first heated – this causes denaturation and separation of the sense and anti-sense strands so that the primers and polymerase can reach the nucleotides and allow replication. The mixture is then cooled slightly to allow the primers to anneal (bind) to the single strands of DNA. The mixture is then heated to the optimum temperature for the polymerase. The heating cycle is then repeated as many times as the user wants amplifications of the DNA, i.e. the first cycle turns one copy of DNA into two, the second cycle turns two into four, and so on.

In your conclusion, you can discuss its practical uses: **Amplification** of small amounts of DNA to a volume that is large enough to be analysed. This is useful in forensic analysis when only trace amounts of DNA are available. **Isolation** of a particular DNA sequence by selective amplification. This is useful to quantitatively assess levels of gene expression for genetic fingerprinting and screening for cancer. **Identification** of a particular DNA sequence in a genome, i.e. PCR will only be successful if the chosen DNA sequence is present. This is useful in screening of bacteria following insertion of DNA sequences (recombinant DNA).

In the case that you have not studied PCR, the interviewer may instead provide you with information on the first two points above, and ask questions aimed to test your logical and lateral thinking skills, such as: 'How do you think PCR works?' In this case, you must use what you know about DNA replication and enzymes, applying it to explain how amplification of a DNA strand could be achieved.

What possible uses can you see for PCR?
In this case, you must use what they have told you about the process and think laterally. PCR is amplification of DNA volume – in what circumstances would you need more DNA? Only the specific piece of DNA is amplified – in what circumstances would you want to target specifically one piece of DNA?

Imagine a frequency graph of three different viruses over a 30 year period. One gradually increases and decreases, one peaks every other year and one peaks three times within a 30-year period. Why? (past question)
With a question like this, the information comes in graphical form but you are not actually supplied with a graph. A good approach would be to draw the graphs, as follows:

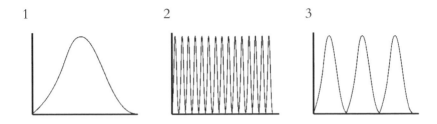

It would then be wise to check with the interviewer they agree that the graphs represent the information given. Do not be afraid to ask for clarification and if you need more information, ask the interviewer.

Next, outline the factors that could affect frequency of viral infection in a population: **climate** – changes in temperature, humidity, seasons etc, **mutation of the virus** – could improve transmission, give resistance etc, **other viruses** – competition or symbiosis (e.g. infection with the influenza virus weakens the immune system and increases chance of other infections), **the discovery of a vaccine or other control methods.**

A good approach would then be to look at each graph in turn and apply the above factors to each situation, asking the question 'what could cause the change seen in each graph?' As far as possible, use examples to illustrate your hypotheses:

1. Discovery of a vaccine could explain graph 1. An example of a virus dramatically affected by the invention and implementation of a vaccine is smallpox. Another possible explanation of graph 1 is environmental change affecting a virus. For example, if the UK climate warms to the extent that malarial mosquitoes can survive here, this would introduce an upsurge in the disease which might only be tackled by a strong response to the virus.

2. A virus that recurs biannually could be due to mutations that increase infection rates coupled to a constantly evolving treatment –for example, the influenza virus mutates every year and humans

produce a new vaccine every year. A biannual recurrence might be caused by a slightly slower mutating virus.

3. It could be the same factor that occurs three times in 30 years, such as three particularly harsh winters or wet summers. It could also be three different factors causing three independent recurrences.

How would you go about setting up a blood bank in a developing country? (past question)

Please note: a question like this would not be out of place in an interview for Medicine or Biomedical Sciences. With a question like this, you are being asked to use your biological knowledge in conjunction with geographical, sociological and economical factors. As an interviewer you will be looking for a coherent plan-of-action that takes into account anything you know about blood donation systems in the UK or abroad.

To start, you might want to clarify the meaning of the term 'blood bank,' and once again, if you are unsure, ask your interviewer to clarify. A blood bank is a store of blood or blood components gathered from donations for later use in transfusions.

You can then move onto listing the factors you would need to consider in planning your approach: set-up and running costs; how to get donations; staff; safety of donating blood; location and logistics of storage; and transportation.

A good applicant would then move on to consider each factor in more detail:

Set-up and running costs: there will be a large initial cost associated with acquiring the necessary facilities needed, however, it would be equally important to consider how the project would be funded in the long-term. You might suggest approaching the government, WHO and charities for funding.

How to get donations: the National Blood Service in the UK relies on charitable donations, however other countries pay people for their donations. You could propose establishing a service in return for a donation. Due to the shortage of healthcare in many developing world countries, an effective strategy could be to offer a free health check-up to blood donors.

Location: the National Blood Service in the UK has multiple static and mobile facilities. The majority of developing countries have less well-developed infrastructures and fewer hospitals. Therefore, although mobile teams would make donating more accessible, you might consider multiple static teams working from existing hospital facilities across the country.

Staff: setting up the blood bank will provide new jobs for nurses, transport workers, administrators, etc.

Blood safety: there are two safety aspects to consider – donation safety and blood safety. Donation safety is vital so that nurses receive proper procedural and safety training. Any blood that may be used in a blood transfusion must be clean from transfusion-transmitted diseases. In the developing world, the main culprit is HIV/AIDS, although malaria, hepatitis B and C and many more are also present. As many developing countries have tropical climates and poor living standards, the frequency of many of these diseases is higher. A blood donor would first need to be questioned and then tested for all of the diseases relevant to that area/country.

Transportation: a storage site would have to be acquired and fitted with refrigeration/climate control systems. It would have to be manned. The location should also be within easy access of the hospitals that will require blood for transfusions. The transportation of blood would require refrigerated trucks.

You might also go one step further and suggest that the blood bank is used to gather information about the population's health, as well as using blood for transfusions. A good way to end this question would be to give a brief conclusion, stating that safety is the most important factor to consider, although all factors would need research before a comprehensive plan could be formulated.

Top tips

It's very important that you know your A level syllabus as answers may require/benefit from factual knowledge you have already acquired. Be prepared to discuss species that you have not encountered before and in these instances, apply knowledge that you have as well as lateral thought. Many successful applicants find watching nature documentaries and regularly visiting the Scientific American and New Scientist websites helpful to keep abreast of their subject and its wider context. As one graduate said, 'there's nothing like a bit of David Attenborough to inspire you!'

Experimental Psychology/Psychology, Philosophy & Linguistics

Questions to get you thinking...

Who is the most intelligent: the straight-A Oxbridge candidate or the young mechanic living in Africa who left school at 14?

How do we test memory in animals, and can we apply the findings to humans?

Can you teach creativity?

What use is psychological study for society?

Why do we have handedness? (past question)

Questions like this, that contain unknown material, invite you to speculate, so make sure you are clear that you are indeed speculating rather than stating your opinions as fact. The interviewer may prompt you to aid debate, don't think that this is a negative action or that you are not saying enough, they just want to understand better how you think or the method behind your reasoning. Strong answers to questions like these would clearly take one or two approaches to psychology, attempting to explain how handedness can be explained by them, and then weigh up the two approaches against one another.

The biological or physiological approach to psychology may suggest that handedness occurs to conserve energy. If only one side of the body has to develop higher levels of dexterity to perform tasks efficiently then there seems to be little benefit in both sides of the body developing to the same and complex degree. It may also be that because language is located in one side of the brain – the left hemisphere – this part of the brain already has in place more complex neural connections, and therefore has a better capacity to form the dominant hemisphere. This is supported by the fact that the majority of people are right handed (which corresponds to having a dominant left hemisphere).

On the other hand, the question of handedness can also be explained from a behavioural perspective. There are two ways of explaining this. Firstly, modelling behaviour could occur when an infant sees their caregiver using one particular hand to do certain tasks; they copy this. Secondly, conditioning may play a part. Perhaps, an infant uses a certain hand to pick up a cup of juice because it is on one side of their highchair. They then drink the juice and are rewarded by the good taste. The action of using this hand and being rewarded are linked in a form of classical conditioning.

You then might conclude that although both of these approaches have valid points, the biological approach punches more weight. It has been proven that handedness is linked to a particular cerebral hemisphere, and therefore seems logical that only one side of the brain should hold the capacity for handedness.

How would a psychologist measure normality? (past question)

'Very strong answers would include ways of measuring more than one type of normality,' says one Oxford Experimental Psychology graduate. They would also then give an opinion of which approach they feel is superior and why.

As we learn in mathematics, deviation from statistical norms is measured using the bell shaped curve of normal distribution (see image). The x axis shows the frequency/level of a behaviour/characteristic, and the y axis the proportion of people in the population displaying that frequency/level. Arbitrary norms are set for the lower and upper limits, and a person outside of these norms is considered to be abnormal. An example would be levels of anxiety. Very high levels of anxiety are abnormal, and may lead to a diagnosis of an anxiety disorder. Very low levels of anxiety may also be indicative of a mental health problem.

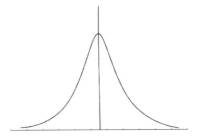

Another method of measuring normality is to define abnormal as causing distress to self/others. Whereas two people might engage in the same level of behaviour, for example checking their watch frequently, one may do this as part of their routine because they like to know the time, and are not overly distressed if they cannot access the time. The other may find it crucial to check their watch, infringing on their day to day happiness, and experience great distress/panic if for some reason they cannot check the time. This would be measured by a self-report diary, where the individual charted their feelings alongside their day to day experiences. It could also be measured through observations.

You might argue that monitoring the distress caused to self or others is a better way of measuring normality. This could be because it takes into account personal experiences of the sufferer, and therefore forms more of a basis for identifying and treating the condition. However, the statistical approach allows larger numbers of people to be more quickly identified, which could be advantageous.

Top tips

Ask questions: some interviewers will want you to assume certain things to formulate your answers, whereas, for others, part of the exercise will be for you to ask the correct questions to find out more about the situation. By asking a preliminary question you will be able to determine which of these situations you are in, and not deprive yourself of useful information. In answering questions, try to show logical development throughout your answer. Use terms commonly used in Psychology if they help you. For example, if looking at the question 'why would a 5-year old refuse to speak with you?', you could frame your answer by looking at factors which are internal (due to the child), external (due to the environment), stable (a problem that is always there), or unstable (a problem that is only due to this situation). Try to include a variety of factors in your answer. Perhaps also try to include a biological, physiological, social or behavioural factors. Do try to show your breadth of knowledge at all times.

Human Sciences

Questions to get you thinking...

Are human beings still evolving?

Are there too many people in the world?

What is the purpose of religion?

Should gorillas have human rights?

Human Sciences blends creative and scientific thought. For the purposes of this exercise, we asked Human Sciences graduates to create different types of interview questions, based on their experiences of the interview.

What makes HIV/AIDS an interesting disease from the perspective of a Human Scientist?

A good answer to this question would be one that, in the first instance, addresses the biology of the disease. You could start by mentioning the fact that HIV/AIDS affects the immune system and renders the person more vulnerable to infection from other diseases. You could also mention that it's difficult to treat because of the ability of the virus to develop resistance to drugs rapidly. Don't be afraid to ask about the biological aspect of HIV/AIDS if you don't know the science of the disease because the tutors will appreciate a demonstration of your interest.

To address the question from another angle, you could discuss where geographically HIV/AIDS is a significant problem (giving your definition of significant in your answer). Sub-Saharan Africa currently has a high number of HIV/AIDS cases as do parts of Asia. In these countries, the disease is often transmitted via sexual networks which include prostitutes and drug users. Transmission of the disease has been linked to poverty in the countries which have high prevalence rates. As an example, women driven to prostitution may be unable to refuse sex because it may be their main source of income. If condoms are unavailable or considered undesirable, these women may be at great risk because of cultural or religious factors.

HIV/AIDS creates problems within societies because it leaves orphans in its wake when parents die of the disease. Further, the disease may be transmitted to babies during pregnancy creating HIV positive children at birth. This means that governments need to find ways of caring for orphaned HIV positive children, who require general everyday care and treatment for the disease.

There are interesting instances of misinformation about transmission of HIV/AIDS. For example, some men believe that their disease can be cured by sexual intercourse with virgins, an act which may infect the women that they have sex with. Also, the use of condoms is avoided by certain people because they are associated with the infection itself. HIV/AIDS is stigmatised in many communities, therefore infection is often traumatic both for the patient and their family.

With your answer it is a good idea to show that you understand that HIV/AIDS is more than a biological disease; it has much wider social, cultural and economic implications which play an important role in the transmission, treatment and prevention of the disease.

What is the difference between marriage and mating?
This question tests your ability to identify ways in which human behaviour might differ from that of animals because of the existence of culture within human society.

You could answer this question by explaining that mating is natural, and likely to be driven by physiological desires which you could say are genetic or 'innate'. These desires are likely to be influenced by natural selection, and, consequently, behaviour which improves the reproductive fitness of an individual (the number of offspring they produce) is likely to spread within the population.

You could then go on to say that marriage in humans is determined by culture. Although men and women might have natural or innate preferences, the people they actually mate with are largely determined by who they marry. Rules about what makes a good marriage partner are often subject to cultural preferences, so for example in the West a woman may choose a marriage partner who has good levels of education, whereas in a more 'traditional' society a good marriage partner might be a man who is good at hunting. Another good point to add would be to raise the question of whether or not humans are still subject to natural selection because of the fact that our culture determines our behaviour?

It is important to demonstrate in your answer that humans are different to other animals, and that human behaviour is difficult to study because our culture influences our behaviour.

Top tips

You may be presented with graphical information in your interviews. If the graphs demonstrate a correlation between two variables, it's important to remember not to jump to a conclusion which assumes a causative relationship. Two factors can be associated without any real connection between them. For example, ice cream sales are high in July. However, July does not cause a peak in ice cream sales; it is the hot weather in July which drives the purchase of ice cream.

Keep reading the news so that you are aware of developments such as the sequencing of the Neanderthal genome, which has revealed that humans interbred with this extinct hominin species. The BBC news website has a great, trustworthy science section, so you can get some excellent talking points from there.

You may be asked to explain the purpose or function of an object shown to you in the interview. Remember that the interviewers may be assessing your ability to analyse objectively without assuming that objects have the same meaning for you as for people in other cultures. Objectivity is a skill which is essential in anthropology. Tutors aren't expecting you to have any specific knowledge about the object in question.

Medicine

Questions to get you thinking...

What is the purpose of DNA?

How would you design a brain?

What are ulcers?

Why do we see things in the colours we do?

Having spoken to many successful Medical applicants, interviews for Medicine tend to be a mix of scientific and ethical questions. Our medical minds have therefore created some sample questions below, based on their own interview experiences, which they believe would be helpful to any aspiring Medicine applicant to think about in advance of their interview.

If there was only one bird flu vaccine left, who would you give it to between you and me?
A good way to start this sort of question is to mention briefly what the bird flu vaccine is and what you know about the potential consequences of not receiving it. For example 'the majority of healthy people are able to recover from having the flu having experienced only normal flu-like symptoms such as a mild fever etc.'

You could then start looking at who should get this vaccine. Consider whether the person asking you the question is, for instance:

- In a position of having a lowered immune system so less able to cope without the vaccine if he or she contracted the flu: pregnant, elderly, on any other medication, suffering from any other illnesses such as AIDS.
- A person who has already recovered from the flu before and would be in a much better position to recover from the flu again. You could perhaps slip in here your knowledge of the primary and secondary immune response.
- A person who has dependents who would be affected if the person was to suffer from flu: children or a disabled person for whom they are caring.
- A person who spends/has spent/will spend a lot of time in a high-risk environment for the flu or around people who have, perhaps in a country where there is an epidemic at the moment.
- Suffering from any condition that may affect his or her life expectancy.

Having considered these factors you can reach a conclusion. With a question like this, however, it is very difficult to reach an informed decision, and a number of our medical graduates do believe it would be acceptable to conclude that 'without further information about your health and general circumstances I could not make an informed decision'.

In contrast, however, if you are one who would rather not sit on the fence, you could equally say that 'assuming that we are both of the same health and have the same circumstances, then, I may give it to myself because I am younger than you'.

If you were the new Secretary of Health, how would you want to improve the NHS?
Questions like this are very common, and admissions tutors are looking for an awareness of the problems currently facing the NHS, as well as the proposed reforms, which would radically change the way the NHS operates.

One issue that all students should be aware of is the problem of the superbug MRSA and C-difficile. This is the sort of thing you could talk about here.

A good way to start this question would be to talk briefly about the problem caused by MRSA being resistant to antibiotics due to resistant strains mutating via natural selection etc., as well as talking about the problem this poses – patients come into hospital with a broken leg and may leave it with a deadly disease! The main problem with this is the lack of good hygiene in hospitals with visitors and staff not using the alcohol gels enough or properly as well as improper sterilisation of equipment used. As the Secretary of Health you may wish to improve training for the staff in hospitals to keep the environment clean and put more money into cleaning measures.

You might also say that you would like to put money into computerising a lot more of the work that doctors and their team do so that it is easily transferred and for safe-keeping. It is ALWAYS a good idea to mention something that you have picked up at work experience here. Be as specific as possible, drill down into detail!

One of the really big issues currently facing the NHS is the rise in obesity and its links to diabetes and coronary heart disease. Thus you might argue that more money should be spent on preventative measures to cost the NHS less in the long run. For example, increasing government campaigns to reduce childhood obesity by encouraging healthy eating and an active lifestyle – along the lines of what we are already seeing on TV and in the press at the moment. Again, you can strengthen your answer by referring to your work experience.

Work experience
Medical interviews tend to be different from other interviews because they are often carried out by practising doctors, rather than academics and therefore they expect you to be informed about the job of a doctor. Remember at the end of your course this is what you will be and your interviewer will partly be assessing your suitability for the role as well as for the course. Consequently, work experience is very important and it is highly likely that it will form part of any medical interview.

When it comes to asking about your work experience, questions tend to be along the lines of 'tell me about your work experience'. Many students can fall into the trap of simply listing all the different hospitals and surgeries they have visited, thinking that this sounds impressive. What's more interesting however is not the quantity of experience you have, but the quality. Tutors want to hear about an experience where you learned about what it means to be a doctor, and the relationship a doctor can build up with his/her patient.

Good students might therefore approach this type of question by mentioning their observation of the importance of good communication – seeing a doctor smiling as he/she greeted the patient, the tone of the voice used (which helped to make the patient feel more relaxed). Indeed, one of the many difficult aspects of being a doctor is to make the patient feel relaxed enough in a consultation to give you all the information that you may need to know. Initially, doctors often do not know what they are looking for and must rely on the openness of the patient. You may have also noticed how a doctor spoke in simple, layman terms, refraining from using medical jargon to ensure the patient understands what is going on at every step of their treatment to ease worry and stress.

It may be that during your work experience you observed how important the wider team of other medical staff are to the role of a doctor, for example nurse and radiographers and doctors and how essential it is that a doctor has the confidence to work independently but also as part of a team. You might have seen certain negative aspects of being a doctor, including the amount of paper work involved or the strain of having to deliver bad news to a patient. You may have seen how important it is that a doctor be able to detach him/herself emotionally from the case.

Your answer will very much depend on your experiences. Really think about what you learned, and how it changed, strengthened or indeed weakened certain viewpoints or opinions of the role of a doctor that you previously held.

Top tips

'From my experience,' says one Cambridge Medicine graduate 'students are best off knowing the whole A level syllabus because admissions tutors may ask you about topics ahead of the level that your school may have got to. This was certainly the case for me but won't apply to all applicants. Of course, if it is something that you have not covered yet you should always say you don't know something, but they may expect you to attempt the question anyway using logic, common sense and an application of the knowledge you already possess.' Be willing to give each question a go – show you are open and willing to consider new ideas.

Veterinary Medicine

Questions to get you thinking...

What do you think about kidney transplants in cats?

Why do animals have two ears (i.e. why not one or four)?

Is selective breeding tantamount to genetic modification?

Why do dogs behave badly?

What is the time difference from sound reaching one ear and the other? (past question)

The time difference between sound reaching the first and second ears is called the interaural time difference. The time difference varies depending on the location of the sound source. If the sound comes directly from in front of the face, say at eye height and equal distance from either ear, then there is no time difference in the sound arriving. We would describe this as sound arriving at a zero degree azimuth (the angle of the signal in relation to the head), the interaural time difference being zero also.

If the sound comes directly from the right or left (i.e. a 90 degree azimuth), then clearly the sound will arrive at the nearest ear first, having further to travel to the second ear, and the interaural time difference will no longer be zero.

It can be calculated as follows:

$T = D/V$

where

D = distance between the ears (probably in the region of 20cm or 0.2m)

and

V = speed of sound (roughly 343m/s)

So in this case the interaural time (T) would be

$0.2/343 = 0.00058s$

If the sound is coming from a smaller angle than 90 degrees (or between 90 and 180), there will be a smaller difference between the distances sound has to travel to either ear (i.e. D is smaller) and the time difference will be reduced. The variation in the interaural time differences does not seem large, but it is detected by the brain when processing sound and is a key source of information in sound localisation.

How would you have solved the Foot and Mouth crisis? (past question)
A good way to approach this question, is to firstly show to the interviewer that you understand what Foot and Mouth Disease is – it is a highly infectious viral disease which affects cloven hoofed animals such as cows, sheep and pigs. Next, you could refer to past Foot and Mouth crises – explaining how in the past, the virus has spread rapidly and beyond control, decimating the UK farming industry. It is therefore important to take the threat seriously and act quickly and decisively.

You can then move into the 'meat' of the argument (no pun intended). Assuming it has only been reported on one farm, you could suggest that the affected farm and the surrounding area be immediately quarantined and that the animals that had been in direct contact with any sufferers culled. The virus can be destroyed by heat, sunlight and certain disinfectants, but it can survive for long periods of time in the right conditions. Thus the affected farm would have to be completely gutted and disinfected before the farmer could even consider going back to normal. The virus does not affect humans, but can be spread on vehicles and boots and so on, so movement from affected to non-affected areas should be strictly limited. Ideally any roads that neighbour the affected property should be shut until the virus has been controlled. Wild animals which could carry the disease between farms, for example deer, should be controlled (probably culled) if/when they are seen.

When the Foot and Mouth crisis hit in 2001, farmers were hesitant to use vaccinations due to difficulties that would later arise in selling the animals overseas. However the rules have since been changed to allow vaccination as an emergency measure in the event of an outbreak. There are several strains of Foot and Mouth Disease, so once the strain has been identified, you could propose recommending the vaccination of all cloven hoofed farm animals in an even wider area than the quarantined area – say county-wide. Airborne spread is known, so if conditions are right (i.e. windy, not too hot) then animals should be kept inside.

As an outbreak of Foot and Mouth Disease can be so devastating, you might point out that you do not think you can overreact to another outbreak. As much as possible should be done to prevent the virus spreading, and if it does the affected farms need to be identified immediately. Clear information should be given to the press and to farming bodies with what to look for in affected animals and who you should call if you suspect you have found a new case. The emphasis is on speed of reaction, and on ensuring that the movement bans/quarantines/culls (if necessary) are strictly adhered to.

Top tips
Make sure you know your personal statement inside out and that your knowledge is thorough and technical. If you don't know something, ask the interviewers – don't try to make up an answer. There is nothing worse than an interviewee desperately fumbling for an answer, after having claimed that they have understood something. Be honest about your ability and this will help the interviewer to assess your potential. You are not supposed to have all the answers now – that's why you are applying to university!

9 LIFE AFTER OXBRIDGE

—— ⟨⟩ ——

WE TALK TO RECENT OXFORD AND CAMBRIDGE GRADUATES TO FIND OUT WHAT THEY HAVE BEEN UP TO SINCE LEAVING UNIVERSITY AND HOW THEIR UNDERGRADUATE DEGREES HAVE INFLUENCED THEIR CAREER CHOICES

Lucy, Oxford Law graduate

❝ Since university I have done a lot of academic stuff – two sets of graduate courses, both law-related. I'm currently working in medical law, which I really do find interesting. I love my subject, and although in practice, law is very different to studying it as an academic discipline, I can't imagine myself working in any other field. So my degree really has influenced my career choices. It is also a good degree for forcing you to learn how to deal with a large workload, think logically, argue persuasively, and problem solve – all valuable life skills.

My advice to prospective Law applicants would be: if you are really interested in working as a lawyer in the future, but you don't enjoy the academic side of law, an undergraduate Law degree might not be for you. You would be far better off doing an undergraduate degree in a subject that you know will interest you, and then converting to law in the future – only around half of all currently practising lawyers completed an undergraduate Law degree.

You do need to be quite stubborn and determined to make it through a law degree at Oxford (and do well!) as well as in the legal profession today. Having a close circle of non-lawyer friends has also definitely helped keep me sane over the years of exams! ❞

Jack, Oxford History graduate

❝ I spent most of my time at Oxford (aside from socialising) acting in plays and performing as part of an improvised comedy troupe. On leaving Oxford, I acted in a Noel Coward play for 5 months with Robert Bathurst. I am now a producer at Channel 4 News, specialising in politics and Europe. My History degree taught me to weigh evidence, treat most things with scepticism and how to write a story – all very useful skills for a journalist. ❞

Jeremy, Cambridge Physical Natural Sciences graduate

❝ After leaving Cambridge, I completed my PGCE at Oxford, before spending two years teaching at a state comprehensive in Wembley, followed by more teaching at a private school in Ealing, where I currently work. I'm also doing a part-time masters in Social Research Methods.

Doing a broad base of sciences at Cambridge is really useful when you walk into a school and have to teach general science. It's also given me flexibility – I'm actually now a Physics teacher despite my Chemistry degree. I also instinctively use maths and logic to solve problems, with varying degrees of success.

My advice to people considering a career in teaching is: don't be a teacher just because you can't think of anything else to do. Teachers have the second most important job in the world – you need to really want to do it. If it is actually something you want to do, go and visit some schools. If it's still what you want to do, train, get a job and do it. It is the best job in the world. I found what I wanted to do by trying it (I've been tutoring since I was 17, then did some work experience in a school and knew teaching was for me) so I guess trying lots of things out and seeing what works for me has been useful (I've ruled out a few along the way – chef, stand-up comic and absolutely anything in an office for various reasons). I'm pretty sure some of the stuff I did whilst an undergrad has been useful – when you've been heckled off stage by 200 people at a May Ball (hence ruled out stand-up comedy) 30 teenagers aren't going to scare you. ❞

Michaela, Cambridge Economics graduate

❝ After graduating, I started working at the Financial Services Authority (now the Financial Conduct Authority). Whilst there, I spent my free time as a member of a semi-professional dance troupe and I also spent a lot of time working as a mentor in Tower Hamlets and helping to establish a mentoring programme for local schools. I left the FSA and started working part-time in the House of Lords for a Baroness and for two Conservative Party organisations. I began tutoring A level Economics as well and I became the Governor for a Special Needs school in my local area. I also joined the Management committee for the Conservative Friends of India. I joined the board of a large charity promoting female and child empowerment and I started writing political and economic blogs and opinion pieces for newsletters and websites.

In July 2013, I began working as an Economic Advisor for a Member of Parliament and I continued to work for one of the political organisations – Women2Win which promotes women in Parliament and Public Life. In December 2013 I became an approved member of the Candidates' List for the Conservative Party and hope to fight a seat in the 2015 General Election.

My degree has instilled in me a solid work ethic and a strong interest in how politics and economics interact. It also gave me great practice at juggling various commitments and at dealing with deadlines.

My advice to anybody wanting to pursue a career in politics would be to make sure you're informed about political and economic events and try and gain work experience through your local MP. Try and read about issues from different news sources so that you understand all points of view, even if you strongly disagree with them. Consider all routes in, whether that's through your local MP or joining APPGs (All Party Political Groups), working for a political think-tank or even simply joining your local association. 〞

Ellen, Cambridge Biological Natural Sciences graduate

❝ I'm currently studying the graduate Medicine course at Imperial College, London. Natural Sciences is a great platform for so many careers in the medical profession and further scientific fields. It's worth remembering that you don't necessarily need to study undergraduate

Medicine to become a doctor. Arguably, studying a broad base of sciences gives you a better grounding in medical science later on. You get to develop your analytical skills and spend a lot of your degree problem solving. The most useful skill I developed is time management; as a Natural Sciences student you constantly have to juggle lots of things. If I could do it all again, I would worry less and say yes more. As an undergraduate, university is a unique place to discover what you want to do – get involved! **""**

Tom, Oxford Engineering Science graduate

"" I followed my final year with a four month placement as a research assistant at the Chinese University of Hong Kong, and am currently studying a PhD in Biomedical Engineering at Imperial. A lot of my success has been due to trying things outside my comfort zone, persevering if something sounds exciting and worthwhile even if it may be very difficult. You may regret not taking chances! I use my degree every day for my research, not only the theory but also ways to approach problem solving and collaborating across disciplines. I would advise Engineering applicants to try to gain as much work experience as possible, and keep an eye on engineering developments in the news and on the internet (it's a rapidly changing and exciting field!). **""**

Freya, Cambridge Law graduate

"" I loved my time at Cambridge; the Law tripos is designed not only to build great lawyers, but to develop you into a challenging and strategic thinker. I found it to be a very human subject, dealing with all of life's big questions: from same-sex marriage, and the legal regulation of the family, through to international conventions regulating war and banning torture.

Cambridge also offers an unrivalled opportunity to try new things outside of academia. In the three years I was there I got involved in rowing, costume design, musical theatre, the jazz dance society, the law society, student journalism, Amnesty International and the Cambridge Union Society. It was a pretty busy three years...

Since graduating I have studied for my Masters degree in Law at University College London, and then gone on to work in business development for Unilever, and more recently for a start up food enterprise. I ultimately decided not to pursue a legal career, but I have found the strategic mindset which my degree has gifted me to be invaluable in a commercial context – I actually work alongside two other Cambridge Law graduates which just goes to show that the course is an ideal grounding for a career in business! 〞

Charlie, Oxford English graduate

❝ Having spent the previous few years working towards getting there, I must admit that when I started at Oxford I found it slightly disconcerting not having a medium-term plan, at least beyond getting my degree. I decided to investigate careers to give myself something to work towards.

I have always been interested in current affairs and I come from a family of lawyers, so I very quickly settled on a career in law. I got involved with the Oxford Law Society and attended various presentations and other events. I did work experience – less formal days in Scotland and vacation schemes in London.

After my undergraduate degree, I read for the Graduate Diploma in Law and the Legal Practice Course. I also took some time out to teach in a prep school. Throughout this time, I ran my own tutoring and educational consultancy business. I think it was my tutoring which was the best preparation for life as a commercial solicitor. It taught me the basics of running a business, especially managing relationships with clients.

I enjoy language and problem solving. At its heart, the law is about solving problems through precise use of language. English obviously deals with language and understanding it precisely. More generally, my undergraduate degree taught me how to deal with deadlines, manage pressure, and analyse and understand large quantities of new information – although English does not have a monopoly on these skills.

Aspiring lawyers often put too much emphasis on the academic side of the profession: the best lawyers are the ones who have real world experience and understand the practical side of their clients' problems. Sometimes the best advice you can give a client has very little to do with the law. "

Caroline, Oxford PPE graduate

" After graduating, I worked at Oliver Wyman as a management consultant for 18 months. I then worked at The Economist for two years, before moving to Germany to join a start-up, where I'm currently working. I'm also in the process of setting up my own business.

My time at Oxford benefitted me hugely: the friends and connections I made, the confidence I gained that even if something seems really hard I can manage it, and widening my horizons to aspire to things that seem very ambitious but are attainable if you try.

Most of my "organised" spare time activities were in second year, e.g. JCR Overseas Officer, rowing in the college team, peer support training. Other than that I loved going to the Oxford Union and other societies' speech events, drinks events and college balls! I did an internship at a small management consulting firm between my first and second year, an internship at Oliver Wyman between my second and third year, and volunteered in India and Niger – the latter with TravelAid.

I think my success has been down to hard work! And doing things I enjoy. Enjoying your work makes it so much easier, and making sure to do things that relax you in your spare time also makes you more effective when you do work.

My advice to PPE applicants would be read widely and have a genuine passion for what you do. "

Alex, Cambridge English graduate

❝ I have worked as an actor and filmmaker for the last four years. Whilst at university, I spent most of my time acting in plays, running the college drama society and going to poetry readings and conferences. The friends I made at Cambridge and the ambition of everyone I was around helped me to believe in my potential and meant there were always exciting people to work with and turn to for advice and help. That has continued out of Cambridge and also helped me to believe in my own value and take risks that maybe I would not have otherwise.

The work ethic you develop as an undergraduate is probably the key thing I've taken away from university. Learning to concentrate on a variety of tasks for 12 hours a day, being able to shift focus quickly and to set your own goals and priorities is something that comes from navigating your way through a Cambridge humanities degree. Those are invaluable for beginning a career as a freelancer or entrepreneur. Also the English degree teaches you to question and reformulate everything around you whilst maintaining an eye for detail. It teaches you to problem solve and bring things together that you usually might not see as compatible. These are invaluable in a creative industry where a lot of the time you are trying to make something from nothing.

My advice to prospective applicants is take as much as you can from university. It is a unique time to make mistakes and try things out. If you are thinking about directing films, get some other students together and make one. There are usually societies that you can join that support student projects and if there isn't then start one. Universities are such supportive places for people trying to be creative and they have the money to allow you to experiment and you have the people around you with whom you can collaborate. Don't miss that opportunity. If you want to act, produce, direct, design, be an agent, or run a company you can do that in miniature at university and see if it's for you, As long as you balance some of that with hard-time in the library, you'll probably be ok. ❞

Rebecca, Oxford Music graduate

" Upon leaving Oxford, I joined a small education business which gave me some experience in presentations, events management, marketing and sales. From there I went into a brand new Marketing and Brand agency, where I worked for two years to grow it into a team of five and clients including National Geographic and No7 (Boots). I then decided I wanted to go into a business rather than work across a number of different clients so I am now Marketing Manager at the UK's leading art supplies retailer.

My advice to graduates would be you should always be willing to support small ventures – there is so much pressure out of university to go for the most well-paid job. The smaller the organisation, the more responsibility you will have from day one and the more you will learn. It makes you all the more employable in jobs two and three.

Music was essentially a course around the History of Music, studying context, reception and audience reaction to music. It really does define how I think about the customer today, and I think I am a better Marketer for the tutorial-based system at Oxford where you take the time to think of multiple ways to tackle a question. I was a Choral Scholar in Lincoln College Chapel Choir, Secretary of Turl Streets Arts Festival two years in a row and directed two musicals in college with a university-wide cast. It was managing the festival, coordinating its launch ball and creating all the posters etc. for the musical that first got me into marketing.

If you're thinking about applying for Music make sure you know the course you are applying for. Oxford and Cambridge are very different. Cambridge is based more around the aural and practical skill you have when you apply, whereas Oxford looks at your basic analytical skills and how they could be enhanced on the course. If you are then looking to go into Marketing, be aware – if you promote any event via social media, write copy for a student paper, or organise events and problem-solve how to get people to turn up – then you are already getting experience in Marketing. "

Meet the Team

Lucinda Fraser
MANAGING DIRECTOR

Classics and German,
Somerville College, Oxford

Since joining Oxbridge Applications
in 2010, Lucinda has delivered our
fundamental aims of inspiring students
to aim high and delivering excellent,
accessible support. Lucinda oversees all
our support, as well as delivering talks
and workshops to students
and professionals around
the world.

Chloe Hillier
PROGRAMME MANAGER

English,
St Catharine's College, Cambridge

Chloe runs our academic support programmes,
looking after UK and international students on
our Premier Service, and students in receipt
of a government bursary on our Access and
Scholarship schemes. Chloe also oversees
our extensive research and publications,
including editing the edition of
Tell me about a banana you're
currently reading.

Alicia Luba
SENIOR CONSULTANT

English Literature,
St. Hilda's College, Oxford

As an expert in the application process,
Alicia meets with parents and students to
provide full assessments and guidance.
She also ventures abroad for missions in
the Middle and Far East and attends
major global education conferences
worldwide, providing talks and
one-to-one consultations.

Olivia
MARKETING MANAGER

English Literature,
Lincoln College, Oxford

Olivia graduated with a first in English at
Lincoln College, Oxford. With a background
in digital communications and media, she
joined the team early in 2013 to lead on
marketing strategy, public relations and all
communications with our clients.
Olivia regularly writes on Oxbridge and
the admissions process and last year
was featured in the Huffington
Post and the Telegraph.

Rebecca Nicholls
SCHOOLS & EVENTS MANAGER

Geography,
Regent's Park College, Oxford

Rebecca heads up Oxbridge
Applications' Courses Team, developing and
delivering our wide range of academic
courses throughout the year as well as our
popular Schools Programmes, working
with schools all around the country to
make sure their Oxbridge hopefuls
are getting the support
they need.

We'd love to hear from you...

f facebook.com/oxbridgeapplications 🐦 ApplytoOxbridge ✉ info@oxbridgeapplications.com ☎ +44 (0)20 7499 2394

www.oxbridgeapplications.com
